INTRODUCTORY

LESSONS ON MORALS,

AND

CHRISTIAN EVIDENCES.

BY

RICHARD WHATELY, D.D., LL.D.

CAMBRIDGE:
JOHN BARTLETT.
1857.

CAMBRIDGE:
ELECTROTYPED BY METCALF AND COMPANY.

PREFACE.

The special merits of the following treatise on Practical Ethics will be found to be simplicity of method, general clearness of style, a good absence of technical terms and artificial classifications, a singular aptness and familiarity of illustration, respect for common sense in the development of principles, the doctrines it exhibits of the essential unity of virtue, of the nature of conscience, and of the determining efficacy of motives, frequent appeals to Scriptural sanctions, and the uniform practice of referring the quality of actions to the spiritual state in man out of which they proceed. It is mainly for these traits that this work has been selected from among the many presented to the public notice, and is now republished here as a text-book for elementary instruction.

The only "Morals" that the educating plans of Christian nations can finally concern themselves much about are, in the high and broad acceptation, Christian morals. It is but a limited and partial service, though an actual one, that science, in the ordinary sense, can render to the moral life. It is certainly true, that there is such a thing as a science of man's moral nature, legitimate and justified; as it is also true, that psychology may be treated under ethical aspects. But traditionary notions of categorical processes, and the ambition of system-builders, have often hindered a vital apprehension of the simple and sublime laws of the soul working, under the Spirit, towards the absolute right and good. Divine truth creates its own modes, and imposes its own conditions. It needs only to be welcomed, in the clear shining of its own light, — only to be studied in a teachable temper and according to the natural necessities of experience, — that it may reveal its reality and beauty. The grand ethical attainment is to come into right, genuine relations with the Creator. Man learns his duties, not by rules and formulas, but through a pure attitude towards the Infinite Father. The subject is to be unfolded, not as an agglomeration of facts, but as a living power. It accosts the understanding less than the will. It proceeds less by analysis than by sympathetic communications of purpose and aspiration. There is but one root for all excellences in disposition or deed. The best system of ethics would grow out of the Sermon on the Mount. In the great New Testament maxim, "Love God and man," lies the central and germinal idea of all true policies, economies, commonwealths, duties. The life of Christ is the norm of all morality. For ethical science the spiritual order is the only logical order. The proof of this profound principle is in the readiness and facility with which it joins moral ideas to actions, informs circumstance with intention, and applies doctrine to all the exigencies and shapes of life; — because what is most true is always most practical. When this is realized, a comprehensive, consistent, and complete philosophy of human character and conduct may be written.

The subsequent discussion of Christian Evidences appears to present what is most important to a primary investigation of the grounds of belief, in a lucid arrangement, unencumbered with extrinsic matter. The author's treatment has also the advantage of actually investing the array of outward proofs with something of the attraction and interest of the internal testimony, — not confusing the two departments, yet not raising too sharp a distinction between them.

In affixing the name of Archbishop Whately to both parts of this work, — although they were first published anonymously, — we follow the common opinion as to their authorship, — an opinion not contradicted on his authority.

F. D. H.

CAMBRIDGE, August, 1856.

CONTENTS.

LESSONS ON MORALS.

LESSON I.

CONSCIENCE.

LESSON II.

THE DIVINE WILL.

LESSON III.

ENCOURAGEMENTS TO DUTY IN SCRIPTURE.

LESSON IV.

OFFICE OF SCRIPTURE IN REFERENCE TO MORAL CONDUCT.

LESSON V.

MODE OF MORAL TEACHING OF SCRIPTURE.

LESSON VI.

MORAL DISCIPLINE.

LESSON VII.

PROPER OFFICE OF CONSCIENCE.

LESSON VIII.

REGULATION OF CONSCIENCE.

LESSON IX.

DIFFICULTIES OF MORAL DISCIPLINE.

LESSON X.

CULTIVATION OF RIGHT FEELINGS.

LESSON XI.

FORMATION OF HABITS.

LESSON XII.

IMITATION OF JESUS.

LESSON XIII.

IMITATION OF THE APOSTLES.

LESSON XIV.

SINGLENESS OF VIRTUE.

LESSON XV.

EASIER AND HARDER DUTIES.

LESSON XVI.

MISCELLANEOUS CAUTIONS. — PART I.

LESSON XVII.

MISCELLANEOUS CAUTIONS. — PART II.

LESSON XVIII.

MISCELLANEOUS CAUTIONS. — PART III.

LESSON XIX.

SELF-EXAMINATION. — PART I.

LESSON XX.

SELF-EXAMINATION. — PART II.

CHRISTIAN EVIDENCES.

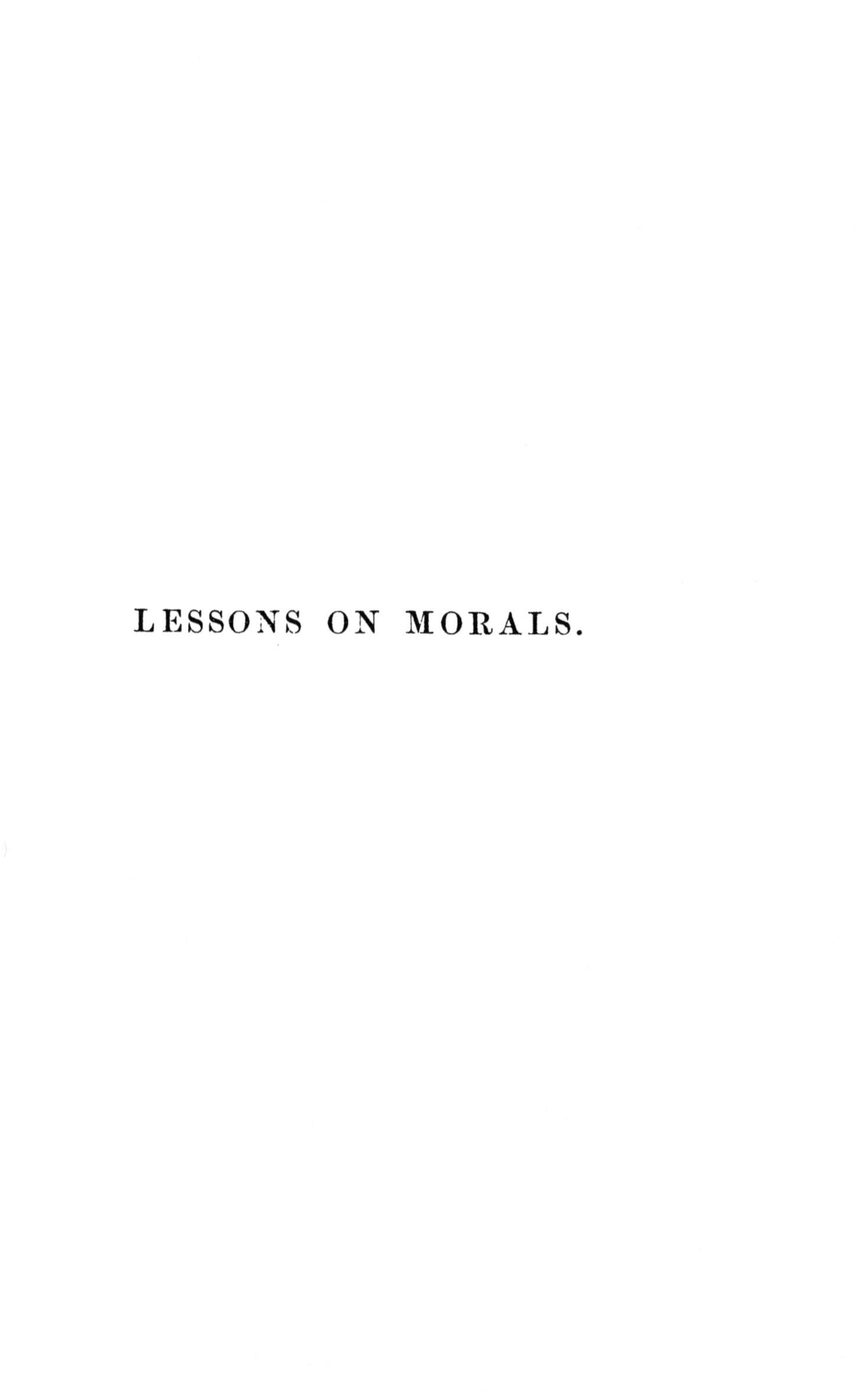

LESSONS ON MORALS.

LESSONS ON MORALS.

LESSON I.

CONSCIENCE.

§ 1.— *The Law of the Land no complete Standard.*

THE law of the land ought not to be made our standard of moral right and wrong. It is indeed our duty to obey the laws, unless there should be a law commanding us to do something absolutely wrong; but this is only a part of our duty, and not the whole. For there are many things to which a good man will think himself morally bound, though they are what no laws make any mention of; such as gratitude to a benefactor, charity to the poor, and many others. Such duties cannot be enjoined by any human laws, because they are what cannot be *enforced;* being in their own nature voluntary. When a man is *compelled* to make repayment to one who has advanced him money, or to contribute to the support of the poor, there is no gratitude or charity in the case. For these consist in *giving* of one's own free will; and no one can be said to *give* what the law obliges him to *pay*. If therefore any one should have been well inclined to contribute a certain sum towards the relief of his poor neighbors, still, as soon as the law *obliges* him to contribute that sum, it is no gift; because what the law requires him to part with is no longer his own.

So also there are many things which every good man would consider wrong, but which the law does not prohibit, because it could not prevent them, or because the attempt to prevent them would do more harm than good. What are called "sumptuary laws" have been, for this reason, abolished in most civilized countries. For though it is wrong for a man to spend more than he can properly afford, in fine clothes, furniture, and feasts, beyond his station, the attempt to prevent this, by legal interference with each man's private expenditure, has always been found to be intolerably troublesome, and almost entirely ineffectual.

§ 2.— *The Law does not control Motives.*

But it was pointed out, in the second place, that even if it were possible for the laws to enjoin everything that is good, and prohibit everything that is wrong, still a man who should act rightly merely in obedience to the laws, and for the sake of avoiding legal penalties, would not be at all what any one would account a good man, because he would not be acting from a virtuous *motive;* and it is entirely on the motives and disposition of the mind that the *moral* character of any one's conduct depends. An action, indeed, which is done from a bad or from an inferior motive, may be in itself right, as being what a good man would be disposed to do; as when a man pays his debts for fear of being imprisoned, or having his goods seized; but this does not make him an honest man.

You can plainly see, therefore, how great an error it would be for a man to make the law of the land his standard of right and wrong, and to be satisfied with himself as long as he did but comply with the laws. For, in the first place, he might do much that is wrong, and might omit many duties, without transgressing any law; and secondly, when he did do what is right in itself, yet not *because* it is right, but merely for fear of legal penalties, though this would be a benefit to the public, it would be no virtue in *him*.

§ 3. — *All Men have some Notion of Right and Wrong.*

All men, except perhaps some few of the wildest savages, have some notion of moral right and wrong, independently of human laws. There is hardly any one who would not account it a good thing to relieve a distressed neighbor, and a bad thing to treat a benefactor with ingratitude; though these are matters which laws do not notice. And every one would allow that whoever has borrowed anything, is bound in duty to repay it, even though there were no law to compel him to do so.

But there are several points in which different nations, and different persons, vary considerably as to their notions of what is morally good and bad. The same things which are condemned by some, are approved by others. And this has led some persons to doubt whether there is any such faculty in the human mind as that which is commonly called "Conscience," or "Moral sense," or "Moral faculty."

But you should remember that every one of our faculties is capable of cultivation and improvement, and is also liable to be corrupted and depraved, and is subject to various imperfections. Human *Reason* is far from being infallible; for many men are deceived by fallacious arguments, and fall into various errors; and there are great varieties in the opinions formed by different persons. Yet no one would on that ground deny that Man is a rational Being. And again, you may occasionally see great variations even in the bodily senses, and in the bodily formation, of different individuals. But we do not consider these variations as doing away with all general rules. Some are born idiots, and some blind; some have been born with only one arm, and some with neither arms nor legs. Yet we speak of Man as a Being possessing reason, and having eyes, and arms, and legs. And again, to a person in fever, sweet things taste bitter; and some have a taste so depraved by disease or by habit as to prefer bitter or sour things to sweet. Yet no one would deny that wormwood is bitter, and honey sweet; or would say that aloes has naturally a pleasanter taste than honey. And it would be equally absurd to deny that there is anything naturally odious in ingratitude, or that justice and beneficence are natural and proper objects of approbation.

§ 4. — *Scripture does not profess to give Precise Rules for Conduct in all Cases.*

Some, however, may be disposed to think that it is of no consequence to Christians what may be the natural faculties of Man in all that relates to moral conduct, or what may have been said or thought on the subject by heathens, since we have in the Holy Scriptures a sufficient guide to teach us all that we are to do or avoid.

But this would be to mistake altogether the whole character of our Scriptures. You may see, even from Scripture itself, that it was never designed to supply a complete set of precise rules as to every part of our conduct; and that the sacred writers do not address themselves as to men that had no natural notion of moral right and wrong. They do indeed notice such errors in particular points as their hearers were the most apt to fall into, and they dwell on such particular duties as had been most neglected. But they do not attempt to go through in detail all things that a Christian is required to do or to abstain from. And they are so far from supposing their hearers to require to be taught the first rudiments of morality, — the fundamental distinction between moral good and evil, — that, on the contrary, they appeal to the moral principles of their people, and call upon them to judge and decide according to those principles. And they appeal to them, not only as Christians, but as *human* creatures; for they speak of the Gentiles before the Gospel had been revealed to them, as "knowing" (when they lived in gross vice) "that they who do such things are worthy of death," and they speak of some who, "not having the [divine] law, do, by nature, the things of the law; their conscience also bearing witness, and their thoughts accusing or else excusing one another." (Rom. ii. 14.)

§ 5. — *Scripture addresses Men as possessing a Conscience.*

Moreover, our Lord says that "the servant who knew not his lord's will, *and did commit things worthy of stripes,* shall be beaten with few stripes; but that he who knew his lord's will and did it not, shall be beaten with many stripes." Now, that one who knew his lord's will and did it not, should receive the heavier punishment, is a rule which one can easily understand; but that one "who knew *not* his lord's will" — that is, who had not received any express command — *could* "commit things *worthy of stripes*," would be utterly inconceivable, if we supposed all notions of right and wrong to have been originally derived entirely from a knowledge of the divine will.

And again, when the Apostles exhort Christians to think on and practise "*whatsoever* things are pure, whatsoever things are honest and lovely, and of good report"; and, "giving all diligence, to add to their faith virtue, and temperance, and patience," and the like, it is plain they could not have been speaking to men who had no notion of what is meant by virtue, and temperance, and purity, &c., and who needed to be taught precisely what is to be accounted good and bad conduct on each point; just as you would inform a blind man that snow has a quality called white, and grass green, and coal black, and the like.

Indeed, the ancient heathen philosophers, who had no belief in a future state of reward and punishment, or in any revelation made to man, used the words which we translate "virtue," and gave, on the whole, much the same descriptions of virtue and vice that any one would do now. And this would evidently have been impossible, if Man had been naturally quite destitute of all moral faculty.

§ 6. — *Moral Goodness attributed to God.*

Moreover, the sacred writers always speak of God as *just* and *good*, and his command as *right* and reasonable. "Are not my ways," says He by a prophet, "equal? Are not your ways unequal?" And again, "Why, even of yourselves judge ye not what is right?" Now all this would have been quite unmeaning if Man had no idea of what is good or bad in itself, and meant by those words merely what is *commanded* or *forbidden* by God. For, then, to say that God's commands are just and good, would be only saying that his commands are his commands. If man had not been originally endowed by his Maker with any power of distinguishing between moral good and evil, or with any preference of the one to the other, then it would be mere trifling to speak of the divine *goodness;* since it would be merely saying that "God is what He is,"—which is no more than might be said of any Being in the universe.

Whenever, therefore, you hear any one speaking of our having derived all our notions of morality from the will of God, the sense in which you must understand him is, that it was God's will to create Man a Being endowed with conscience, and capable of perceiving the difference of right and wrong, and of understanding that there is such a thing as Duty. And if any one should use expressions which seem not to mean this, but to imply that there is no such thing as natural Conscience,—no idea in the human mind of such a thing as Duty,—still you may easily prove that his real meaning must be what we have said. If any persons tell you that our first notion of right and wrong is entirely derived from the Divine Law, and that those words have no meaning except obedience and disobedience to the declared will of God, you may ask them whether it is a matter of *duty* to obey God's will, or merely a matter of *prudence*, inasmuch as He is able to punish those who rebel against Him? Whether they think that God is *justly entitled* to obedience, or merely that it would be very *rash* to disobey one who has power to enforce his commands?

They will doubtless answer, that we *ought* to obey the divine commands as a point of duty, and not merely on the ground of expediency; that God is not only powerful, but good; and that conformity to his will is a thing right in itself, and should be practised, not through mere fear of punishment, or hope of reward, but *because* it is *right*.

§ 7. — *Obedience to the Divine Will is a Duty.*

Now this proves that they must be sensible that there is in the human mind some notion of such a thing as Duty, and of things being right or wrong in their own nature. For, when any persons submit to the will of another merely because it is their interest, or because they dare not resist, we never speak of this submission as a matter of *duty*, but merely of prudence. If robbers were to seize you and carry you off as a slave, threatening you with death if you offered to resist or to escape, you might think it *advisable* to submit, if you saw that resistance would be hopeless; but you would not think yourself bound in duty to do so. Or again, if you were offered good wages for doing some laborious work, you might think it *expedient* to accept the offer, but you would not account it a moral duty. And when a farmer supplies his cattle, or a slave-owner his slaves, with abundance of the best of food, in order that they may be in good condition, and do the more work for himself, or fetch a better price, and not from benevolence to them, every one would regard this as mere *prudence*, and not virtue. And we judge the same in every case where a man is acting solely with a view to his own advantage.

You can easily prove, therefore, that when people speak of a knowledge of the divine will being the origin of all our moral notions, they cannot mean exactly what the words would seem to signify; if, at least, they admit at the same time that it is a matter of *duty*, and not merely of prudence, to obey God's will, and that he has a just claim to our obedience.

LESSON II.

THE DIVINE WILL.

§ 1. — *A Divine Command in any Particular Point creates a Duty.*

SOME persons are apt to fall into indistinctness of language, and confusion of thought, on this subject, from not taking care to distinguish between our moral judgment on some *particular cases*, and our notion of Duty *generally*. On any particular point, a pious man will be ready, if he is convinced that a divine command has been given, to obey it at once without further inquiry; taking for granted that it is right, though he may not see the reason of it. But this is not from his having no notion at all, generally, of *anything* being in itself right or wrong, and knowing no meaning of the word "good," except "what is commanded by a superior power." On the contrary, he acts as he does from his general trust in God's goodness, and just claim to obedience. For, in this or that *particular point*, a divine command may *make* that a duty which was not so before. But this can only be when the command is given to a being endowed with a moral sense, which enables him to perceive that there is *such a thing* as Duty, and that God has a rightful claim to be obeyed, even when the reason of his commands is not perceived.

In like manner, a telescope will enable a man possessing the sense of sight to see objects invisible to the naked eye. But the revelation of a divine command could no more *originate* the notion of duty, generally, in a being destitute of Moral Faculty, and to whom, therefore, the word "duty" would have no meaning at all (though he might be *afraid* to disobey), than a telescope could confer sight on a blind man.

§ 2. — *Moral Precepts and Positive Precepts.*

In order to have a clear view of this subject, you must be careful to observe the distinction (which some persons are apt to overlook) between what are called *moral* precepts [or "natural" precepts] and *positive* precepts. We are bound to comply with both; but "moral precepts" are what relate to things right and wrong in themselves, independently of any command; and "positive precepts" are what relate to things originally indifferent, but which are *made* right or wrong by the command of a Superior who has a just claim to obedience.

Thus, when children are forbidden to tell lies, or to quarrel, these are things forbidden because they are wrong in themselves. And when they are told to improve their minds by learning what is useful, and to be kind and helpful to each other, and the like, these things are commanded because they are right in themselves. But when they are forbidden to go beyond the bounds of the play-ground, and are charged to come in at a certain hour, these are what are called "positive" precepts. To go beyond a certain spot was originally nothing wrong in itself; but *became* wrong, after the rule had been laid down, because it would be an act of disobedience. And to come in from play at twelve o'clock, or at one, is in itself a matter of indifference, but it is *made* a matter of duty as soon as the master or parent has appointed the time.

So also it is a moral duty (as has been above said) to obey the laws of the land when not wrong in themselves; and some of these relate to things originally and naturally right and wrong; others, to things originally indifferent. For instance, to import tea, or wine, or to manufacture candles or malt, is a thing originally indifferent. But when a tax has been laid on these things, then to evade this tax is to rob the revenue, — that is, to rob the nation. And, accordingly, to sell, or to buy, smuggled goods is a thing morally wrong.

The like holds good with private contracts. In these, a person may be bound, as to matters originally indifferent, not by the command of a superior, but by his own act. For it is clearly a moral duly to fulfil one's engagements. Thus, a husband and wife are bound, by the marriage contract they have made, to their mutual duties, though they were not bound to each other before. Children, on the other hand, are bound by an original and natural obligation to honor their parents.

Again, when the Israelites were commanded, in the Mosaic law, to be kind to their neighbors, and liberal to the poor, this was commanded because it was in itself right. But when they were commanded to keep the feast of the Passover, and to perform certain appointed ceremonies, and to set aside certain specified days and years as sanctified, this was right because it was commanded.

So, also, the prohibition of murder and theft were what are called "moral" [or natural] precepts, as relating to things wrong in themselves; but to eat the flesh of the animals specified as "unclean," which is a matter originally indifferent, was wrong for Israelites, because it was forbidden in their law.

In such cases, the command of a rightful Superior makes things morally right and wrong which were not so before the express command was given. And when such a command does exist, we are bound in duty to obey it.

§ 3. — *Moral Precepts to be observed in the Spirit, and Positive in the Letter.*

The distinction between positive duties and [natural] moral duties, it is most important to perceive clearly, and always to keep in mind. For with respect to the latter class, — that of natural duties, — we are left to be guided by our own conscience, according to the best judgment we can form; and we must not expect to have precise rules laid down as to every case that can arise; nor satisfy ourselves that we are blameless as long as we do nothing that is expressly forbidden, and omit nothing that is, in so many words, commanded.

But with respect to the other class, — that of positive duties, — it is sufficient if we do but conform precisely to the commands distinctly laid down for us. We are safe as long as we transgress no express injunctions given to us.

And precepts of this class we are bound to comply with according to the *letter*, without presuming to depart from this, and to plead that we are observing the *spirit* of the command. With moral precepts it is the reverse. For instance, the injunction of our Lord "to wash one another's feet," is usually regarded (and very rightly) as no positive precept, but only an injunction to be kind and helpful to each other. Any one, therefore, would be complying with his command in spirit, and as was designed, by showing such kindness generally, even though he should never literally wash another's feet. And, on the contrary, one who should literally wash another's feet, but should generally refuse all kind assistance and relief, would be in reality disobeying the command, by disregarding the spirit of it.

But, on the other hand, when our Lord said, "Do this in remembrance of me," and commanded his disciples to baptize, He was giving positive precepts; as we learn from the practice of the Apostles, who evidently understood Him (as He must have known that they would, and designed that they should) to enjoin the use of literal water, and bread and wine. No one should presume, therefore, to omit the literal and exact compliance with these commands, and to set up the plea of observing them in the *spirit*.

So, also, when the Israelites were enjoined to sanctify certain distinctly specified days as religious festivals, it was not allowable for them to make any alterations, and to plead that they were observing the *spirit* of the ordinances, by keeping the Passover, for instance, at some different time of the year; or by sacrificing some other animal than the one enjoined; or by sanctifying as a sabbath every sixth day, or every eight; or by fixing on the first, or second, or third day of the week instead of the seventh, on the ground that one day is in itself as good as another. In all positive precepts, in short, an exact compliance with the very letter of the command is required; and is made, *by* the command, a moral duty to those to whom the command is given.

§ 4. — *Compliance with Positive Precepts a Moral Duty.*

The obedience, in these matters, of a pious man to the divine commands, even when he does not understand the reasons of them, and his general trust in the divine wisdom and goodness, — all this is of a piece with what we feel and do towards our fellow-men. A dutiful and affectionate child, for instance, will fully trust (with good reason) in the goodness and the superior judgment of a kind parent, and will comply cheerfully with his directions, even when not knowing why they were given; all the more cheerfully from being convinced that his parent's directions are right; and not as merely yielding to superior power, and calculating on reward or punishment.

So, also, some friend, on whose worth and good sense you fully rely, will perhaps take some measures which you presume, from your knowledge of his character, to be right ones, before you have sufficient knowledge of particulars to judge of the case itself.

And we judge in the same way in other matters also, that have no relation to moral conduct. For instance, if you had read several works of some author, which you greatly admire, you would be likely, when you heard of some new work of his about to be published, to expect, before reading it, that that also would show great ability. It is not that you have no notion of good or bad writing except what is or is not *his;* but you would form your expectations of what you have not seen from that which you have seen.

§ 5. — *Sin implies a Moral Faculty.*

In addition to what has been said, it is important to remark, that *sin*, which the sacred writers so often impute to men, does itself imply the existence of a moral sense. For a being destitute of all power of distinguishing between moral good and evil, as is the case with brutes, however odious his actions might be, could not commit sin. And accordingly, though a wolf, or a swine, or any other brute, may do acts which *would* be sinful in a man, no one speaks of a brute as *sinful*, or imputes to it moral *guilt*. And, for the same reason, no sin is ever imputed to the *acts* of a new-born infant, or a complete idiot. And, accordingly, in some parts of this country, the term used by the common people for an idiot is "an innocent." For, though idiots may be very *mischievous*, it is understood that they can incur no *guilt*, whatever they do, from not having the sense to perceive right and wrong. They, and infants, every one would say, are not *moral agents*, any more than the brutes; and, consequently, the word *sin* would not apply to any of their *acts*. Yet the higher kinds of brutes, such as horses and dogs, can be taught to obey their masters, and to do or to abstain from certain acts, from fear of punishment or hope of reward. But we consider *sin* to consist in doing what one knows, or might have known, to be *morally wrong*; — in short, in transgressing the rules of *duty* which one is capable of understanding. So, also, *folly* we consider as consisting in acting against the dictates of one's *reason*, and consequently as implying a rational nature. And, accordingly, no one imputes folly to a brute, any more than sin.

Of course, when any express command does come from God, or indeed from a parent, or any other rightful superior, this *increases* the sin of those who disobey it. And this is what the Apostle Paul evidently means when he speaks of "the commandment" making sin "*exceeding* sinful."

But in no case can there be any *sin* at all except in a violation of *duty* by a Being capable of understanding what duty is.

LESSON III.

ENCOURAGEMENTS TO DUTY IN SCRIPTURE.

§ 1. — *What Scripture reveals in Reference to Duty.*

YOU have seen, then, that Man has been endowed by his Maker with a power of distinguishing, in some degree, good and bad actions; which is called by some the "moral sense" [or moral faculty], and by some "conscience." And you have seen that the sacred writers always address us as Beings having some notion of what Duty is; and that the moral precepts they deliver always proceed on that supposition. And, moreover, it has been pointed out, that if Man had been a Being quite destitute (like the brutes) of all idea of moral right and wrong, then no revelation of the divine will, nor any expectation of future rewards and punishments, could have imparted to such a Being the notion of Duty. Man might, in that case, have obeyed the divine commands as a matter of *prudence;* just as a slave (and indeed even a brute) may be brought to do what his master bids him. But the notion of being *justly* bound to obey, as a matter of Duty, is what could never have entered his mind.

What, then, you may next ask, is the connection between a divine revelation and moral conduct? If, as we have seen, a knowledge of God's will could not of itself convey any notion of Duty to a Being naturally destitute of a moral sense, and if the sacred writers do not undertake (as it is plain they do not) to give precise directions as to every point of conduct, what is it that revelation does teach us in reference to morality?

§ 2. — *God's Approval of Virtue.*

In the first place, we learn from our Scriptures that our Maker approves of virtue, and disapproves of vice. Now this was either unknown, or very imperfectly known, to the ancient heathen. Their most eminent philosophers regarded those supposed Beings who were called gods (to none of whom, by the way, they attributed the creation)* as wholly regardless of human concerns. And as for the tales circulated among the vulgar about a state of happiness or suffering after death, they derided them as "old wives' fables." They understood what is meant by "virtue," and wrote many admirable things on the subject; but always without any reference, or with very slight reference, to the will of their gods. And as for the vulgar among the ancient heathen, though they were not altogether without a notion that their gods favored the virtuous, and sometimes sent heavy judgments on very great crimes, they trusted chiefly to costly sacrifices, and splendid temples, and images, and to superstitious ceremonies, for making their gods propitious, and atoning for all violations of moral duty.

And, indeed, great part of the worship of several of these gods consisted in gross immorality. Thus, we read in the book of Deuteronomy concerning the relig-

---

* See "Lessons on Religious Worship," Lesson II.

ion of the Canaanites: "Every abomination unto the Lord which He hateth, have these nations done unto their gods; for even their sons and daughters have they burned in the fire unto their gods."

Our religion, on the contrary, teaches, that "in every nation he that feareth God, and worketh *righteousness*, is accepted of Him"; that our great Master came into the world, and lived and died for us, "that he might redeem us from all iniquity, and purify to Himself a peculiar people, zealous of good works." Whenever, in our Scriptures, the unspeakable love and goodness of God towards us is set forth, in sending his blessed Son for our salvation, we are always called on to show our gratitude and love towards Him in return, by a zealous and watchful endeavor after personal holiness. "If ye love me," says the Saviour, "keep my commandments." And he warns us that to those who lead a sinful life, even though they shall have preached in his name, and "in his name done many mighty works," He will say at the last day, "I know you not; depart from me, all ye workers of iniquity."

§ 3. — *Divine Approbation of Virtue an Encouragement.*

Now it is indeed true, as was remarked above, that if Man had been a Being destitute of moral sense [conscience], no knowledge of the divine will could have given him the notion of Duty; and anything we might do, in compliance with God's will, on grounds of *mere* self-interest, would not be at all of the character of Virtue, but would be only Prudence. But Man being such as he actually is, — capable of understanding the difference between moral good and evil, but of a frail and imperfect character, and exposed to many temptations to sin, — such a Being is of course greatly encouraged in virtue, and deterred from sin, by knowing that our Maker requires what is good, and forbids what is evil, and that "He hath appointed a day in which He will judge the world in righteousness," and will "render to every man according to his deeds; to them who, by patient continuance in well-doing, seek for glory and honor and immortality, eternal life; but unto them that obey unrighteousness, tribulation and anguish upon every soul of man that doeth evil."

Such an encouragement in the practice of duty as our great Master has thus mercifully provided, is what Man greatly needs. For, besides the temptations of sin which he is exposed to, it is to be remembered that, when he does resist them, and fulfils his duty, this does not of itself produce any positive pleasure; because it is the very nature of Conscience to show us that good conduct is what we are *bound* to, and as only the payment of a just *debt.* If we fail in this, and act *against* conscience, its reproaches are painful: if we *comply* with its dictates, it then does not pain us, but neither does it afford *positive* gratification; only quiet, and peace, and freedom from remorse. For if a man should pride himself on anything he had done, as if it were something meritorious in God's sight, as being beyond his bounden duty, this thought would be itself a sin.

Though, however, the mere performance of duty does not of itself give positive pleasure, to obtain *approbation* even from our fellow-creatures is gratifying; sometimes, indeed, even dangerously so. And our natural desire of approbation God has graciously thought fit to direct towards Himself; assuring us that He sees, and sees with favor, every struggle against sin, every effort to obey his commands and to improve in virtue. And moreover, He has promised, not only to be a "rewarder of them that diligently seek Him," but to make their reward consist in a fuller knowledge of Him, and a more perfect enjoyment of his presence and of his approbation. "We know," says the Apostle John, "that when Christ shall appear, we shall be like Him; for we shall see him as He is." We have thus, therefore, — what Man so much needs, — a strong encouragement to strive after the improvement of our moral character. For "every one," the Apostle goes on to say, "that hath this hope on Him, purifieth himself, even as He is pure."

§ 4. — *Divine Aid in the Performance of Duty.*

Secondly, Man being by nature weak, and being beset by temptations, our religion holds out the promise of inward divine aid in the practice of Duty, from the Holy Spirit, which "helpeth our infirmities." "I am the vine," says our Lord, "ye are the branches; as a branch cannot bear fruit of itself except it abide in the vine, no more can ye except ye abide in Me: without Me ye can do nothing." And, "It is God that worketh in us," says the Apostle Paul, "both to will and to do of his good pleasure."

As for Man's need of such aid, — that is, his frailty and proneness to fall into sin, — that is but too well known from universal experience. But some persons seem inclined to attribute this entirely to bad governments and laws, faulty education, and bad examples. And they seem to think that improvements in governments and systems of education might put an end to all moral evils. No doubt erroneous education, unwise laws, &c., do exist, and do greatly contribute to increase the faultiness of the human character; but they never could have been the *original* cause of it; since it is from *men* they have all proceeded. Our Scripture history, however, tells us that our first parents, without any bad education, corrupting examples, bad governments, &c., did transgress the only command given them. And as no one of us can be, by birth, of a firmer and purer moral character than they were originally, we may be sure that we, left to our own unaided strength, should have acted, if placed in their situation, no better than they did.

§ 5. — *Scripture Examples.*

Thirdly, we find set before us in our Scriptures the life of our Saviour, who "left us an example that we should follow his steps," and "purify ourselves as He is pure."

And we have also the examples of his Apostles, which are instructive to us, both in their failings which are recorded, and in their recovery through their divine Master's instruction and support, and in the life of devoted Christian virtue to which they were at length brought. For they were evidently not men of superior natural intelligence; nor were they originally exempt from worldly ambition, and timidity, and other failings. And we can trace in the Scripture history the gradual improvement and elevation of their characters, under the training to which they were subjected.

Fourthly and lastly, although, as has been said, there is no such thing attempted by the sacred writers as a complete enumeration of all points of duty, in all possible circumstances, still they afford us much important moral instruction in those points wherein it is most needed. They dwell on such duties as their hearers were the most disposed to neglect; such as kindness to enemies, patience under provocation, forgiveness of injuries, and the like. They correct, from time to time, various errors in moral conduct to which men are liable. And they instruct us, in various ways, how to rectify and improve our moral judgment, and bring it into practice in our lives.

For Man's moral faculty is (as was observed at the beginning) capable, like our other faculties, of cultivation and improvement, and liable also to be depraved and perverted in various ways. And a moral instructor is one who undertakes, not indeed to *create* a moral faculty in a Being quite destitute of it (any more than an oculist undertakes to create eyes), but to *cultivate* and improve the moral faculty, and remove its imperfections, and preserve it from corruption; even as an oculist seeks to *preserve* the eyes, and cure the *diseases* of them.

LESSON IV.

OFFICE OF SCRIPTURE IN REFERENCE TO MORAL CONDUCT.

§ 1.— *The Golden Rule.*

THAT invaluable rule of our Lord's, "To do to others as we would have them do to us," will serve to explain, when rightly understood, the true character of moral instruction. If you were to understand that precept as designed to convey to us the first notions of right and wrong, and to be your sole guide as to what you ought to do and to avoid in your dealings with your neighbor, you would be greatly perplexed. For you would find that a literal compliance with the precept would be sometimes *absurd*, sometimes *wrong*, and sometimes *impossible*. And probably it is through making this mistake that men in general apply the rule so much seldomer than they ought. For the real occasions for its use occur to all of us every day.

Supposing any one should regard this golden rule as designed to answer the purpose of a complete system of morality, and to teach us the difference of right and wrong; then, if he had let his land to a farmer, he m iht consider that the farmer would be glad to be excused paying any rent for it, since he would himself, if he were the farmer, prefer having the land rent-free; and that, therefore, the rule of doing as he would be done by requires him to give up all his property. So also a shopkeeper might, on the same principle, think that the rule required him to part with his goods under prime cost, or to give them away, and thus to ruin himself. Now such a procedure would be *absurd.*

Again, supposing a jailer who was intrusted with the safe custody of a prisoner should think himself bound to let the man escape, because he himself, if he were a prisoner, would be glad to obtain freedom, he would be guilty of a breach of trust. Such an application of the rule, therefore, would be morally *wrong.*

And again, if you had to decide between two parties who were pleading their cause before you, you might consider that *each* of them wished for a decision in his *own* favor. And how, then, you might ask, would it be possible to apply the rule? since in deciding *for* the one party you could not but decide *against* the other. A literal compliance with the rule, therefore, would be, in such a case, *impossible.*

§ 2. — *Application of the Golden Rule.*

Now, if you were to put such cases as these before any sensible man, he would at once say that you are to consider, not what you might *wish* in each case, but what you would regard as *fair, right, just, reasonable,* if you were in another person's place. If you were a farmer, although you might feel that you would be very glad to have the land rent-free, — that is, to become the owner of it, — you would not consider that you had any just claim to it, and that you could *fairly expect* the landlord to make you a present of his property. But you would think it reasonable that, if you suffered some great and unexpected loss, from an inundation or any such calamity, he should make an abatement of the rent. And this is what a good landlord generally thinks it right to do, in compliance with the golden rule.

So also, if you had a cause to be tried, though of course you would *wish* the decision to be in your favor, you would be sensible that all you could *reasonably expect* of the judge would be that he should lay aside all prejudice, and attend impartially and carefully to the evidence, and decide according to the best of his ability. And this — which is what *each* part may fairly claim — is what an upright judge will do. And the like holds good in all the other cases.

§ 3. — *Design of the Golden Rule.*

You have seen, then, that the golden rule was far from being designed to impart to men the first notions of justice. On the contrary, it *presupposes* that knowledge; and if we had *no* such notions, we could not properly apply the rule. But the real design of it is to put us on our guard against the danger of being blinded by self-interest. A person who has a good general notion of what is just may often be tempted to act unfairly or unkindly towards his neighbors, when his own interest or gratification is concerned, and to overlook the rightful claims of others. When David was guilty of an enormous sin in taking his neighbor's wife, and procuring the death of the husband, he was thinking only of his own gratification, quite forgetful of duty, till his slumbering conscience was roused by the prophet Nathan. On hearing the tale of "the poor man's lamb," his general abhorrence of injustice and cruelty caused him to feel vehement indignation against the supposed offender; but he did not apply his principles to his own case, till the prophet startled him by saying, "Thou art the man!"

And we, if we will make a practice of applying the golden rule, may have a kind of prophet always at hand, to remind us how, and when, to act on our principles of right. We have only to consider, "What should I think were I in the other's place, and he were to do so and so to me? How should I require him to treat me? What could I in fairness claim from him?

§ 4. — *Offices of Scripture and of Conscience.*

Besides this most important rule for the *application* of our principles, we find in Scripture (as has been already observed) many precepts designed for the *correction* and improvement of our principles; many cautions against the errors men are likely to fall into, in their moral judgment on various points. For Conscience is far from being an infallible guide, any more than Reason, generally.

One may illustrate the distinct uses of Scripture (in all that relates to morals) and of natural Conscience, by the comparison of a *sun-dial* and a *clock*. The clock has the advantage of being always at hand, to be consulted at any hour of the day or night; while the dial is of use only when the sun shines on it. But, then, the clock is liable to go wrong, and vary from the true time; and it has no power in itself of correcting its own errors; so that these may go on increasing, to any extent, unless it be from time to time regulated by the dial, which is alone the unerring guide.

Even so it is with natural conscience as compared with Scripture, which directs us according to the "wisdom which is from above." In each particular case that may occur, our own heart will furnish a decision as to what is right or wrong; and that in many cases which are not particularly specified in Scripture, though they fall under the general principles of the Gospel. But then our own hearts are liable to deceive us, even to the greatest extent, and to give wrong judgments, if they are not continually corrected and regulated by a reference to the word of God, which alone — like his sun in the natural world — affords an infallible guide.

§ 5. — *Regulation of Conscience.*

While, therefore, you take care, on the one hand, not to do anything that your conscience tells you is wrong, you must beware, on the other hand, of concluding that your conduct is necessarily right because your conscience approves it; or that you yourself at least are free from sin as long as your own judgment does not condemn you. For men may so far deprave their conscience as to bring themselves to mistake wrong for right; like one who should bend the ruler which he is drawing lines by. Thus, our Lord declared to his disciples that those who killed them would think (not merely pretend, but think) that "they were doing God service." And Paul bitterly bewails his own sin in "persecuting the Church," when he "verily thought that he ought to do many things contrary to the name of Jesus of Nazareth." And afterwards, when he became an Apostle, he says, "I judge not mine own self; for I know nothing by myself [against myself]; yet am I not hereby justified; but He that judgeth me is the Lord."

We must be careful, therefore, to regulate both our business by the clock, and the clock by the dial; that is, to regulate our conduct by our Conscience, and our Conscience itself by the commands and instructions which God has given us.

LESSON V.

MODE OF MORAL TEACHING OF SCRIPTURE.

§ 1. — *Difference of the Gospel-teaching from that of the Law.*

THERE is no need to transcribe our Lord's "Sermon on the Mount," or his various instructive parables, and the several moral precepts delivered from time to time by Him and his Apostles. For we are not writing for persons unacquainted with the Bible, or neglectful of its teaching. But it is important to point out some things that are peculiar in the general plan of moral instruction in the New Testament.

1. In the first place, you may observe how greatly it differs from the Law of Moses, in not having, like that, a number of precise rules laid down as to several particular cases. That Law did indeed lay down the general principles of conduct, in those two great commandments on which, says our Lord, "hang all the law and the prophets": "Thou shalt love the Lord thy God, with all thy heart, and thy neighbor as thyself." But besides these general commandments, there is a great number of precepts as to particular points of conduct. For the Israelites were in a sort of half-civilized condition, and needed to be treated in many respects like children. Now children must be subjected, we know, to

many precise regulations and restrictions, on account of their not being fully capable of self-government. And these are gradually relaxed as they grow up, and they are left more and more to guide their conduct by their own judgment. This is not from our thinking that good conduct is less required of a man than of a child; but, on the contrary, because he is supposed to have reached what is called "years of discretion," and may be considered capable of judging for himself what is right or wrong, and of acting accordingly.*

Hence, the Gospel, which was designed for men in a more advanced state than that of the ancient Israelites, gives much less of precise directions than the Mosaic law. It is not that a less degree of moral excellence is required of the Christian, but that the Gospel lays down pure and elevated moral *principles*, rather than exact *rules;* and requires men to conform their lives to those principles.

§ 2.—*Men accustomed to Precise Rules.*

Most men, however, are willing rather to have certain exact rules laid down for them as to particular points, and to be told precisely what they are to do and to avoid, in each case, than to be left to their own discretion, and required to regulate their own conduct for themselves, according to certain principles, and to be made responsible for doing so. And this was particularly the case with those Jews whom our Lord was addressing, because they had been brought up under the Mosaic law, which contains a great number of precise

---

* See Lessons on Religious Worship, Lesson III.

directions. And besides this law, they had among them many pretended traditions (often alluded to in the Gospel history), which claimed to be of equal authority with the written law. These are to be found in a book now extant, called the "Mishna," which contains a multitude of minute precepts; some of them additions to the laws of Moses, and some explanations of those laws, and directions how they are to be observed.

Now, a people who had been trained under such a system would particularly require to have strongly impressed on their minds that Jesus did not design to give them any such exact set of rules as they would be likely to expect.

And here you may observe what a strong internal evidence this affords of the divine origin of our religion. If Jesus and his Apostles had been mere uninspired men they would not have failed — brought up as they had been under the Jewish system — to lay down such precise precepts as the people of that Age and Country were the most willing to receive, and the most prepared to expect. Their proceeding in quite a different way from what would have been both the most natural to themselves (as mere men), and the most acceptable to their hearers, is one of the many marks of their having come from God.

§ 3. — *Principles substituted for Exact Rules.*

How much men did, at first, expect a system of exact rules you may see from several passages in the Gospels. For instance, you find Peter asking his Master, on one occasion, "Lord, how oft shall my brother sin against me, and I forgive him? till seven times?" And you find one who had been told that he was bound to "love the Lord his God with all his heart," &c., and "his *neighbor* as himself," inquiring, "*Who is* my neighbor?" wishing to have a certain exact line drawn between those whom he was, and was not, bound to love and to benefit. And Jesus shows him that by one's "neighbor" is meant *any* one whom it is in our power to serve; giving an example of an *alien,* and one of a *different religion.*

But our Lord, in the general course of his teaching, took an effectual method of showing his disciples that He meant them (instead of satisfying themselves with a *literal* conformity to certain precise *rules*) to cultivate right *dispositions,* and act on right *principles.* This He does by often giving such precepts that a literal compliance with them would be either (1.) impossible, or (2.) irrational and *absurd,* or (3.) *insignificant,* and of too little importance to be worth inculcating for their own sake. For where a literal compliance with some precept would be either impossible or absurd or wrong, it is plain that such a compliance could not be *intended;* and where it would be trifling and unimportant, it is manifest that it could not be *all* that was intended. And thus the disciples were driven — if they were sincerely desirous to learn, and would intrepret rationally and candidly what they heard — to perceive that such precepts were designed to explain and to impress on their minds the *dispositions* they were to cultivate, and the general principles on which they were to act.

§ 4. — *Moral Discretion.*

For instance, when our Lord tells his disciples to

make their prayers and their alms so secret that "their left hand should not know what their right hand did"; and again, "to let their light so shine before men, that they might see their good works, and glorify their Heavenly Father," it is plain that an exact literal compliance with *both* precepts would be impossible, and therefore could not have been designed. What, then, is it, one may ask, that He did mean? Evidently, that when the publicity of our alms and our devotions seems likely to benefit men by our good example, then we should let them see our light shining, "that they may glorify our Father in heaven"; and that, when it is our own glory rather than his that is sought, or that is likely to be the only effect of publicity, then concealment should be preferred. And of this our great Master requires us to judge for ourselves in each case, and to decide according to our discretion.

Again, when He tells us that, in order to be "his disciple," a man must "hate father and mother, and wife and children, and all that he hath," it is plain that this was not meant to be understood and obeyed literally. And, indeed, He himself supplies, in another place, an explanation of it, when He says, "He that loveth father and mother *more than me* is not worthy of me."

But, even independently of that explanation, it is sufficiently clear to any one of ordinary good sense and candor that He was looking to those cases (very common at that time) in which the opposition of parents, or wife, or children, must be encountered by one resolving to be a devoted servant of Christ; and that he must be ready in such cases to account as nothing in comparison the regard felt for those who have the strongest hold on our hearts, when we could not comply with their wishes without deserting our Master's cause. And this he expresses in another place by saying, "If thine eye offend thee, pluck it out"; . . . "if thy right hand offend thee, cut it off and cast it from thee"; that is, if what is most dear and precious to thee prove a hinderance in the path of Christian duty, renounce it at once and completely.

§ 5. — *Principles taught by Instances in Small Matters.*

Then, again, several of our Lord's precepts relate, as has been just said, to such *small* matters, that every candid and sensible person must perceive that a mere literal compliance with them could not have been *all* that was meant, and that the design must have been to give a sample of the kind of *disposition* to be cultivated. When, for instance, Jesus censures those who took possession of the most honorable seats at a feast, and tells his disciples to take the lowest seats, He does indeed mean that his precepts should be literally complied with; since unobtrusive modesty is right, and arrogant forwardness wrong, both in great matters and in small; but He meant to give a *specimen*, in one of the smaller points relating to good manners, of the disposition to be shown in *all* cases; and accordingly He concludes by laying down, generally, "Every one that exalteth himself shall be abased, but he that humbleth himself shall be exalted."

Again, He gives an example and also a precept, both of humility and kindness, in condescending to wash his disciples' feet, and adding, "Ye ought also to wash one another's feet." This was (as is well known), from the peculiar circumstances of the Age and Country, one of the chief refreshments to travellers. This particular service, consequently, was chosen as affording an easy and familiar illustration of the general disposition He designed to encourage, — a readiness to perform kind offices for each other. Now, if the particular office of kindness selected by Him had been one of the most *important* services of life, the disciples might possibly have supposed that the precept related to that *particular service* alone. But this was guarded against by his particularizing one of the commonest and *smallest* services. When He said to them, "Ye ought to wash one another's feet," they must have felt sure that the precept was meant to extend to more than that one small point of hospitality, and to comprehend a general readiness to befriend one another.

These few instances may suffice as specimens (since you may easily find others for yourself) to show how our great Master guarded his hearers against expecting to receive any complete set of precise rules for their conduct; and against satisfying their conscience by the performance of certain specified acts, and by taking care to do nothing that is expressly forbidden.

§ 6. — *Importance of Right Motives.*

Another point on which our Scriptures supply needful corrections of men's moral notions, is the importance of right *motives*. Thus our Lord declares that the alms-giving of the Pharisees was utterly worthless in God's sight, because it was practised through ostentation, "for to be seen of men." "Verily, I say unto you," said He, "they have their reward"; that is, the human praise, which was what they sought, they may obtain; but that is all: the Divine approbation they must not expect. The Apostle Paul, again, tells the Corinthians: "Though I give all my goods to feed the poor, and though I give my body to be burned, and have not charity, it profiteth me nothing."

Men have the more need to be put on their guard as to this point, because it is possible, and indeed common, for a person's acts to be of service to his neighbors, or to the Public (as, for instance, the relieving of the distressed poor), though they have nothing at all of the character of virtue, from want of the right motive.

Every one must perceive, on reflection, that the very same act may be either virtuous, or sinful, or indifferent, according to the motive from which it is done. And so completely does the moral character of any action depend on the motive and intention of the agent, that, when this is fully known, we account him right or wrong (as the case may be), even when no outward act at all has taken place, or one quite different from what was designed. For instance, that attendant on King William Rufus, who discharged at a deer an arrow which glanced against a tree and killed the king, was no murderer, because he had no such design. And, on the other hand, a man who should lie in wait to assassinate another, and pull the trigger of a gun with that intent, would be morally a murderer, not the less though the gun should chance to miss fire.

So also, when our first parents transgressed the divine law in Paradise, their sin was committed as soon as they had fully resolved to eat of the forbidden fruit, and before it had actually entered their lips. Whatever effects may have been produced in them by the actual eating of the fruit, it could not have been to *make* their nature frail, and such as to commit sin; since they had actually committed their sin *before*. And in whatever sense, therefore, they may have been said, before, to have been "very good," it could not have been in the sense of their being originally exempt from this frailty and proneness to disobedience. That their character may have become *worse*, through some effect produced by the fruit itself, is quite possible. But to speak of Man's having *become liable* to sin, through committing sin, would be as absurd as to speak of his having created himself.

§ 7.— *Virtue and Vice depend on the Motives.*

It is plain, then, that though we commonly speak of virtuous and vicious *conduct*, yet, properly speaking, and in the strictest sense, it is not the *actions* themselves that are virtuous or vicious, but the *disposition* of the agent. The outward acts are accounted morally good or evil, merely as being *signs* of the inward disposition. They are generally the best signs we can have of a man's disposition; but we all know that they are not to be relied on as *infallible* signs. If, for instance, any one were making bountiful gifts to the poor, he might, perhaps, be considered as kind-hearted and liberal; but if it were discovered that he was doing this for the sake of securing his election to a seat in Parliament, or for some other object of his own, no one would any longer give him credit for virtue in what he was doing. And (as was formerly observed, Lesson I.) if any one acts honestly, and does what is right in itself, merely from submission to the laws, and through fear of incurring legal penalties, this is evidently mere prudence, and not moral virtue.

You are to remember, however, that when we speak of the *intention* and *design* being what makes a man's conduct morally good or bad, we mean, not an intention merely of doing what *he thinks* right, but what *really is* right. For, as has been above observed, the unbelieving Jews thought they were doing God service in killing the Christians. But this neither justified the *act*, nor made the intention a *good* one.

And you are also to remember, that we are not speaking of intentions and designs to do at some *future time* what is in one's power to do at once; but of such a *full* intention and purpose as will lead to *immediate* action as soon as the opportunity offers. For, "to-morrow," says the proverb, "comes never"; and the same tempter who leads you to put off doing what is right to a "more convenient season," will be as ready to suggest an excuse to-morrow as to-day.

LESSON VI.

MORAL DISCIPLINE.

§ 1.— *Object of requiring Good Conduct.*

THE object aimed at by any moral instructor, and of course by the sacred writers, is to make us good men. And good works, [or virtuous actions,] which are the natural fruit of good dispositions, are required principally as a *proof* of those dispositions, and as an exercise and training to produce a virtuous character.

On the other hand, if a farmer, or any other employer of laborers, endeavors to make his men honest and industrious, in order that they may do his work the better, he is not properly a moral instructor; since his main object is, not the benefit of the workmen themselves, (though he may, in fact, have greatly benefited them,) but the *work done*, which is for his profit.

Now it is plain that our Divine Master can have no need of the services of his creatures; and that, therefore, the good works which He requires of us must be entirely for our own benefit, not for his, in order to our moral improvement. And from this you may see how utterly worthless in his sight must be any good works (that is, good in themselves) not done from a good motive. For "Can a man be profitable unto God, as he that is wise may be profitable unto himself? Is it any pleasure to the Almighty, that thou art righteous? or is it gain to Him that thou makest thy ways perfect?" Job xxii. 2, 3.

§ 2.— *Good Works by Proxy.*

And you may also see what an absurdity those fall into who imagine that it is possible to do good works by *proxy*, and in this way to have imputed to us as ours what is done by another on our behalf. Yet, in some Christian churches, men have been so far deluded as to imagine that it can be acceptable to God to pay a priest to perform religious exercises for them, or to pay a person to go on pilgrimages, and undergo penances, on their behalf and in their stead. Now all this evidently goes on the notion that these supposed good works have a *value in themselves* in God's sight, and are acceptable to Him on their own account, as if they were some benefit to Himself.

But if those prayers and pilgrimages, etc., were really the best possible works in themselves, it is plain that the Most High could have no need of them, and that it is not for his profit, but for ours, that he requires us to worship and to obey Him.*

We do, indeed, find in Scripture several expressions which, taken literally and by themselves, would imply that God is really desirous, for his own sake, of the worship and services of his creatures. He even describes Himself as a "jealous God"; meaning that He will not allow the honor due to Him to be paid to others. But this is to be understood in the same way as when *anger*

---

* See Note at the end of this Lesson.

and *repentance* are attributed to Him; and even eyes, and ears, and hands. All this is meant to impress on us that He *knows* all things,—as we do what we see and hear; and that we ought to dread disobeying Him, as we should some great earthly king who would be really angry at our rebellion; and that we should be as careful to honor Him as if He really could be gratified by our honor.

Bút it is plain that He cannot really have any need of our services; and that it is for our own sakes, and that of our brethren, not for his, that we are commanded to "do all for the glory of God."

§ 3.— *Works required for the Sake of the Works.*

The distinction we have been speaking of, which it is most important to keep in mind, may be thus illustrated; if a man offers for sale any article—for instance, a map—to a publisher, it is no matter to the purchaser whether the man drew it himself or got some friend to draw it for him. Provided the map is honestly the seller's property, and is well executed, that is all that is to the purpose. On the other hand, if a schoolmaster sets a boy to draw a map, by way of practice, in order that he may *learn* to be a good draughtsman, then, if the boy should get a schoolfellow to do it for him, and should show it up as his own, he would be reproved and punished. For the task was set him, not for the sake of the *map*, (which the master could have drawn better for himself,) but as an exercise for the improvement of the learner.

Now you cannot doubt that this latter case answers to ours in reference to our Divine Master, and that, as "no man can be profitable unto God," and He cannot stand in need of our services, it must be a mere groundless fancy to think that another person can perform our duty in our stead, and that his good works — real or supposed — can be imputed to us, and considered as done by ourselves.

A like illustration from the case of a school will serve to explain another point also, on which some persons have fallen into perplexity or mistake, — that of the *rewards* promised in Scripture, and the *merit* which some suppose good works to possess in God's sight.

Suppose, for instance, some rich and liberal man should found a school for the children of his poor neighbors; and suppose that, besides building a school-house, and providing teachers and school-books, he should also propose *prizes* for such of the scholars as should behave well, and make good proficiency in their learning. Every one would understand that the children and their parents ought to be very grateful to such a patron for his kind bounty. And the children would easily be made to understand that they ought to show their thankfulness by taking pains to profit by the advantages afforded them. They would readily understand that any of them who should behave ill, or refuse to learn, would be expelled; and that those who exerted themselves would obtain the prizes. And when it was said that the prizes were to be the *reward* of good behavior, no one would be so stupid as to think that those who gained them could claim them as something *earned* by themselves as a matter of right, and for which they owed no thanks to any one. All would understand that the *proposing* of the prizes was from the free bounty of the kind patron; and that the proficiency in learning of the children thus rewarded was no benefit to *him*, but only to them; and that it was entirely for *their* sakes that they were encouraged to take pains in learning.

But they would fully calculate on receiving the promised rewards in case of good conduct, though not as what they had originally any claim to, but *because* it had been *promised*. For, though the *offer* of the prizes came from the patron's free bounty, the *fulfilment* of a promise once made is a matter of justice.

§ 4. — *Righteousness of God.*

And, accordingly, we read that "God is not *unrighteous* [unjust] to forget our work and labor of love": not that He was originally bound in justice to reward any good works of ours, or that they can be a benefit to Him; but because He has graciously *promised* to be a "rewarder of them that diligently seek Him." The *offer* of a reward to any of his creatures is a free *gift* of his bounty; but we may trust to his *justice* to make good what He has said.

If you could imagine the patron of a school, such as we have been describing, to have supplied to the children not only a school-room, and teachers and books, but also the eyes with which they read the books, and the ears with which they hear what is said to them, and the brain by which they understand it, then the case would answer more closely to that of ourselves in reference to our Maker, "in whom we live and move and have our being." For He has supplied to us all our powers of mind and body, and He requires us, as He certainly has a full right to do, to employ these in leading a Christian life and devoting ourselves to his service. And He has held out to us the promise of the "*prize* of our high calling," — the "crown of glory," which the Lord, the *righteous* Judge, will give, at that day, to all them that *love* his appearing. To this we could have no natural claim; and though we may fully rely on his justice for the fulfilment of his promises, all that we can receive from Him is not the less a free and bountiful gift, since the promises themselves proceed from his bounty alone.

§ 5. — *Good Conduct has no natural Claim to Reward.*

Some, however, are apt to speak as if they thought that virtue is, in itself, naturally entitled to reward; and that, if any Being *could* lead a life (though none of us does so) of perfect, unsinning virtue, he might then justly claim [though *we* cannot] to be rewarded with immortal happiness.

But you may easily perceive, from considering what is the nature of *duty*, that such a notion is quite groundless. For it is evident that a *duty* must be something that is *due*, — a debt which we are *bound* to discharge. That is the very meaning of the word. And no one can be justly entitled to reward for merely paying his debts. If a man *fail* to pay what he was bound to pay, he is liable to punishment. If he does pay his debts, he is exempt from punishment; and that is all he can claim.

Reward is what a man is justly entitled to, only for doing something *beyond* what he was bound to, — something which he could not have been liable to punishment for not doing. For instance, if a man devotes his own private property, and time, and labor, to the effecting of some great public benefit, when he was not required to do so, the nation will think such a man worthy of being rewarded by some public honors bestowed on him. And when any one bountifully relieves, out of his own private purse, his distressed neighbors who had no claim on him, this is a *merit* as regards *them;* and he is justly entitled to their gratitude, and to any services they may be able to do him in return.

But the Most High has evidently a just claim to the obedience of his creatures; and all that they can do in the keeping of his commandments can have no claim of merit in his sight, being only the payment of a debt due to Him.

And, accordingly, our Lord tells his disciples that when they have "done all things that He has commanded them, they are to say, We are unprofitable servants: we have done that which it was our duty to do." And thus also the Apostle Paul speaks of "death being the *wages* of sin, but eternal life the *gift* of God through Jesus Christ."

§ 6. — *Reward and Punishment when due.*

Some persons, however, are accustomed to speak of the rewarding of virtue and the punishment of vice, as if the two naturally went together. But they may perceive, on reflection, that this is not at all the true state of the case. For no man is *punishable* for omitting to do something which he was *not bound* to do. And for doing anything that he *was* bound to do — such as paying a debt — he has no natural claim to reward, only to exemption from punishment. If, indeed, a reward has been *promised* him for doing his duty, he may look for that reward on the ground of the promise made, and on that ground alone. But the merit which claims reward, as in itself rightly due, must be for some things *beyond* what a person was *bound* to do.

And, accordingly, those Churches which teach that the supposed merits of saints may be transferred from them to us, always represent these merits as consisting in what are called works of "supererogation"; that is, something beyond their duty, over and above that which was required of them. But such a notion is utterly groundless, and contrary both to Scripture and Reason. For Scripture teaches that we are "to love the Lord our God with *all* our heart, and soul, and strength." And Reason teaches that nothing we can do that is acceptable to Him can be more than his just due. There may, indeed, be something which, from peculiar circumstances, is a duty to one man and not to another. And thus one man may go beyond what is required of some *other* men; but no one can go beyond his *own* duty.

It is plain, therefore, that no human virtue can have merit in God's sight, or any natural claim to reward, independently of express promise. In reference to your fellow-*men*, indeed, you may have merit, and may justly deserve from them gratitude and reward, for having done them some service that is in itself *valuable to them*, and which is also beyond what they had any right to require. But it is plain that nothing of this kind can be the case in reference to our Maker.

And as for Man's attaining heavenly happiness by the performance of good works, even in unsinning perfection, no such thought can enter the mind of any one who has any just notions either of the nature of Virtue, or of his Religion. For Reason teaches us that the idea of a man's raising himself to immortal life, is as absurd as that of a brute's exalting itself into a man; and that the performance of duty cannot (as has been just said) entitle us, of itself, and independently of express promise, even to any reward at all. And the Christian Scriptures teach us that "by grace [*i. e.* favor] we are saved; and that not of ourselves: it is the gift of God."

NOTE.—If any one should ask you, "Since the Most High can have no need of any one's services, or, again, of any one's *sufferings*, how can it be that the sufferings and death of Christ could procure Man's salvation, and that He should have suffered in our stead?" If any one should ask this question, you should answer that you *do not know;* since it is a point on which Scripture gives us no explanation; and that you cannot clear up either that or any other part of the *one* great mysterious difficulty (of which this is a branch), the existence of *evil* in the universe. We know, as a fact, from the plain declarations of Scripture, that "Christ died, the just for the unjust," and that "by his stripes we are healed"; and we must suppose that if it had been possible for us to understand, and needful for us to know, the reasons *why* this was necessary, and *how* the death of Christ avails us, the Scriptures would have told us. But they do not. They merely tell us the fact. And if, again, Scripture had plainly declared that it is possible to be virtuous by proxy, and that another person's good works would be accepted by the Most High as ours, then we should have been bound to believe this, though unable to explain it. But as it is, the Scriptures tell us no such thing. We are left on this point to the light of Reason; and nothing can be more contrary to Reason, than that one man's virtue should be accounted another's,—that a barren branch of the vine should be reckoned fruitful, on account of the fruitfulness of another branch.

It is for us to take Scripture as we find it; not presuming to add on doctrines of our own devising, or attempting to explain mysteries

5

which Revelation has left unexplained. It is for us to seek to know as much, and to be content to know *only* as much, of heavenly things as Scripture tells us; and to remain willingly ignorant of what our all-wise Master does not think fit to teach us. According to the wise saying of Scaliger, —

> "Nescire velle quæ Magister optimus
> Docere non vult, erudita inscitia est."

> "Be willing and contented not to know
> What our Great Teacher thinks not fit to show:
> This is Man's truest wisdom here below."

LESSON VII.

PROPER OFFICE OF CONSCIENCE.

§ 1. — *Foundation of our Moral Notions.*

You may have seen, then, that (1.) the law of the land is not to be made the standard of moral right and wrong; both because it cannot enforce *all* duties, or prohibit everything that is wrong; and also because it is only concerned with outward *acts*, and cannot control *motives;* though it is on these that the whole moral character of any action depends.

(2.) You have seen that Conscience [or the moral faculty] is a part of the human constitution; since without such a faculty it would have been totally impossible to form the notion of such a thing as *duty*, or such a thing as *sin;* though we might have submitted to the divine commands as a matter of prudence.

(3.) You have seen that Conscience being (like the rest of our faculties) liable to corruption, capable of improvement, and requiring sometimes to be corrected and sometimes to be fortified; hence, God has been pleased to afford us in the Scriptures much important moral instruction, both by precept and examples, and also the promise of divine aid in the performance of duty, and, lastly, the promises and warnings relating to the Day of Judgment.

And (4.) it was pointed out, that, since the Most High can have no need of our services, it is plain that good works are required, not as a benefit to Him, but as an exercise to *us*, in order to our own moral improvement; and can have no merit in his sight, nor can claim reward from Him, except on the ground of his free promises.

In order, then, to form a virtuous character, two things are requisite: — (1.) that we should steadily act on principle, — conforming all our conduct to the dictates of Conscience, and keeping all our faculties and tendencies under its control; and (2.) that we should regulate our Conscience itself; guarding against the errors to which it is liable, and taking care, while acting on *principle*, to keep *that* a *right* principle.

In short, we must (according to the illustration in Lesson IV.) proceed as a man of sense does in the disposal of his *time*. He continually consults his clock or watch, and regulates all his occupations by that; taking care, however, to regulate his watch also, when opportunity offers, by the sun-dial.

§ 2. — *Two Things requisite for Virtuous Conduct.*

Both of the two things we have mentioned are equally indispensable. For a man who should have the most perfect knowledge of his duty, and the most correct moral judgment on every point, but whose passions should prevail over his reason, and cause him to act against his own judgment, would be only tormented by his conscience, and not guided by it. And he would be in the condition of some nation whose laws were wise and good, and its rulers able and upright men; but in which the subjects were in rebellion against their rulers, and set the laws at defiance.

On the other hand, a man acting constantly according to the dictates of conscience, but of a mistaken conscience, and proceeding on wrong principles, would be in the condition of a nation in which the rulers were strictly obeyed, and the laws rigidly enforced, but whose laws were absurd, and the rulers unwise or unjust. And it is plain that neither of these nations would be in a prosperous condition.

Conscience is, as we have said, a mere tormenter to one who does not act according to it. And the more conscientious any one is, and the clearer and juster his moral judgments, and the better he is acquainted with God's commandments, the more he will suffer the misery of self-reproach, if he is leading a life of sin. And, accordingly, the Apostle Paul gives a vivid and touching description of a man in this condition; of one, that is, who knows the divine will, and in his judgment approves of what is right, but who is enslaved to ["sold under"] his passions, and acts against his conscience. "I delight in the law of God," — he represents such a man as saying, — "after the inward man; but I see another law in my members, warring against the law of my mind, and bringing me into captivity to the law of sin, which is in my members. O wretched man that I am! who shall deliver me from the body of this death?" Rom. vii. 22–24.

It is plain that the same sort of description would apply to any one who is acting contrary to his judgment of what is right; whether his knowledge be derived from a divine revelation, or from the light of nature.

5 *

And, accordingly, several of the ancient heathen writers give nearly the same picture of a man wanting in self-control, and sinning against his own better judgment. In particular, the most celebrated and the soundest of the ancient moralists, Aristotle,* has a passage agreeing in substance, and almost in words, with what we find in the Apostle Paul, describing the wretched state of the man in whose mind there is, he says, a continual inward "civil war" between his conscience and the passions that enslave him.

§ 3.—*Man under the Law and under the Gospel.*

Of course, the Apostle, though using the first person, is not describing his own actual condition, or that of those he was writing to, but that of one who has a knowledge of what is right, but wants strength of purpose to act on that knowledge. That he is not speaking of himself individually — nor indeed of the Roman Christians at that time — is plain, from his going on to say immediately after,† "There is therefore now no condemnation to them which are in Christ Jesus, who walk not after the flesh, but after the Spirit. For the law of the Spirit of life in Christ Jesus hath made me free from the law of sin and death." (chap. viii. 1, 2.)

And, moreover, he had just before been saying to the

---

* See Note at the end of this Lesson.

† You are to remember that the divisions into chapters and verses were not the work of the sacred writers, but were made long after their time, for the sake of reference.

It happens, unluckily, that the break between the 7th and 8th chapters comes in the midst of an argument, and almost in the middle of a sentence.

Romans (chap. vi.), "God be thanked, that ye *were* the servants of sin, but ye have obeyed from the heart that form of doctrine which was delivered to you. Being then made free from sin, ye became the servants of righteousness." (v. 17, 18.)

And, in the First Epistle to the Corinthians, he describes himself as "keeping under his body, and bringing it into subjection"; which is a complete contrast to the state of a man "*sold* [as a slave] under sin," and "brought into *captivity* to the law of sin."

But he is describing (in Rom. vii.), first, the condition of a person situated as the Gentiles had been, who had no revelation of God's laws, and were left to the imperfect guidance of mere natural conscience. "I was alive," says he, (that is, had not incurred — or, at least, was not aware of having incurred — the penalty of death,) "without the law, once."

Now Paul himself, we know, was born and educated a Jew, and never had been "without the law"; but he is speaking (though in the first person, which is a very common mode of expression, not only with Paul, but in our common conversation) of a *Gentile*, in ignorance of the law. And then he proceeds to point out how the "coming in of the law" — that is, the knowledge of it — caused "sin to enter in" (Rom. vii. 9); that is, caused that to be — and to be perceived to be — sin, which had not been so before.

And then he goes on to describe the condition of a person having a knowledge of the divine will, but wanting self-control, and "sold under sin." And, lastly, he describes (ch. viii.) the situation of those on whom the Gospel has bestowed the inestimable gift of divine grace, not only to show them what is right, but to strengthen them for the performance of it, and thus to make them "*free* from the law of sin."

§ 4.—*Depraving of Conscience.*

Many persons, however, are apt to seek an escape from the reproaches of conscience by bringing their conscience to conform to their conduct. They try to satisfy themselves that they are right in following their own wrong inclinations and prejudices, and that their faults are not faults, or not faults in *them;* or, at least, that they are quite trifling and excusable faults. Many a man takes more pains to justify his faults than it would cost him, with God's help, to cure them.

Those who labor thus to blind their own judgment, and to satisfy their conscience by perverting it, will generally succeed, sooner or later, in this self-deceit. And then they rejoice in the thought that they are free from self-reproach, and are acting agreeably to the dictates of conscience, when perhaps the truth is, that they are not doing so, *because* they think it right; but, on the contrary, have brought themselves to think it right, because they were inclined to do it. It is not that they omit such and such duties from being originally ignorant that they *are* duties; but they have persuaded themselves that they are not duties, because their inclination is against them.

It is a proverbial remark, and a just one, that "a liar will sometimes repeat the same falsehood so often, that at last he will come to believe it himself." He did not originally say it because he believed it; but, by saying it, has brought himself to believe it. The like takes place with many other sins besides lying. And a man will often succeed in thus convincing, not only himself, but others, of his "sincerity." When they are satisfied that he believes what he says, and thinks it right to act as he does, they will often take this as at least some excuse or palliation, even when they think him in the wrong. And so it is, if a man speaks and acts as he does, properly in *consequence* of his judging it to be right; but if it be, that, in consequence of his so acting, he has at length brought himself to judge it right, this kind of "sincerity" is the last stage of moral corruption. For this is not taking conscience for one's guide, but making one's self the guide of conscience.

And, thus, a person who begins by committing the one of those two errors above mentioned will end by committing the other. If you begin by neglecting the warnings of conscience, and acting against your own moral judgment, that judgment will in time become depraved, and you will act on wrong *principles*. For when any country (according to the illustration above given) has long permitted rebellious subjects to disobey the legitimate governors, and transgress the laws, it is likely that in time those rebels will themselves become the real governors, and will make such laws as they please.

Even the teaching of Scripture, which was designed for our guidance and correction, will not serve that purpose, to any one who reads it with a biassed mind, and searches in it for a confirmation of his own opinions and a justification of his own conduct. His reading will be like a man's looking at objects through a colored glass, which shows them not as they really are, but tinted with the hue of the glass. And such a person is not really following Scripture, but making Scripture follow his prejudices.

§ 5. — *Misapplying of Scripture.*

The Apostle Paul, for instance, before his conversion, " verily thought that he ought to do many things " against Christianity. Yet he was familiar with the Old Testament Scriptures; those Scriptures from which he himself afterwards " proved that Jesus is the Christ." But he had been in the state of mind which he afterwards describes as that of many of his countrymen, who, he says, in reading the books of Moses and the Prophets, have a " veil on their hearts."

And, again, you may find persons convinced that they are bound to receive all the doctrines and decrees of their Church, even when plainly contrary to the written word of God, because our Lord said — in speaking of the case of a *dispute between two private individuals* — that, if any one " refuse to hear the church," he is to be regarded " as a heathen man."

So, also, (to refer to the passage of Scripture above mentioned,) men, leading a profligate life, and given up to the practice of vices which their moral judgment condemns, may flatter themselves that they are just in the condition of the Apostle Paul, and as safe as he was; because they will insist on it that he was speaking of *himself* individually in his actual state, when he said, " I am carnal, sold under sin," etc.

Again, the words of the Prophet Isaiah (lxiv. 6), " All our righteousness is as filthy rags," may be interpreted, taken by themselves, to signify that our practice of righteousness is not all acceptable to God. For the sacred writers — or indeed any writer — may be made to say anything by thus picking out a sentence, or half-sentence, here and there. But if you look to the whole of the passage, you will see that the prophet is not speaking of persons who had been obedient to God's laws, but of those who had been most emphatically *un*righteous. "Behold," says he, "thou art wroth, for *we have sinned.* . . . . We are all as an unclean thing, and all our righteousness is as filthy rags; and we all do fade as a leaf, *and our iniquities like the wind have taken us away*, and there is none that calleth on thy name." His expression is only another way of saying, "We are quite *destitute* of righteousness," even as the same prophet (ch. i.) described a like condition by saying, "Thy silver is become dross."

There are many other parts of the Bible that may be thus perversely interpreted, so as to sanction what is absurd or wrong. And thus may men, as the Apostle Peter warns us, "wrest the Scriptures to their own destruction." Such students of Scripture resemble (to recur to a former illustration) a man who should pretend to regulate his clocks and watches by the sun-dial, and should go to it in the night with a *candle*, and thus throw the shadow whichever way he would.

NOTE. — Aristotle, in the subjoined extract from his *Ethics*, agrees, as you will see, in substance, and almost in words, with what Paul says in Rom. vii. Many other passages to the same effect will be found in several of the ancient writers. But there are some persons so ignorant of what the heathen authors have said, and so unconscious of their own ignorance, as to imagine that no one not enlightened by the Gospel could have used such expressions as those of Paul. The passage here given, from Aristotle, will serve as a specimen to show how greatly they are in error.

And the error is a dangerous one; because those who teach that the Apostle is speaking of himself in his present state, nullify all the moral instruction they may give elsewhere. All their descriptions of Christian virtue will be regarded as something very beautiful in theory, but quite impossible to be realized in practice. For no one will ever presume to think of becoming a better man than the Apostle Paul. And any one who is living a life of gross vice, while acknowledging and admiring the excellence of a virtuous life, and who is, in practice, "brought into captivity to the law of sin in his members," will consider all attempts at reformation as hopeless, and will think himself in a safe state, as being in the very same state with a most eminent Apostle. There is, moreover, a danger of this misinterpretation leading to infidelity, or at least to a disparagement of Paul's authority. For if you compare the sixth chapter of this epistle, and also the eighth, with the seventh, you will see, that, supposing him to have been speaking of himself throughout, he is made, according to the plain sense of his words, to fall into the most gross and absurd self-contradiction; such as no inspired writer, nor even any man of good sense, could have been guilty of.

Extract from Aristotle's Ethics, B. ix. c. 4.

"Some define 'a friend' one who *keeps company* with you, and has the *same preferences, and sympathizes* with your sorrows and joys, etc., etc.

"Now all these things exist in the virtuous man, in reference to himself. . . . . Such a one *agrees* in sentiments with himself, and seeks the same objects in *every part* of his mind. And he wishes for and acts for what is *good* for *himself*, and what appears so; namely, for the *rational* portion of himself, which is what is most properly each man's self. . . . . He likes his own *company;* for the recollection of his past actions is agreeable, and he has good hopes for the future. And he, above all others, *sympathizes* with himself in pains and pleasures. For the same things are painful and agreeable to him *throughout his whole* mind, and not one thing to one portion of him and another to another; for he is, so to speak, exempt from regrets and changes of mind. . . . . But nothing of this kind is found in worthless characters. For they are at *variance* with themselves, and have a *craving* for one thing and a *deliberate will* for a different one, as is the case with those destitute of self-command: for they prefer to that which they themselves think *good for them*, pleasures which are *hurtful* for them. Some, again, through cowardice or indolence, draw back from such actions as they themselves know to be best for them. And those who have committed many dreadful deeds, and are hated on account of their wickedness, fly from life and make away with themselves.

"Bad men, again, seek for some persons to keep them company, and fly from themselves. For when left to themselves, they remember many things that are odious, and look forward to such conduct in future; but in company with others, they are enabled to forget themselves. And having in them nothing amiable, they have not towards themselves any of the feelings of a friend. They do not *sympathize* with their own pleasures and pains; for their mind is in a state of discord, and one portion of it is, on account of its evil nature, *pained* at abstaining from certain things, while another portion is *gratified* by such abstinence; and one part draws one way and another the opposite, as if pulling the man asunder, ... for bad men abound in regrets.

" A bad man, then, seems not to have the feelings of a friend, even towards himself, from having nothing in him worthy of friendship.

"Now if such a state be an excessively miserable one, we ought earnestly to strive to avoid wickedness, and endeavor to become virtuous. For so will a man become a friend to himself, and obtain the friendship of others."

LESSON VIII.

REGULATION OF CONSCIENCE.

§ 1.— *Conscience never to be opposed.*

You have seen that, as man's conscience is not infallible, you must not at once conclude that you are right when you are acting according to the dictates of conscience. And yet you may be sure that you are wrong if you are acting *against* it. For if you do what you believe to be wrong, even though you may be mistaken in thinking so, and it may be in reality right, still you yourself will be wrong.

And this is what the Apostle Paul means when he says, "Happy is he that condemneth not himself in that thing which he alloweth," Rom. xiv. 22; and, "Whatsoever is not of faith, is sin"; that is, whatsoever is not done with a full *conviction* [faith] that it is allowable, is, to him, sinful; and he condemns himself in doing it.

And on this principle he alludes (in 1 Cor. x.) to the case of some of the "weaker brethren" [the less intelligent] among the early Christian converts, who thought that the flesh of animals which had been offered in sacrifice to idols was unclean, and not to be eaten. He does not at all himself partake of this scruple; considering it a matter of no consequence, in a religious or moral point of view, what kind of food a man eats. But he teaches that those who do feel such a scruple would be wrong in eating that flesh, and "their conscience being weak is defiled; for to him who thinketh it unclean, to him it is unclean." And he teaches also that it would be wrong for any one to induce others to do what *they* think sinful, though it be something that is not sinful to one who does not think it so.

In such a case as this, both parties are acting rightly, if the one eats what he is convinced is allowable, and the other abstains from what he thinks is not allowable; provided always that neither of them uncharitably censures or derides his neighbor. "Let not him that eateth," says Paul, "despise him that eateth not; and let not him that eateth not, judge him that eateth." And, "Let every man be fully persuaded in his own mind." Rom. xiv. 5.

§ 2.—*A Wrong Principle makes it impossible to act rightly.*

But there are some cases in which a man who has been brought up in some wrong system, or who in any way has taken up some false principle, may hold himself bound in duty to do what is in itself wrong. And in such a case he cannot but go wrong, whichever course he may take, till his moral judgment has been set right.

For instance, if a jury have formed a false opinion as to some cause tried before them, either from their having been biassed by their feelings and prejudices, or from not having listened with sufficient attention to the witnesses and the arguments on both sides, it is impossible for them, while in this state of mind, to give a right verdict. For a verdict according to the wrong opinion they have formed would, of course, be a wrong one; and yet no one would say that, while they do hold that opinion, they would be right in giving a contrary verdict.

So the Apostle Paul himself "verily thought that he ought" to persecute the Christian Church; and in doing so, he acknowledges that he was guilty of a grievous sin. He had not studied the ancient prophecies with sufficient care, and candor, and humility, to perceive from them, in conjunction with the rest of the evidence, that Jesus was the true Christ, and not, as his enemies maintained, an impious pretender. But it is plain that, while Paul did hold this erroneous belief, it would not have been right for him to become a disciple of Jesus, whom he then regarded as a false prophet.

Again, the doctrine has been distinctly maintained (in a *Protestant* book, published a few years ago), that "the magistrate who restrains, coerces, and punishes those who oppose a true religion, and seek to propagate a false one, obeys the *will of God*, and is not a *persecutor*." Now suppose any magistrate to have embraced this doctrine, believing — as of course he must — his own religion to be true, and those opposed to it false, he will, of course, hold himself bound in duty to establish a system of what, in the ordinary sense of the word, is called "persecution"; though he may satisfy himself by not calling it by its real name. And if, through tenderness of feeling, he should spare any whom he accounts heretics, he will consider himself as disobeying God's will. Such a man, therefore, as long as he is in this state of mind, "not knowing what manner of spirit he is of," cannot possibly be right, whichever course he may take.

Any one, therefore, whose conscience has been in any way depraved, and who is proceeding on some wrong principle, cannot possibly act rightly, whether he act according to his conscience or against it, till he is cured of that defect in his moral judgment.

If, however, any one has *done his best* to form a right judgment, and acts accordingly, but has fallen into error through unavoidable ignorance, or weakness of understanding, we may hope that his all-seeing and merciful Judge will pardon this involuntary error. But as *no more* is required of us than to do our very utmost to avoid error, so no *less* is required, if we would stand acquitted before Him. And what mortal can know, with complete certainty, who has, or has not, done his utmost? You should never therefore allow yourself to pronounce with full confidence, that your neighbor has *not* done this, or that *you* yourself have.

§ 3. — *Careful Study needed for Good Conduct.*

You can see plainly, therefore, that one who is sincerely anxious to lead a virtuous life has need of diligent study and care, to learn what his duty is in each case, as well as of firm resolution in keeping steadily to the course his conscience points out. You must not be satisfied with doing what you think right, — that is, with thinking that to be right what you do, — unless you have also taken pains to form a right judgment. Nor must you be satisfied with opening the Bible at random, and taking for your direction any passage that happens to meet your eye; or again, looking out for some passage that may be so interpreted as to justify the course you are inclined to take. And you should not listen to any one who would persuade you that no careful study is needed in order to learn and practise your duty; and that any such Lessons as these now before you may be thrown aside as useless; and that if you have but a right faith, and pray for divine guidance, your religion will at once make you a good man, without any pains or watchfulness as to your moral character being required.

The Scriptures themselves, if you will listen to them, will teach you quite otherwise. Our Lord bids his disciples "*watch* and pray, lest ye enter into temptation." We must *pray* as if *nothing* depended on ourselves; and we must *watch* as if *everything* depended on ourselves. And He and his apostles exhort us to "strive," to "run," to "give all diligence" in our Christian course, and to "work out our own salvation with fear and trembling," that is, with anxious care, on the very ground that it is "God that worketh in us, both to will and to do of his good pleasure."

§ 4. — *Divine Blessing bestowed on Diligent Care.*

And it is thus that every man of common sense proceeds in all the concerns of ordinary life, when he is thoroughly in earnest. A gardener, for instance, knows very well that the fertility of the earth, and the life of all his plants, are God's gift; and that, without the rain and sunshine from heaven, his trees would bear no fruit. But he does not satisfy himself with merely praying for favorable seasons, and then leaving his garden to the care of Providence. He digs and manures the ground; and he not only takes care of the *roots* of his fruit-trees, but also endeavors to protect the blossoms from blighting winds and noxious insects. And even so we are bound, not only to take care about a right *faith*, which is the *root* of Christian virtue, but also to bestow vigilant care on the moral character itself.

So also, if any one is endeavoring to learn some art or trade by which to maintain himself, though he will, if he be a pious man, beg the divine blessing on his exertions, he will not omit those exertions. He knows, indeed, that his hands, and eyes, and ears, and understanding, are all divine gifts; but he knows also that he must diligently and carefully *exercise* all the faculties that have been bestowed upon him, and lose no opportunity of gaining useful instruction in his business. Now, to improve one's moral character is the business of *every* man. And as no one can think this a matter of less importance than any of the various arts of life, so we have no reason to expect that, in this great concern, God will bestow that blessing on the negligent which, in everything else, He reserves for the diligent.

LESSON IX.

DIFFICULTIES OF MORAL DISCIPLINE.

§ 1.— *Moral Improvement a Laborious Task.*

It is important to observe, that one who earnestly sets himself to the task of moral improvement, must not expect to obtain at once the comfort of an easy and quiet conscience. On the contrary, he will sometimes find that, as he proceeds in his task, his conscience will even give him increased uneasiness. But this should not discourage him, if the case be that the pain felt is not from increased sinfulness, but from increased consciousness of it; not from his conduct having become worse, but from his moral judgment being more enlightened, and his perception of what is wrong, and his abhorrence of it, stronger than before.

When a strong light is admitted into a room which had been left in a slovenly state, and partially darkened, the stains on the walls, and the dirt on the floor, which had escaped notice in a dim light, will now strike the eye of every one. This will be likely first to shock and disgust the occupiers of the room, and next to set them upon cleaning it. Even so, a person who has been laboring to purify and to raise his moral character, and to advance in the knowledge and practice of virtue, will often perceive more and more of blemishes which he had before overlooked. He will perhaps find in himself faults which he had thought himself free from; and he will reproach himself for having omitted duties which had not formerly occurred to him as duties. But he must consider the increased pain caused by a more enlightened conscience as a step towards improvement, and as something that ought rather to encourage than to dishearten any one who is really bent on amending his life.

§ 2. — *No direct Pleasure from Conformity to Conscience.*

But after all, (as was remarked above,) the most enlightened conscience, and the most exact compliance with its dictates, will never of itself afford us directly any positive pleasure, though it will save us from a vast amount of pain. For it is the office of conscience to point out what is our duty; that is, what is *due*, — what we are bound to do, as a man is, to pay his debts. Now no one can claim reward or praise for paying a *debt*, — only, exemption from punishment. And when any one is considered as deserving from his fellow-men some reward, this is always for doing something *beyond* what they had a right to *require* of him, — something which they could not have justly punished him for *omitting* to do. And from our Maker, therefore, no creature can claim praise or reward, except on the general ground (as was pointed out in Lesson V.) of his free and bountiful *promise*.

In this respect, then, the moral faculty [or "moral sense," or "conscience," or "sense of justice"] differs from our other faculties, sentiments, and propensities.

For each of these, when strong, not only gives pain if its exercise is impeded, but affords positive pleasure when its action is freely called forth. For instance, a *benevolent* man not only is pained by the sight of suffering which he cannot relieve, but feels *delight* in doing good, and is positively pleased with the view of another's gratification. So again, one in whom the sentiment of attachment to friends is strong, not only is distressed at the absence or loss of friends, but greatly enjoys their society; and one in whom the love of approbation is strong, is not only pained by censure or contempt, but also highly gratified by praise. Any one, again, in whose character there is a great deal of firmness (the propensity of which the faulty excess is blind obstinacy), is gratified by the very act of holding resolutely to his purpose, against solicitations, and threats, and difficulties of any kind. A great calculator delights in the work of calculation. One who possesses in a great degree the faculty which phrenologists call "constructiveness," will take pleasure either in building and in constructing machines, or in framing systems, devising plans, composing books, or, in short, in some way putting *things together*, so as to form a *whole*. And so it is with the rest of our faculties and propensities.

But the moral faculty — which some call conscientiousness — is an exception. When it is strong, it is capable of giving, if opposed, great pain; but, as has been above explained, no direct, positive pleasure, if complied with. It then merely says to us, "You are an unprofitable servant; you have but done that which it was your duty to do."

§ 3. — *Indirect Gratifications from the Discharge of Duty.*

But then God has been graciously pleased so to order things, that indirectly (though not directly) virtuous conduct does afford the very highest gratification. He has declared his own favor and approbation (as was remarked above) of those who seek earnestly to do his will; and this affords a high gratification of that *love of approbation* which is a part of the human character. Again, he has also enlisted our self-love in the same cause, by graciously promising to be "a *rewarder* of them that diligently seek Him." And *hope* is a portion of the human character which is capable of affording very great pleasure.

Moreover, though the discharge of duty, simply as duty, affords no positive pleasure, there are some duties which are in themselves agreeable. The sentiment of benevolence, for instance, when strong, affords in its exercise (as has been just said) much gratification: and the more we exercise ourselves in doing good, — which is a great part of our duty, — the more will the sentiment of benevolence be strengthened. Again, the sentiment or propensity (whichever it may be called) of firmness, which is a portion of man's nature, affords, when it exists strongly, a pleasure — and a very allowable pleasure — in the very act of standing firm against temptation, and surmounting difficulties in the performance of duty. And there are also several other natural feelings which may become sources of much gratification in the practice of duty, and which will thus indirectly make virtue conduce to the greatest happiness even in this life.

§ 4. — *Supremacy of Conscience.*

And it may be added, that, though conscience is not in itself a source of positive gratification, every kind of enjoyment is, in a certain sense, dependent on it; that is, the approval of conscience is, to a right-minded man, a necessary *condition* of every kind of gratification. He cannot find real, unmixed pleasure in anything that his sense of duty forbids, since anything which might be in itself agreeable would bring him more pain than pleasure if attended with self-reproach. For conscience (or the moral faculty) is to be regarded as a kind of *absolute sovereign*, to whom everything must be kept in subjection, and without whose permission nothing is to be done. All our mental powers, and inclinations, and sentiments, and actions, are to be thus under the supreme control of conscience, and to be exercised and indulged, or restrained, according to its dictates.

The Creator has not, indeed, implanted in the human mind anything that is, originally and in itself, evil. But, on the other hand, there is no part of our nature that does not become bad if not controlled and regulated by an enlightened conscience. Some of Man's dispositions indeed are of a more amiable character than others; such as gratitude, compassion, benevolence, attachment to our friends, and love for our children. But even these are so far from being necessarily virtuous, that they become mischievous and wrong whenever they are not under the control of conscience guided by right reason. For instance, if your attachment to a friend, or your gratitude for services received from him, should lead you to give a wrong decision in his favor, and to do injustice to others, (which you may often be strongly tempted to,) this would be a manifest violation of duty; and so it would be, if your compassion for some one in distress should lead you to give him what is not your own; that is, what you owe to a tradesman. The tradesman may perhaps be less in *want* of the money than the other, or than you yourself; but he has a *right* to it, which you have not.

Or again, pity for a criminal might tempt you to pardon and let loose on society a villain who might do unspeakable mischief. Or, on the other hand, indignation against injustice and cruelty, which no one would consider a feeling bad in itself, may be carried to such a faulty excess as to become itself unjust and cruel. The desire of knowledge, again, and of wisdom, no one would call bad in itself; and yet it was this that tempted our first parents in Paradise to disobey the divine command.

§ 5. — *Amiable Feelings to be under Control.*

Again, a man's fondness for his children may tempt him to spoil them by foolish indulgence, or to do unjustifiable acts for the sake of enriching them. And even piety — that is, the disposition to venerate a superior Being — is far from being anything good and virtuous, unless it be rightly directed. Indeed, the very first of the ten commandments is directed against the worship of false gods. And (as was before remarked, Lesson III.) great part of the worship paid by the ancient heathen to their gods consisted of acts the most abominable. And many of the heathen idolaters of the present day offer human sacrifices. Indeed, one may say pro-

7

fessing Christians have done nearly the same, when they have thought to do God service by burning heretics at what they call (*auto da fé*) an "act of faith." And such Christians may be considered as, in a certain sense, worshippers of a *false god;* since, though they use the name of the true God, they give a totally false representation of his nature.

Benevolence, again, when not under the control of reason and a sense of duty, causes some people to do much more harm than good, by giving indiscriminate relief to the idle and worthless, and thus drawing men off from honest industry, and encouraging beggary.

Over all our feelings, therefore, and all our conduct, a conscientious sense of duty, under the guidance of sound judgment, must be allowed to reign supreme.

LESSON X.

CULTIVATION OF RIGHT FEELINGS.

§ 1. — *Feelings not under the direct Control of the Will.*

WHEN you are told, that not only your actions, but your sentiments, inclinations, and feelings of every kind, ought to be under the control of conscience, it may, perhaps, occur to you, that our *actions* only are directly subject to the Will, and that *wishes* and *feelings* of all kinds are involuntary. It may be in your power, for instance, to do another person a service if you will; but it is out of your power to make yourself, by an act of the will, to feel affection for him. So, also, a man may be induced, by the offer of wages or otherwise, to undergo hard labor, and wounds, and cold, and heat, and other hardships; but it would be absurd to speak of hiring him to *feel* no fatigue, or cold, or pain. He may resolve to submit to abstain from food; but to resolve not to be hungry or thirsty would be absurd. And so it is with the rest of our feelings as compared with our actions.

There is something of the same kind in the different functions of the different parts of the bodily frame. Some of them depend directly on the will, and others nct. For instance, a man can open or shut his eyes, or move his limbs as he will; but the circulation of the blood, the process of digestion, and the secretions of the liver and other glands, are not under the control of the will. You may tell a man to walk, or run, or sit down; but to tell him to alter the pulsations of his heart, or the digestion of his food, would be as idle as to bid him "add a cubit to his stature."

But although many of the actions of the bodily frame are not under the control of the will *directly*, they are so, to a certain degree, indirectly. Though it would be in vain for a man to will that the circulation of his blood should be raised or lowered, he can take some medicine that will have such an effect. It is not in your power to feel hot or cold at pleasure; but you may be able to warm yourself by exercise, or by coming to a fire. So, also, merely to have a will to sleep would have no effect; but it may depend on your will to swallow an opiate which will cause sleep; and so in other cases.

§ 2. — *Feelings under the Control of the Will indirectly.*

Now something corresponding to this takes place with respect to all our sentiments, inclinations, and feelings of every kind. They are under the control of the will indirectly, though not directly. A skilful orator, if he wishes to excite in his hearers some feeling — suppose pity — does not think to effect this by telling them to feel pity; because, even if they were desirous to comply with all his directions, it does not depend on their will; but he puts before them a vivid description of sufferings undergone, and of every touching circumstance of the case, and dwells on these till the feeling of pity arises in their hearts, whether they will or no.

It is the same with indignation, admiration, or any other feeling. He acts, in short, the part of a physician, who does not *tell* his patients to digest their food better, or to quicken their circulation, etc.; but tells them to use such and such a diet, or medicine, which will aid their digestion or circulation.

Now a good man on many occasions has to act the part of an orator towards himself. If at any time he is conscious that he does not feel, or does not feel sufficiently, the love, or veneration, or gratitude, or whatever else it may be, which he is sensible he *ought* to feel, and which the case calls for, it would be in vain for him to say to himself, I *will* feel so and so; but he recalls to his mind, and dwells upon, all the circumstances that are likely to excite and to heighten such a feeling. He thinks over, for instance, all the services and kindnesses of a benefactor, and the great need he had for them, till, by dwelling on these, the feelings of gratitude and love arise in his heart.

So, also, if he wishes to *allay* in himself any emotion, — suppose that of resentment, — though it is not under the direct control of the will, he deliberately sets himself to reflect on all the softening circumstances of the case, such as the provocation the unoffending party may suppose himself to have received, his ignorance, or weakness, or perhaps disordered state of health; he endeavors to fancy himself in the other's place; and, above all, he meditates on the parable of the debtor, who, after having been himself forgiven, exacted payment with rigid severity from his fellow-servant.

And in all this he is proceeding just as we do with respect to those bodily functions before alluded to. We cannot, by a direct exertion of will, quicken or retard the pulse; but we can, by an act of the will, swallow a medicine that shall produce that effect. And this is the only possible way in which you can proceed, either with yourself or with another, in what relates to the feelings.

§ 3. — *How to influence one's Feelings.*

But people often deceive themselves (though it may seem strange that they should), by imagining that they feel what they do not. They mistake for the *feeling* of compassion, or gratitude, or veneration, etc., the *conviction* of their understanding that the case is one which calls for such a feeling. And they say, perhaps, without the least intention to deceive, that they are "very glad" of this, and "very sorry" for that, without really feeling the gladness or the sorrow, but only a belief that they ought to be glad or to be sorry.

But those two things — the conviction of the understanding, and the actual feeling — are as different from each other, as a blind man's full belief that grass is green, and coals black, is from the actual perception of those colors by the eye.

It is plain, therefore, that you must proceed differently in regulating your actions and your feelings. In bringing your *conduct* into subjection to conscience, you must have a resolute will to *do* what conscience requires; but in bringing your sentiments and *inclinations* into this subjection, a mere will to do so is not sufficient; you must, with prayer for divine assistance, bring before your thoughts, and dwell upon, all the circumstances that may tend to excite or to allay, as the case may be, the feelings which you ought to cherish or to repress.

And it is thus that the sacred writers proceed. "Thou shalt love," says Moses, "the Lord thy God, with all thy heart," etc.; for "*consider how great things* He hath done for thee." And thus also do the Apostles teach us the duty of love to our Saviour: "For when we were yet without strength, in due time Christ died for the ungodly; for scarcely for a righteous man will one die, yet peradventure for a good man some would even dare to die. But God commended his love towards us, in that, while we were yet sinners, Christ died for the ungodly." (Romans v. 6, 7, 8.) "We love Him," says John, "because He first loved us": and there are many other passages to the same effect.

§ 4. — *Control of Feelings gradual.*

You will perceive, then, that the work of bringing about any change in your sentiments and inclinations is one of some difficulty, and only to be effected gradually. On the other hand, a man who is resolutely bent on *acting* differently from what he had done before, may do so immediately. "Let him that stole," says the Apostle, "steal no more"; but rather "let him labor, working with his hands the thing that is good, that he may have to give to him that needeth." Now any one who was fully determined to obey this admonition, and reform his life, would at once renounce theft, and betake himself to honest industry. But he would find that his former habits of idleness and dishonesty had left in him evil dispositions and wrong wishes, which could not be at once subdued. He would indeed comply at once with the commandment not to *steal*, but not with that which forbids us to *covet*. For his former thievish practices would cause him to feel for a time strongly tempted to commit acts which a man who had always lived honestly would not so much as think of. And steady industry will at first be much more irksome to such a man than to one who has been always used to it, and who perhaps would even be uneasy without it.

Again, any one who had been habitually intemperate, though he might firmly resolve — and, through divine grace, keep steadily to his resolution — to reform his life at once, yet would, for a time, suffer much pain from the craving after his accustomed indulgences; which craving would never be felt at all by one who had been always of sober habits. And so in other cases.

But any one who is earnestly striving to reform or to improve his character, may be encouraged by the thought that the chief difficulty is in the first step, and that his path will become smoother and easier the longer he treads in it. He must not be discouraged at finding bad thoughts and wishes force themselves occasionally into his mind, provided he does not cherish, and indulge, and retain them there, but strives to get rid of them. His evil propensities will gradually become weaker by being continually checked and restrained, on a right principle.

For it is on a *right principle* (as will be explained presently) that he must act, if he would acquire a virtuous *habit;* and he will more and more acquire a liking for many good actions which at first were distasteful to him.

The process of reforming the corrupt nature of Man, by establishing a Christian moral principle, may be compared to that of *grafting* a wilding tree — such as a crab-tree, or wild plum — with scions of a good fruit-tree. The younger the stock — the tree to be grafted — is, the more easily is this complete change in its nature brought about; because, when it is once grafted with a single scion, this will become the main stem of the tree, and all the branches it puts forth will be of the right sort. But a wilding tree may be successfully grafted at a considerable age; only, in this case, you must put on perhaps twenty or thirty scions, grafting *each branch;* and, afterwards, you must be continually on the watch to cut off the fresh shoots sent forth by the wild stock.

Even thus, a person who has been early trained in right principles will be likely, in the whole of his conduct, to put forth, as it were, branches of Christian virtue; and, on the other hand, one who has long lived a different kind of life will have to unlearn a number of distinct evil habits, and to ingraft, as it were, each branch with a fresh scion of virtue.

§ 5. — *Right Acts lead to Right Inclinations.*

But in carrying on such a work of reform or improvement as we are speaking of, you must begin by *acting* in such a way as conscience tells you is right. You must not wait till you are completely in a proper frame of mind; and defer doing what a virtuous man would do till you have all the dispositions and inclinations of a virtuous man. On the contrary, it is only *by* so acting that you can acquire those dispositions. Virtuous actions are, indeed, the fruits of virtuous habits; but they are also the means of acquiring those habits. They are the seed produced by the tree which springs from that seed. To wait, therefore, till you have become a virtuous man before you begin to lead a virtuous life, would be like resolving not to go into the water till you were able to swim ; or not to mount a horse till you were a good rider. It is only by practising virtue that you can bring yourself to delight in virtue.

Suppose, for instance, a man who had been given up to selfish gratification, and indifferent to the welfare of others, should, by God's grace, be brought to a conviction of the sinfulness of such a life, and the duty of beneficence, he ought at once to set about the work of doing good to his fellow-creatures. At first, and for some time, he will, perhaps, be exercising a painful self-denial in giving up some personal gratifications he had been accustomed to, or in parting with money that he highly prizes, for the relief or benefit of persons he does not much care about, and in taking trouble to serve them. He will only enjoy the satisfaction of doing his duty. But, by degrees, the sentiments of compassion and benevolence will be cherished in him by beneficent acts, and will become stronger and stronger. His feelings will in time overtake his reason. He will come to feel an interest, more and more, in the welfare of others, through the exertions he makes for their benefit; till at length it will be felt as a greater self-denial to withhold his good offices than to perform them. His selfish inclinations will be weakened by being continually repressed, and will at length become odious to him. He will gradually cease to "give grudgingly, and of necessity," and will become the "cheerful giver" that God loveth. And the like takes place in the formation of other virtuous habits.

§ 6. — *Right Actions must be what are done on Right Principles.*

But then, as we said above, it is necessary that good actions should be done from a good principle. For it is only by *virtuous conduct* that a virtuous habit can be acquired; and your conduct is *not* virtuous in *you* (though it may be beneficial to others), if you do not act from a good motive. If a man (as was observed in Lesson I.) pays his debts punctually, and is fair in all his dealings, merely through fear of legal penalties, or for the sake of keeping up a good character, that he may prosper the better in his business, there is no virtue in all this; nor is he even in the way to acquire any virtue. For, though it is true that, according to the proverb, " Honesty is the best policy," he who acts altogether on that motive alone is not an honest man; nor is he training himself to become such. His conduct, indeed, is in itself honest; but it is in him only a matter of *policy*. He will indeed have been forming a habit, but only a habit of prudence, not of justice. And, accordingly, he will be very likely to wrong and defraud his neighbor if ever he has an opportunity of doing so with impunity.

So, also, a man of a violent and revengeful temper will sometimes exercise great self-control from motives of prudence, when he sees that he could not vent his resentment without danger or loss to himself; such self-restraint as this does not at all tend to subdue or soften his fierce and malignant passions, and to make him a mild and placable character. It only keeps the fire smouldering within, instead of bursting out into a flame. He is not quelling the desire of revenge, but only repressing it till he shall have an opportunity of indulging it more safely and effectually. And accordingly, he will have to exercise the same painful self-restraint again and again on every fresh occasion.

But to exert an equal self-restraint, on a good principle, with a sincere and earnest desire to subdue revengeful feelings, and to form a mild, and generous, and forgiving temper, this will produce quite a different result. A man who acts thus on a right motive, will find his task easier and easier on each occasion; because he will become less sensitive to provocations, and will have been forming a habit of not merely avoiding any outward expression of anger in words or acts, but also of indulging no resentful feelings within.

And the like takes place in the controlling and regulating of all our feelings. By *doing* what is good, at once, on a right motive, you will gradually come to have good sentiments and inclinations. Your *conduct* will first be, in each particular act, virtuous; and this will, in time, form in you a virtuous *character*.

LESSON XI.

FORMATION OF HABITS.

§ 1.— *What is practised, that will be learnt.*

YOU have seen, then, that it is by the practice of what is good on a right principle, that good habits are formed. Mere reading, and listening, and talking on the subject, will no more make you a virtuous man, if you do not earnestly set yourself to practise, through divine help, the duties you know, than listening to a physician's advice, and looking at his medicine, without taking it, would restore a sick man to health.

The patient would, in this case, be neither the better nor the worse for the physician's advice. But it is not so with one who has been accustomed to hear moral and religious discourses without acting upon them. He will be much the worse for them; because he will have become *hardened* against receiving any profitable impression from discourses that might strongly impress a person hearing them for the first time. "Familiarity," says the proverb, "breeds contempt." You may observe, in travelling on a railroad, how the young cattle run away in terror from the engine; while those that have often seen it pass, go on quietly grazing, and do not regard it. And even so, one who has been accustomed to be a "hearer of the word, and not a doer," will acquire more and more of the same kind of "familiarity."

It might seem unnecessary to remind any one, that "what you practise, that you will learn." But so it is, that many persons seem to expect to learn one thing by practising another very different thing. What misleads them is, that they speak loosely of being *accustomed* to such and such a thing, and forget that two persons may have been both of them conversant about the very same *objects*, and yet may have acquired opposite *habits*, from being accustomed to *act* in opposite ways.

Suppose, for instance, that there is in your neighborhood a loud bell that is rung very early every morning to call the laborers in some great manufactory. At first, and for some time, your rest will be broken by it; but if you accustom yourself to lie still, and try to compose yourself, you will become in a few days so *used to it*, that it will not even wake you. But any one who makes a point of rising immediately at the call, will become so *used to it* in the *opposite* way, that the sound will never fail to rouse him from the deepest sleep. Both will have been accustomed to the same bell, but will have formed opposite habits from their contrary modes of action.

And we may see the same thing even in the training of brute animals. For instance, of sporting dogs, there are some, such as the greyhound, that are trained to *pursue* hares; and others which are trained to *stand* motionless when they come upon a hare, even though they see it running before them. Now both kinds are accustomed to hares; and both have originally the same instincts; for all dogs have an instinctive tendency to pursue game. But the one kind of dog has always been encouraged to run after a hare, and the other has always been chastised if it attempts to do so, and has been trained to stand still.

§ 2.— *Opposite Habits acquired among the same Things.*

In like manner, of two persons who have been accustomed to the sight of much human misery, one, who has been used to pass it by without any effort to relieve it, will become careless and hardened to such spectacles; while another, who has been in the practice of *relieving* sufferers, will acquire a strong habit of endeavoring to afford relief. These two persons will both have been accustomed to the same objects, but will have acquired opposite habits. So, also, if you are accustomed to talk about virtue, and to listen to discourses on the subject, and to peruse, for instance, such Lessons as these now before you, without acting on what you say, and hear, and read, you will acquire a habit of talking, etc. without acting.

Whoever, therefore, is not the *better* for such studies, will assuredly be the worse for them. And if you are accustomed to read the Bible, either without careful attention, or without striving to bring into your daily life what you learn from it, you will become insensible to what it teaches. If, on the contrary, you make a practice of applying in your own conduct what you hear and read, you will acquire a *practical* habit. By talking, or listening, or reading, you will learn to talk, or to listen, or to read; by attending, you will learn to attend; and by acting, you will learn to act.

A person who has acquired a habit of letting all his

religious and virtuous sentiments evaporate in words, instead of being brought into practice in his life, resembles the "barren fig-tree," which was blasted by our Lord's command, to furnish an instructive emblem. A tree that is in a torpid and leafless state in the winter frost, may be roused into vigorous life and fruitfulness by the summer sun and warm showers. But much more hopeless is one which is in a state of active vegetation, yet bears "no *fruit*, but leaves only." Such a tree is a picture of the man who is not ignorant or thoughtless respecting morality and religion, but who lets all his knowledge and his thoughts on such subjects be wasted in barren talk, — "leaves," without fruit. Such persons, however, sometimes attract more notice, and gain more admiration from the inexperienced, than those who talk less, and do more. For you may observe that, in a steam-engine, the steam makes a much louder whizzing when it is *let off*, and the wheels are standing still, than when it is quietly acting on the machinery.

Again, the custom of being present at public worship, with an earnest and devout attention to the Service, tends to cherish a habit of devotion; but the oftener a person is present at a Service which he does not attend to, the more he will acquire of a habit of inattention to that Service. And those who have been made familiar with the words of Scripture, without being accustomed to attend to the meaning, or to bring its lessons into practice, will acquire a habit of such unprofitable reading.

Such habits are often acquired in childhood, by those who have been habitually brought to church at a very early age, before it was possible for them to take part in, or to understand, what was said: and who have used the

Bible as a mere reading-book; or have been accustomed to read it as if there was some virtue in the mere act of perusal. And these will have, in after life, a troublesome and difficult task in unlearning such a habit. This difficulty is created by the course pursued by well-meaning friends, whose wish is to *accustom* them early to pious exercises, and who overlook that obvious truth, that "what you practise, that you will learn"; and that you cannot learn one thing by practising another quite contrary to it.

In the smaller affairs of daily life, hardly any one ever commits such blunders as are often made in the most important matters. Every one would see, for instance (to recur to the examples given just above) the absurdity of expecting that by being accustomed to hear a bell, and to lie still at the sound, he would acquire the habit of immediately rising whenever it rung.

§ 3. — *Progress in forming a Virtuous Character.*

You will perceive, then, that it must be a work of some labor and difficulty to form good moral habits, — especially for those who have to *un*learn evil habits. The chief part, however, of this difficulty will be (as was above pointed out) in the *beginning* of a right course. Many things which at first cost much and painful self-denial, will afterwards, when the habit has been formed, be practised with ease, and even with pleasure.

And each particular act will then become less an *act of virtue*, while at the same time the *character of virtue* will have been the more confirmed. For instance, take the case of a youth who had been brought up among thieves, and had been accustomed to pilfering, and encouraged in it by his vile associates, but who has been received (as many have been) into one of the ragged schools, and has there received a good moral and religious training. He will, for a time, have, of course, a great inward struggle against his former habits. Such a youth was on one occasion intrusted by the master, by the way of a trial, with some gold to get changed; which he could easily have carried off. When he honestly brought the change, his schoolfellows were overjoyed; and we have reason to believe that the holy angels rejoiced with them, at this victory over evil habits. (Luke xv. 10.) It was in him — brought up as he had been — a great act of virtue to resist the temptation. But to a person who had been always honestly brought up (and probably to that same youth, a few years later) there would not be even any temptation. Such a one would not so much as think of stealing; and therefore it would not be accounted an act of virtue in him to refrain from it. But this would be, not from his being a less virtuous character, but, on the contrary, from his being fully confirmed in that character.

§ 4. — *Virtue a Struggle of Good against Evil.*

And so it is with other habits. Virtue, therefore, appears to consist in a struggle, and a successful struggle, of good against evil. Moral *goodness* is not called *virtue*, where there is no temptation to be resisted, — no evil tendency or weakness to be overcome. And accordingly, while we attribute to the Deity the highest *moral perfection*, and speak of his *goodness*, it would shock any one to speak of Him as a *virtuous* Being.

It would sound degrading, as implying some *evil* tendency to be resisted, or at least some weakness to be overcome. But Man, in this his state of trial and discipline, can never so completely extinguish all faulty tendencies, and throw off all infirmities, as to be exempt from the need of care, and vigilance, and self-control, and firmness against temptation. Man's *goodness*, in short, must, in this life, consist in *virtue*.

Accordingly, our estimate of the virtue displayed in any act, depends much on the difficulty to be surmounted, the temptations to be withstood, etc. If, for instance, any one decides justly in some cause in which he has no interest, and where both the parties are strangers to him, we think little of the virtue of justice displayed by him. But if he decides fairly in some case where he has to sacrifice his own interests, or do violence to his feelings; or if he reduces himself to poverty by giving up an estate to one whom he thinks entitled to it, when he might safely and without discredit have kept it, this we commend as a virtuous act. And thus the person commended by the Psalmist is, "He that sweareth to *his own hurt*, and changeth not." (Ps. xv. 4.)

So also we hardly account *veracity* as virtuous, when a man tells truth in some case where there is nothing to be gained by falsehood, but only when by telling the truth he exposes himself to loss, or danger, or discredit. And the like in other cases. And hence the great advantage of our having placed before us the example of the Apostles and other early disciples, who were, as they tell us, "men of like *passions*" with us; that is, subject to the same infirmities and trials.

§ 5. — *Imitation of our Heavenly Father.*

We are, indeed, told to imitate our Heavenly Father. But then it is only the divine *acts* that Man can imitate. We are told to be "merciful even as our Father in heaven is merciful," and to be — as He is — "kind to the unthankful and the evil."

The greatest difference in the *nature* of two Beings is no reason against the *acts* of the one being held up as an example to the other. Indeed, the acts of some brute animals (such as the ant and the bee) are often referred to for Man's imitation; though no one supposes those creatures to act from any such *rational calculation* as guides the conduct of an industrious and prudent *man*. And indeed, even the very precept, "Thou shalt *love* thy neighbor as *thyself*," relates only to *acts*, not to inward feelings. For no one can have an *affection* for himself, of the same kind with what we feel for another person whom we love. Self-love is a desire for our own welfare, which no rational Being can be destitute of, whether he is or is not of an affectionate character. But the meaning of the precept is, that as we seek for our own welfare, as an end, and without any further object, so we should, in like manner, seek for our neighbors'. So also our Lord, in the parable of the "Unjust Steward," sets before us for imitation an example of prudent forethought; though no one can suppose that it was meant that we should imitate his dishonesty, or act on his motives.

But in the case of the Apostles, we can imitate, not merely their actions, but their inward dispositions also, throughout. We see them resisting strong temptations, and struggling against and subduing their worldly and ambitious desires, and their timidity, and their feelings of resentment; we see them giving, when it impoverished themselves, and refusing gifts which they stood in need of, and facing dangers which they naturally dreaded. In short, we see them practising *virtue.* And though we have not their miraculous powers, there is no reason for thinking that we are less required, or less enabled, than they were, to practise Christian virtue.

As for their miraculous powers of healing, etc., these were given them for the advantage of *others*, not for their own. Miracles were necessary as a proof of the divine origin of the Gospel. But these superhuman gifts neither *implied* that the possessors were good Christians, nor necessarily *made* them so. *All* the Apostles, Judas Iscariot among the rest, wrought miracles during our Lord's abode on earth. And some of the Corinthians abused their miraculous powers for the purposes of vain display, and made them a subject of rivalry and contention. But, on the other hand, when Paul tells the Romans (who had then had no *miraculous* gifts, Rom. i. 11), that, "if any man have not the Spirit of Christ, he is none of his," (Rom. viii. 9,) and when he says to them, "As many *as are led by the Spirit* of God, they are the sons of God," it is plain he is speaking of a far different, and far more valuable kind of spiritual gift, — the moral guidance of the conscience, and improvement of the character. And this is what is equally needed by all Christians in all ages, and which all may equally obtain.

But some people fall into the mistake (which you

should carefully guard against) of imagining that there is something virtuous in the mere barren *admiration* of some eminently virtuous character, and deep reverence for it, without any effort to imitate it.

Sometimes, indeed, a man will even flatter himself that there is a laudably *modest humility* in not aspiring to the same high moral excellence with some eminently virtuous men that are mentioned in history, or actually living among us. And yet perhaps you may hear these spoken of as men of *exemplary* character; though it is plain no one can be, to *us*, *exemplary*, unless we endeavor to *follow* his example. The more we admire any virtuous conduct, if we do not strive to copy it, as far as is suitable to our situation, the more we condemn ourselves. And it is not humble modesty, but rather presumptuous confidence, if we are *satisfied* without doing our utmost to attain the highest degree of moral excellence that is within our reach.

LESSON XII.

IMITATION OF JESUS.

§ 1.—*Example of our Saviour.*

As for the imitation of the Lord Jesus himself, to which we are exhorted in the Scriptures, that is something intermediate between the imitation of the *divine* goodness (spoken of above), and the imitation of mere human Beings. So far forth as He was a divine person, we can imitate only his *acts;* but considered as to his human nature, we are told, "Let the *same mind* be in you which was also in Christ Jesus"; and thereupon we have his *humility* and *obedience* held up for our imitation. And again, we are told that we "have not a high-priest who cannot be touched with a feeling of our infirmities, but was in all points tempted like as we are, yet without sin."

Now, though of course He had no *evil* propensities, we should remember, that, if He had not those human feelings and inclinations which are not in themselves evil, He could not have been "tempted [*i. e.* tried] like as we are"; or indeed tempted at all.

And it is to be observed, that there are many human feelings which *become* evil when wrongly indulged, but which are not so when properly controlled. For instance, it is no sin for one who is fatigued by labor of any kind, to long for repose; only, he would be wrong to indulge this desire when duty calls on him to rouse himself to exertion.

So also, it is no sin for any one to be glad of the love and approbation of his friends and countrymen; provided he does not sacrifice duty for the sake of their favor, or do anything *on purpose* to gain applause for its own sake. And the like in many other cases.

§ 2. — *Jesus had Human Feelings.*

There is no reason, therefore, to suppose that the Lord Jesus was indifferent to the good opinion of his countrymen; which He might have obtained by falling in with their wishes and expectations. And they would have welcomed Him with open arms, if He would have allowed them to "make Him a king," to deliver them from the yoke of the Romans, and found a triumphant and splendid temporal empire. Instead of this, He exposed himself, by disappointing their hopes, to their hatred and scorn, to insults and tortures, and a most ignominious as well as cruel death.*

We have no reason to think that He did not feel all this, even more than his bodily sufferings. And, accordingly, we are told that He "endured the cross, *despising the shame*"; and we are exhorted to "consider Him that endured such contradiction of sinners against himself." (Heb. xii.)

Again, if any one should feel weariness and disgust in laboring long and painfully at the task of instructing ignorant, narrow-minded, and perverse learners, and slow-

---

* See Lectures on Good and Evil Angels.

ly overcoming their prejudices; this would be no sin, provided he did not shrink from the task, if duty imposed it, nor suffer any impatience to break out. And when, therefore, we see our blessed Master condescending to labor, day after day, and year after year, in gradually enlightening the minds of humble fishermen and peasants, and in correcting their errors, we have here an example, in all respects for our imitation, of patient and humble assiduity.

Again, there is nothing sinful in feeling displeased with persons who manifest stubborn ingratitude, and repay kindness with bitter insult and cruel persecution. The sin would be in allowing ourselves to indulge revengeful feelings; "rendering evil for evil, railing for railing." And accordingly, the Apostle Peter holds up to us the example of our Lord Jesus in this point also, who "did no violence; who, when He was reviled, reviled not again; when He suffered, He threatened not"; and who, as we read in the Evangelists, prayed for his murderers.

These points are here noticed merely as specimens. There are many others which every attentive reader of the Gospels cannot fail to be struck with, in which the excellences of our Lord's character as a *man* plainly appear, and are suitable for our imitation.

§ 3. — *The Nature of the Lord Jesus mysterious.*

But some persons, though far from indifferent to the subject of religion, do not pay sufficient attention to that important portion of it which is now before us, — the example of Jesus as set forth in Scripture for our imitation. Instead of this, they have occupied themselves in discussing questions as to several mysterious points on which Scripture reveals nothing. *In what manner* the divine nature was united with the human in the person of our Saviour, — and what was the precise character of his *inward feelings,* — all these and other such questions are what the Sacred Writers have left unexplained. And we cannot doubt that, if an explanation of these had been possible, and needful for us, it would have been given. Yet these are questions which some persons presume freely to discuss; as if the speculations of human reason could enlighten us on matters not revealed to the Apostles; or at least not revealed *by* them. And such rash *speculations* have often drawn off men's attention from what is *plainly* set forth in Scripture for our *practical* benefit.

How the human body and mind act on each other, we cannot explain or understand; but we know that they do; and we can make a practical use of that knowledge. We know not the nature of the sun; we cannot explain how it is that it continues to throw out light and heat without being, as a candle is, consumed in so doing: but we can *see* by its light, and enjoy its warmth.

And even so, we can benefit by the teaching and the example of the Lord Jesus, though we have a very dim and imperfect notion of his real nature. To turn aside from a practical benefit that is placed *within* our reach, and occupy ourselves instead with speculative inquiries about matters *beyond* our reach, would be like the folly of our first parents, who, when permitted to "eat of the tree of life," turned to the forbidden "tree of *knowledge*."

Some people, again, allow their veneration for Christ

and his Apostles to vent itself on tangible objects, such as "relics," or on supposed holy places, to which they make pilgrimages. We are told that our divine Master left us an "example that we should follow his steps," instead of which they go to Jerusalem to tread literally on the ground He trod. Instead of "putting on Christ," as the Apostle exhorts us, they venerate a *tunic* He is supposed to have worn, or bits of wood of the supposed "true cross"; or procure a bottle of water from the river Jordan, for baptizing their children. Instead of being "followers of the Apostles, even as they were of Christ," they bow down before fragments of their bones, or locks of their hair, etc.

All this is as if some one, when shown a tree bearing delicious and wholesome and nourishing fruit, should neglect the *fruit*, and try to feed on the leaves or bark; or as if, when he had received a package of most valuable goods, he should lay them by, and make no use of them, but wear with much pride *the canvas wrapper* in which they were packed up.

§ 4.—*Jesus a Faultless Model.*

The great advantage of our Lord's example, as compared with any description of an imaginary person—an ideal perfect man—is its *reality*. We know that He did actually live on this earth, and that what is recorded of Him is not fiction or supposition, but what was really said and done.

But again; his example has the advantage over those of all other *actually existing* persons, of being absolutely *perfect*. The greatest, and noblest, and purest of all merely human characters have their imperfections; and these an imitator might be led into, through his admiration of their excellence.

And it may be observed, by the way, that this is a mistake some people may be in danger of, in reference to the characters in the Old Testament history. They may suppose that every person mentioned with any degree of commendation, and especially those who were endowed with any prophetical powers, or received any other mark of divine favor, are to be looked on as perfect models,—held up for our imitation throughout; though many of them were undoubtedly guilty of faults deserving much censure, even considering the rude age in which they lived. And all of them did live in such a half-civilized, half-barbarian state of society, as requires great allowances to be made for those brought up in it. Their comparatively gross and uncultivated intellectual and moral condition is what our Lord alludes to in his expression "hardness of heart." (Matt. xix. 8.)

Even the best, however, of these men, are not to be imitated as if they could be reckoned faultless. But in imitating our divine Master, whatever errors we may fall into by our own injudicious imitation, we cannot be led into any, by imperfections in the model itself.

And in studying the life of our Lord, in conjunction with that of the earliest disciples, we have the advantage of seeing not only a perfect model, but also an example of the *copying* of that model. We not only see the original pattern, but are also shown *how* it was first imitated. "Be ye followers," says the Apostle Paul, "of me, even as I am of Christ Jesus." We thus have, as it were, before us, not only a perfect human *figure*, but also a *statue* made from it by a first-rate sculptor.

§ 5. — *Danger of Erroneous Imitation.*

But, as has just been said, it is possible to fall into mistakes by our own injudicious and improper imitation of a faultless example, or indeed of any example. If some one's conduct is perfectly right for *him*, or under his circumstances, *we* may be altogether wrong in copying it if we are placed in quite different circumstances.

If a king, for instance, or any one else in high authority, conducts himself in the best possible manner, it would be absurd, and a criminal usurpation, for a private citizen to pretend to follow his example by assuming regal state and power. And so it would be, if a pupil were to take upon him the office of a master, and pretend to give instruction in the school where he is placed to receive it. The way in which a subject should follow the example of a *good king*, is by conducting himself as a *good subject;* and then each of them alike will be acting in a manner suitable to his own position.

Accordingly, there are many parts of our Lord's conduct which would have been unsuitable for the Apostles to imitate; and many parts, both of his conduct and theirs, that would be unsuitable for us.

For instance, we read " that He taught as *one having authority*, and not as the scribes "; that is, instead of confining himself to the expounding of the Mosáic law, and reasoning upon that, (which was the practice, and the proper office of the scribes,) He spoke as having a direct commission from Heaven, saying, " *I* say unto you " so and so; and appealing not to arguments, but to the miracles He wrought, as a proof of his coming from God.

And again, you should observe that He does not use the language of the prophets, who had been accustomed to say, "Thus saith the Lord," each of them having been charged with certain specific messages; but God gave not the Spirit by *measure* unto *Him.* He came not only with authority, but with full, unlimited authority; and his language was, "I say unto you."

Now, of course it would be profane as well as absurd for any one of *us* to teach as "having authority"; that is, as demanding assent and submission to what we say, *because we* say it.

LESSON XIII.

IMITATION OF THE APOSTLES.

§ 1.—*How far the Apostles are to be imitated.*

As for the imitation by the Apostles of their divine Master, and again *our* imitation of *them*, you must remember that they were in some respects in a different position, both from Him, and again from us. They spoke and acted as his *messengers*, (which is the meaning of the title "Apostles,") and commissioned by Him as ambassadors. They accordingly kept closely to the instructions they received from Him, either by word of mouth, or by the inspiration of his Spirit. Thus, we find Paul saying that on one point "he has no commandment from the Lord"; and again, in another place, that it is not he that gives the commandment, but "the Lord." And the reality of this their commission from Christ, they prove by the miracles done in his name, which they expressly call the "signs of an Apostle."

Now, any one among *us* may indeed be allowed to bring arguments to convince the Reason, that so and so is the meaning of a certain passage of Scripture, or that his views on some point are right. But if, instead of this, he demands assent to what he says, on his bare word, declaring that he is inspired [or "moved"] by the Holy Spirit of God to say it, you may fairly ask him to prove this by the display of some sensible miracle.

This demand was made — and justly made — of Jesus and his Apostles; and they did display miraculous powers. But any one who thus pretends to inspiration, and yet fails to give this necessary proof of it, is imitating the Apostles only in the same way in which a man might be said to imitate a real ambassador from some king, by *pretending* to have a commission from him, when he had no *credentials* to produce.

§ 2. — *How far the Example of our Lord is not to be followed.*

Again, our Lord spake to the multitudes in parables, which most of them did not understand, and reserved the explanation of "the mysteries of the kingdom of heaven" for his disciples. And this was, in his case, quite reasonable; since his disciples were — *all* who chose to be so — all who were convinced by his "mighty works" that He was a real prophet, and that therefore they were bound to place themselves under his instruction, even before they understood it. "We know," says Nicodemus, "that thou art a teacher sent from God; for no man *can do these miracles* which thou doest, except God be with him."

All that were thus candid and docile *became* his disciples, and received the explanations they needed; while those who "were without" the circle of his disciples, and came to listen out of idle curiosity, or with design to watch for occasions of accusations against him, were left uninstructed. For "he that hath," said Jesus, "to him shall be given; and he that hath not, from him shall be taken away even that which he hath."

The Apostles, however, by their Master's direction, spoke not in parables, but declared openly and plainly to all, what they were commissioned to teach. "If our gospel be hid," says Paul, "it is hid to them that are lost,"—["in the way to be lost," according to the original,]—"whom the god of this world hath blinded"; and again, "I am pure from the blood of all men; for I have not shunned to declare unto you all the counsel of God." And this was in conformity with our Lord's injunction, "What I have told you in secret, that preach ye openly; and what ye have heard in the ear in closets, that proclaim ye upon the house-tops."

§ 3.—*False Imitation of the Lord Jesus.*

It would be doubly absurd, therefore, for any religious or moral teacher among *us* to think of imitating our Lord's example by delivering obscure precepts to the people, and offering to give explanations of them to those who would enroll themselves as his disciples. "Why *should* we," they might answer, "become your disciples? We have no means of judging whether what you teach is right or wrong, till we understand what it is, unless you give, like Jesus, a miraculous proof of a divine commission." For He said, "If I had not done among them the *works* which none other man did, they had not had sin."

But if any one pretends to infallibility without giving such proofs of it, the sin would be, not in denying his claim, but in admitting it. His imitation of our Lord is like the imitation of a true coin by a piece of base metal, which will not stand a trial by the touchstone.

You see, therefore, that men may fall into grievous

mistakes by endeavoring, or pretending, to follow some one's example, while they do what is for *him* quite right, but for them, who are in a different situation, quite wrong.

§ 4. — *Mistakes as to the Conduct of the Apostles.*

But besides the danger of this kind of error, there is also another to be guarded against. For some people make mistakes as to what the conduct really is, of the model they wish to copy; and therefore imitate it improperly, even in points wherein it ought to be followed exactly.

For instance, we find the Apostles and other early disciples submitting to stripes and imprisonments, and encountering hunger and thirst, and dangers and persecutions of every kind, in their Master's cause, and while engaged in preaching his Gospel (2 Cor. vi. 4 – 10). And we admire, very justly, the patient fortitude they displayed. And in all cases, the more hardships and privations and sufferings of any kind a man encounters in the *discharge of his duty*, the more we admire his virtue. Now the admiration of such virtuous fortitude has led many persons, in various ages and countries, to imagine that there is something virtuous in *self-inflicted* sufferings, that have no further object; and that to expose one's self to various hardships and privations, merely as a display of fortitude, is something in itself acceptable to the Deity.

Among the Hindoo idolaters, for instance, there are many devotees who plunge iron hooks into their flesh, and practise a variety of even more extravagant penances, which they imagine to be an acceptable service to the gods they worship. If we go to the opposite side of the globe, we find tribes of American Indians practising like cruelties on themselves. And in many Churches professing to be Christian, persons who aspire to be "saints" place great part of their service of God in scourging or half-starving themselves, lying on beds of rugged stones, shutting themselves up in uncomfortable cloisters, wearing filthy garments, and in various other ways inflicting self-torture; as believing the endurance of suffering for its own sake, and without any further object, to be a Christian virtue.

Now all this is as great an error as if any one should think to attain the character of a good soldier by wantonly shooting or stabbing himself. We admire, and with reason, the valor of a soldier who boldly mounts a breach amidst a shower of bullets, or rushes on a line of bayonets, at the command of his leader, in the service of his country. But this is because he encounters the danger in doing his *duty*, and could not avoid the danger, except by shrinking from duty. But to expose himself to wounds or death *for no object*, is far from being a soldier's duty.

§ 5.— *The Apostles never tortured Themselves.*

And such self-torturers as we have been speaking of are equally far from really imitating the conduct of the Apostles. For *they* never exposed themselves to persecution, or suffering of any kind, needlessly and wantonly; though there was none that they shrunk from, in the discharge of their duty. They submitted to cruel scourgings, rather than forego the preaching of the Gospel; but they never scourged themselves. Paul himself repeatedly pleaded his privilege as a "Roman citizen," to save himself from illegal scourging. And when shipwrecked on the island of Melita, he took all the careful precautions for safety, that the most timorous lover of life could have done; ready as he was "not only to be bound, but also to die, for the name of the Lord Jesus." All this is what the Apostles understood, and doubtless rightly understood, by their Master's declaration, "If any man will be my disciple, let him deny himself, and take up his cross and follow me"; *his* cross, — that which is laid upon him by his Christian duty, — not one of his own imposing

And the "mortification" to which Paul exhorts his converts, is not self-torture of any kind, or at all what the word "mortification" means, in its ordinary use among us now; but the *putting to death* (that is the exact sense of the word in the original) of evil habits and desires. "Mortify," says he, "your members which are upon the earth, fornication, uncleanness, inordinate affection, and covetousness"; and "they that are Christ's, have *crucified* the flesh with the affections and lusts."

But as for hair-shirts, and beds of flints, and all kinds of gratuitous suffering purposely undergone for its own sake, there is nothing, either in the teaching or the examples of the Apostles, to show that they practised or recommended, or at all approved, of anything of the kind.

§ 6. — *Goods of Christians not Common.*

Again, there have been persons who have imagined that Christians ought not to possess any private property, but to "have all things common"; as a supposed imitation of what is recorded (in Acts) of the earliest "believers."

But it is quite a mistake to suppose that any such system was established as a general rule for Christians, even at the very first. This is plain from the words of Peter to Ananias; whose sin the Apostle declares consisted, not in retaining his property, but in "lying to the Holy Ghost." As for the land, that, he reminds him, and the price of it, has been "his own," and "in his own power"; which clearly shows that he was not required to give it up on becoming a disciple.

The case, no doubt, was this: that our Lord's *immediate attendants* while He was on earth, and also those who after his departure were *engaged in the ministry,* were required to throw any property they might possess into a common stock, from which all so engaged were maintained, and the poor relieved out of the surplus. And it need not be wondered at, — considering the immense work then to be begun, of preaching the Gospel to many millions, — that *all* the very earliest of the converts should have been needed, and all ready, to take part in this ministry.

Ananias and his wife seem to have designed to *partake* of *this common stock*, while they fraudulently retained a portion of private property; the resigning of which was a *condition,* not of their embracing Christianity, but of their being entitled to maintenance out of the common stock.

But it is quite clear that no such system as a general community of goods among Christians ever existed. This is proved, not only by what was said to Ananias, but also by the "charge" given to "them who are *rich* in this world, to be ready to *give*, and glad to distribute"; and from many other passages of Scripture: among others, one already mentioned, "Let him that stole, steal no more; but rather let him labor, that he may *have* to *give* to him that needeth."

Those therefore who would forbid men's possessing private property, would not be really following the example of the Apostles.

These instances may serve as specimens, to show what errors men may commit by inconsiderately and unwisely attempting to imitate the best examples.

LESSON XIV.

SINGLENESS OF VIRTUE.

§ 1.— *Various Treatises on Morals.*

THERE are several treatises on Morals, by various writers, in several languages; in which you will find an enumeration of what are called the different *virtues;* such as fortitude, temperance, justice, liberality, gentleness, etc. And there is much that may be studied with profit in some of these treatises. But in studying them you must be very careful to avoid the mistake of supposing these virtues to be so many *distinct habits*, independent of each other, like the several different sciences and arts.

What is likely to tend to this mistake is, that they are, like the several sciences and arts, conversant about different *kinds of things.* As Arithmetic, for instance, relates to numbers, and Grammar to language, and Music to certain sounds, etc., which are things of quite different kinds; so, Fortitude is concerned about dangers and pains, and Liberality, about money and other property, and Temperance, about sensual indulgences, etc. And hence a person might fall into the mistake of considering each virtue to be a habit as distinct from the rest, and unconnected with them, as Music, for instance, from Grammar or Mathematics.

A man may, we know, be a mathematician without being a classical scholar; or he may be a painter without understanding music; and so of the rest. And those who do possess a knowledge of several different arts or sciences, will usually have learnt them from so many different teachers. But it is not so with what are called the different moral habits. These, though conversant about different kinds of things, are, properly, only *branches* of the *one* habit of virtue; which is, as has been above explained, the habit of doing whatever is *right;* of regulating our whole conduct and character by an enlightened Conscience, and keeping every part of our nature in subjection to that.

§ 2. — *Virtues not distinct, like the Arts.*

When we apply the word "art" to Agriculture, for instance, and to Navigation, and to Architecture, etc., we are only using that term to denote a class which comprehends several things of different kinds, each of which may be properly called "*an art,*" and is independent of the rest. But we ought not, strictly speaking, to say that temperance, for instance, is "*a* virtue"; it is, in truth, a *part* of virtue: it consists in performing one portion of our duty; and duty extends to the proper regulation of our actions and inclinations throughout; in short, to the whole character.

As for the various arts and sciences, they not only are conversant about different kinds of things, but they depend on *different faculties* in the mind; and *this* it is that makes them quite distinct and independent of each other. The power, for instance, by which a man calculates, and that by which he learns a language, and that by which he constructs a machine, are quite distinct. You may, if you will, apply the one *word* "understanding" or "intellect" to every one of these faculties; but this would be only applying one *name* to several different kinds of powers. In like manner, the one word "sense" may be applied to hearing, sight, and smell; but they are quite *distinct* senses; and we could not use the eyes for hearing, or the ears for seeing. But conscience is *one* faculty, not several; and we are bound to keep *all* our various appetites, desires, affections, etc., different as these are from each other, under the one control, of that one which we have called conscience.

§ 3.—*Apparent, but not Real Virtues.*

But what helps to mislead people as to this point is, that we may often see what *appear* to be virtuous habits quite unconnected with each other. For instance, a man who is sober, from being convinced that intemperance would bring sickness, and perhaps poverty, may appear to be practising the virtue of temperance; and yet he may be a cheat, and a liar, etc. He may, perhaps, be a member of what is called a "Temperance Society," the rule of which binds a man as to one point only; and he may never think at all of that society called a "Christian Church," the members of which are bound to "fight manfully under the banner of Christ crucified against *sin*"; and which, accordingly, is both a "Temperance Society," and also an "Honesty Society," and a "Veracity Society," and a "Benevolence Society," etc.

Or, again, take the instance of courage; a man of constitutional intrepidity and firmness, with a great desire of glory, and perhaps a strong attachment to his country, will be likely to make a good soldier, though he may be covetous, and cruel, and tainted with many other vices. And accordingly the most formidable armies have been often made up of men whom no one would call virtuous characters. But the courage of such a man is only an apparent, not a real virtue. For virtue consists in doing one's *duty*, *because* it is duty, and on a right *principle*,— a principle which extends to *all* points of duty alike. A man is rightly called "an artist" who is master of even any *one* art, though he may be ignorant of the rest. But no one is a good man who does not strive to do what is right, and abstain from what is wrong, *throughout*.

§ 4.—*The Sacred Writers, and the Heathen Philosophers, agree on the Oneness of Virtue.*

And this is in conformity with what the Apostle James says: "Whosoever shall keep the whole law, yet offend in one point, he is guilty of all. For that law which said,* Do not commit adultery, said also, Do not kill. Now if thou commit no adultery, yet if thou kill, thou art become a transgressor of the law." (James ii. 10, 11.) He does not mean that a single sin is as bad as many, or that all sins are equal. Nor can it be supposed that, when our Lord bids us "be perfect," (or rather, according to the original, "complete,") "even as our Heavenly Father is perfect," He means that nothing short of god-like, sinless goodness would be accepted.

---

* This is the marginal reading of our Bibles.

But He and his Apostles meant only, that a man acting on a right principle, according to the best of his own moral judgment and discretion, (what James calls the "perfect law of liberty,") will not pass over altogether, and wilfully neglect, any portion of duty; since the same principle extends to the whole; and, consequently, every transgressor is a "transgressor of the law" altogether. But if, on the contrary, there were as many distinct, independent, and unconnected rules laid down, as there are things to be done and to be avoided, then, a man who should have violated *one* of these rules would have done nothing against the rest. As it is, our obedience to the law of conscience, however *imperfect*, in one sense, it may be, is not, they teach us, to be *partial* and *limited*.

So, also, the Apostle Paul tells us that "he that loveth another hath fulfilled the law" (meaning, of course, as far as regards one's neighbors). "For this, Thou shalt not kill, Thou shalt not commit adultery, Honor thy father and thy mother; and if there be any other commandment, it is briefly comprehended in this, Thou shalt love thy neighbor as thyself. Love worketh *no* ill to his neighbor; therefore love is the fulfilling of the law." Rom. xiii. 8–10.

It is remarkable that the very same doctrine, in this respect, with that of the Apostles, is maintained by the most eminent of the ancient heathen moral philosophers. A man cannot, according to Aristotle (Eth. Nicom. b. vi.), be said, in the strictest sense, to possess *one* virtue, and to be destitute of the rest; since the principle which he calls right Reason [*phronesis*], on which a truly virtuous man acts, must extend to *every* point of duty.

§ 5. — *Consistency.*

Whatever principle, then, or system of conduct, you lay down as morally right, you should go through with it, and follow it out consistently, without making arbitrary exceptions according to your own taste and convenience. It might indeed be said, that, strictly speaking, *any* fault, however small, is an "inconsistency" in a man whose life is on the whole virtuous. But what we mean when we speak of an inconsistent character is, that his *course of life* is inconsistent. It might be said, in like manner, that *every single weed* in a cultivated field, or in a whole farm, is an "inconsistency"; and yet you would hardly find, even among the best kept farms, any one that had not a single weed. But a farmer would then, and then only, be reckoned inconsistent, if he attended carefully to one portion of his crops, and left another to be spoiled through neglect; or if he sowed one half of a field with wheat, and the other half with thistles and rag-weed.

Act, therefore, *throughout*, on whatever principle you have adopted as right; or, if you find that to do so would lead to something wrong or absurd, you should take this as a proof that the principle itself which you had adopted must be erroneous, and requires to be changed. But a person who does fairly follow out even an erroneous rule of conduct, which he has mistaken for a right one, is in a fair way to discover in time his own mistake. And moreover he is deserving of less blame than one who (as the phrase is) "plays fast and loose" with his principle; acting on it in one case, and laying it aside in another just as suits his inclination.

If, for instance, you are fully convinced that such precepts as "Resist not evil," etc., are to be taken literally and strictly, as forbidding all self-defence, then you should make a point of never resorting to the aid of *law*, or of any magistrate, officer of law, or civil governor of any kind. For it is plain that all human laws and human government must rest ultimately on physical *force*. The ruler "beareth not the *sword* in vain," but "is ordained for the *punishment* of evil-doers." A law that should merely *exhort* men to pay their just debts, but should denounce no penalty for non-payment, nor be supported by any power of arrest or seizure of goods, would be a mere jest. On the above principle, therefore, you would be bound to leave it to the choice of your tenants and other debtors whether they should pay you or not. Nor would it be allowable for you to call in the police to help you against robbers. For it would be absurd to pretend, that, though it is a sin to employ force *yourself*, it is no sin to *employ others* to do it for you.

Again, if you are convinced that the Mosaic law, or that a certain portion of it, is binding on Christians, then you should observe every one of its commandments, or every one of that portion of its commandments, exactly as they were given, without presuming to leave out or to alter any particle. Or if you find that this would not be right, or that it would lead to some absurdity, then you should not *profess* to take the Mosaic law for your rule.

§ 6. — *Men apt to trust in one Supposed Virtue.*

It is worth remarking here, by the way, that none are

so likely to fall into the error (formerly noticed) of thinking to deserve and *earn* reward by the supposed merit of their good works, as those who consider each (so-called) virtue to be a separate habit; and that they may, and do, practise some one or two virtues, on which they rely and pride themselves. They trust to these as not only compensating for all failures in other points, but as entitling them to reward. For a man is called "an artist" (as was observed just above) who is master of any *one* art; and a tailor, for instance, may say, "I know nothing about cultivating the land, or building houses; those matters are no business of mine: making clothes is my trade, and that is enough; it is by that I *earn my living*." And a carpenter or a smith, etc., might say the like. And so also those who altogether mistake the whole nature of moral virtue, consider that a man may, in like manner, be considered virtuous who practises any one virtue. To guard against such a mistake, it is best to avoid the kind of language that leads to it, and, instead of speaking of several distinct virtues, to say that there are so many distinct *branches of duty;* and that Virtue consists in earnestly setting one's self to the performance of *every* duty.

LESSON XV.

EASIER AND HARDER DUTIES.

§ 1. — *Differences in Men's Dispositions.*

YOU have seen, then, that no one should think of such a thing as possessing one virtue and not others. But it is, nevertheless, true that different parts of duty will be easier or harder to practise, some to one person, and some to another, according to each man's original disposition or early education. Suppose, for instance, the case of a person who is naturally of a covetous disposition, but of a calm, mild, and gentle temper; and another, who is naturally careless of gain, and liberal, but irritable and passionate. The one of these will have to exercise much self-control, in acting always honestly and liberally, which would cost the other little or no effort, though he would scarcely at all feel such provocations as the other would find it very difficult to bear with patience.

One man, again, may find it cost him a severe struggle to resist the temptations presented by a desire for applause, and dread of censure, but will encounter pain and danger readily; while one of an opposite disposition will find it much easier to forego applause, and even to undergo scorn, than to face danger. And there are many other such differences.

Any one who is disposed to complain of the labor and pain it costs him to do what some others do with ease, should reflect that, on the other hand, *they* perhaps find a great difficulty in something that is, to him, much easier.

§ 2. — *Analogy of Bodily Constitutions.*

There are much the same kind of differences in what relates to bodily health. One, for instance, can perhaps undergo much bodily labor, and be even the better for it, but has a weak digestion, and is obliged to be very particular about his diet; while another may find scarcely any kind of food disagree with him, but is easily over-fatigued. And the like in many other cases.

But no one would consider himself in *good health*, if some part of his body were disordered, though the rest might be quite sound and healthy. Nor, in like manner, can any one be in a healthy moral state, if he allows himself in any kind of sin, or neglects a portion of his duty. For as a good digestion, for instance, is not *good health*, but only a *part* of good health, so (as was above remarked) Temperance, or Fortitude, etc., is not virtue, but only a part of virtue.

And, again, you may observe, that, with respect to bodily health, every prudent man is especially careful to guard against those particular diseases to which he knows his own constitution is the most liable. But in moral conduct there is a temptation to reverse this course; — to bestow the chief attention on those duties which are most agreeable to our own nature, and to feel the least dread of the faults we are the most inclined to. A man, for instance, of an open-handed and benevolent disposition, but inclined to indolence and to sensuality, will be likely to regard these as far less odious faults than avarice. And one who is naturally disposed to be active, frugal, and temperate, but parsimonious, and fond of gain, will abhor sloth and intemperance much more than love of money. And the like in many other cases.

And it may sometimes happen that your having some strong tendency in your own character will cause you to perceive it not in yourself, but in your neighbors. If, for instance, you are disposed to covetousness, your over-anxiety to buy cheap, and sell dear, may make you think others covetous; because they will ask more, and offer less, than, to you, will seem reasonable.

If, again, you are of a quarrelsome temper, this may cause you to think others quarrelsome; or even to *make* them so, in their dealings with *you;* because you will be apt to say and do such things as are likely to irritate them.

Or if you are disposed to be obstinate and opinionated, or proud and overbearing, others will appear to you to be obstinate, etc., because they will not give way to you as you will think they ought.*

And it is the same with Vanity, and several other kinds of disposition.

§ 3. — *Care of Bodily Health and of Moral.*

And, again, a person whose natural tendency is to-

---

* A man of this character is said to have complained of his ill-luck, inasmuch as, whenever he was placed on a jury, he always found himself joined with *eleven obstinate men* who would not hear reason.

wards some extreme — suppose, an excessive desire of applause and dread of censure — will perhaps take great pains in proving (what no one denies) that it is neither right, nor possible, to root out completely this feeling; and that we ought not to be, nor can be, wholly indifferent to the good opinion of our neighbors. He might be answered, "It is for you to take all possible care to keep down that feeling; and be assured there is no fear but you will have *enough of it left*. Treat it as you do the grass on a lawn, which you mow down as close as you can every week; not with the hope, or the wish to destroy the grass, but quite secure that it will grow up again fast enough."

Some again excuse or palliate their faults by saying that such conduct is *natural* to persons of their age, or station, or bodily constitution, etc. As if nothing could be a sin to be guarded against, except something to which we are not naturally inclined!

You should imitate, then, the conduct of a prudent man in the care of his health; using double watchfulness and exertion in guarding against those faults in particular which your own character is the most prone to, and in fulfilling those duties which you are the most inclined to neglect. And you should imitate the procedure of builders in straightening a piece of timber that is warped; who bend it a *little* beyond the straight line in the contrary direction.

Some people, indeed, carry this too far, and, in their excessive dread of one extreme, fly to the opposite; to penuriousness, for instance, in their dread of prodigality; or to rashness and hurry, through dread of over-cautiousness and hurtful delay; or the contrary. This kind of error you should of course avoid; but still your first and chief care should be to guard against the extreme to which your own disposition most inclines you.

And as the advice of a good physician may be of use in helping you to understand your own bodily constitution, so a judicious friend may perform a like service in the important point of self-knowledge. For many a one deceives himself as to what really are his own natural tendencies. For instance, one who is somewhat inclined to the love of money, may fancy himself remarkably liberal; because every act of liberality will have cost him such an effort, that he will think much of it, as a most heroic sacrifice. A man, again, who has much self-esteem, may fancy himself peculiarly modest and humble; because he will view, as it were, through a magnifying-glass, any act of condescension; and will seem to himself to be lowering his own just pretensions when he is taking upon himself less than he thinks he has a fair claim to, though, in reality, more than is right. And so in other cases.

A wise and candid counsellor may help to guard you against this kind of self-deceit.

§ 4. — *Enumeration of Virtues not necessary.*

As for such a set of precise rules as should at once apply to every case that can arise, it is what not even the longest Treatise could contain. And an enumeration of what are called the several "Moral Virtues" — that is, the *branches* of virtue — would be unsuitable for introductory Lessons like these; and, for the reasons above given, cannot be necessary.

If, indeed, each Virtue were a distinct Habit, independent of the rest, and if Man had no Moral Faculty to guide his conduct in each kind of matter, but depended wholly on the particular instruction he received on each particular branch (as is the case with the several Sciences and Arts), then, to omit the description of any one Virtue, would be to leave the learner, as far as regarded that one, entirely at a loss. Thus, if in training a youth for the Medical Profession, for instance, you were to teach him Chemistry and Botany, etc., but to leave out Anatomy, his course of study would be imperfect. Or if, again, in a treatise on Agriculture, you were to find full instructions for the cultivation of corn, but nothing said about green crops, or about cattle, you would find fault with the work, as imperfect.

But in what relates to moral conduct, since Man does possess a Faculty which is designed to be applied to the guidance of the whole life, no one can justly complain that he has received imperfect or insufficient moral instruction, on the ground that some particular point of duty, or some particular sin, has not been specified. If you have been supplied (to refer to a former illustration) with a *Clock* or Watch, and also with a *Sun-dial* by which to regulate it, together with directions (such as are to be found in Almanacs) as to the *allowances* to be made of differences between them, there is no need that you should be reminded again and again of each of the several engagements you have at such and such hours.

§ 5.—*Mode of Instruction in the New Testament.*

And accordingly, the New Testament Writers (as was above observed) do not undertake to enumerate all points of Christian duty, and to enjoin and forbid each kind of right and wrong act; but exhort men to the cultivation of good dispositions and the practice of Virtue, generally, and to the imitation of their Divine Master; giving, however, some particular admonitions on those points on which the particular persons they happened to be addressing were the most likely to fail.

And they designed, no doubt, that, in after ages also, Christian moral teachers should pursue a like plan; explaining the principles of Morality, and giving also such particular cautions as might seem best suited for their own Age and Country, and for the class of hearers they were instructing.

And a few cautions of this kind will be all that are necessary in these introductory Lessons. Let the Christian dwell on what the Lord Jesus said and did, and act with a full sense that *his* eye is upon us, and that He requires us to love and to imitate Him, and has promised to "come unto such followers, and to make his abode with them," and has gone "to prepare a place for them"; and then the Christian will not seek, or need, any set of exact and full-written rules for each particular point of conduct.

LESSON XVI.

MISCELLANEOUS CAUTIONS. — PART I.

A few miscellaneous hints and cautions, as to points on which mistakes are apt to arise, may be more useful (for the reasons above given) than an enumeration and description of what are usually called the several Moral Virtues.

§ 1. — *The Matter to which our Conduct relates should be well understood.*

You must remember that you are bound not merely to do what appears to you to be right in each case, but also to take pains to understand the subject relating to each duty you are called on to perform. It would not be enough, for instance, for a man holding some public situation, merely to have a desire to promote his Country's welfare; he is bound, also, to take all possible care to learn in what that welfare consists, and what are the best measures for promoting it. For if, through want of such care, he does mischief instead of good, it is no sufficient excuse to say that "he meant well."

Or again, — to take one of the commonest and most obvious cases, that of charity to the poor, — you are bound not merely to seek to relieve distress, but to inquire diligently, and consider attentively, in what way you can do this the most effectually, so as to do the most good, and the least harm. For there can be no doubt that careless, indiscriminate almsgiving does far more harm than good; since it encourages idleness and improvidence, and also imposture. If you give freely to ragged and filthy street-beggars, you are in fact *hiring* people to dress themselves in filthy rags, and go about begging, with fictitious tales of distress. If, on the contrary, you carefully inquire for, and relieve, honest and industrious persons who have fallen into distress through unavoidable misfortune, you are not only doing good to those objects, but also holding out an encouragement, generally, to honest industry.

You may, however, meet with persons who say, "As long as it is my intention to relieve real distress, my charity is equally virtuous, though the tale told me may be a false one. The impostor alone is to be blamed who told it me; I acted on what he said; and if that is untrue, the fault is his, and not mine."

Now this is a fair plea, if any one is deceived after making careful inquiry; but if he has not taken the trouble to do this, regarding it as no concern of his, you might ask him how he would act and judge in a case where he is thoroughly in earnest, — that is, where his own interest is concerned. Suppose he employed a Steward, or other Agent, to buy for him a house, or a horse, or any other article, and this Agent paid an exorbitant price for what was really worth little or nothing, giving just the same kind of excuse for allowing his employer to be thus cheated; saying, "I made no careful inquiries, but *took the seller's word;* and his being a liar and a cheat is his fault, and not mine";—the employer would doubtless reply, "The seller indeed is to be condemned for cheating; but so are you, for your carelessness of my interests. His being greatly in fault does not clear *you;* and your merely intending to do what was right, is no excuse for your not taking pains to gain right information."

Now on such a principle we ought to act in our charities: regarding ourselves as Stewards of all that Providence has bestowed, and as bound to expend it in the best way possible, and not shelter our own faulty negligence under the misconduct of another.

And here it may be remarked, by the way, that you should never allow any one — least of all, yourself — to put forward the very common excuse of "*it* is such a one's fault"; as if only *one* person could be in fault in any *one* transaction. Thus, when you point out to some ignorant people something erroneous in their religious belief or practice, they will often reply, "Well, this is what the Church teaches and orders, as the Priests tell me; if there is anything wrong in it, *they* must bear all *the* blame, and not I. I say and do just what they bid me; and they must answer for me." This is just the sort of excuse that Adam resorted to for his transgression of the Divine command. He laid *the* blame upon "The Woman"; and the answer he received was, "Because *thou hast hearkened* unto the voice of thy wife," etc.

§ 2. — *Right Principles not to be reserved for Great Occasions.*

Do not reserve the exercise of virtuous principle for *grand occasions,* neglecting small matters of daily occurrence; but remember that there may be great faults in relation to small things, and an important exercise of virtue in matters of little importance in themselves.

Do not, for instance, satisfy yourself with generously forgiving some great injury, while you allow yourself to be impatient and irritable under the various petty provocations that are perpetually occurring. And be not content with making some grand sacrifice of your own interest or enjoyment to a sense of duty, yet giving way to unjust selfishness, and disregard of the rights and the feelings of others, in every-day matters. For you should remember, that it is for the sake of *our own* moral discipline and improvement that virtuous conduct is required of us, not for the *intrinsic value* of any good works of ours; and that it is by frequent practice, rather than by some great and rare efforts, that a habit is acquired.

§ 3.— *Self-love and Selfishness.*

The mention of *Selfishness* leads me to remind you not to confound that with *Self-love,* which is quite a different thing. Self-love is (as was formerly remarked) a rational, deliberate desire for our own welfare, and for anything we consider likely to promote it.* It exists in various degrees in different persons; but it is impossible to conceive a rational Being completely destitute of it. No one can be completely indifferent about

* Sometimes the word self-love is used to signify *self-partiality,* —a tendency to overrate the excellence or the importance of our own performances. But properly, and according to the usage of those who are the most accurate in their language, it signifies "the desire for our own welfare, as such."

his own happiness, who is but capable of forming an idea of happiness.

And Self-love, you should observe, is quite distinct from all our other desires and propensities, though it may often tend in the same direction with some of them. One person, for instance, may drink some water because he is *thirsty;* and another may, without thirst, drink — suppose from a mineral spring — because he believes it will be *good for his health.* This latter is impelled by self-love; but not the other.

So, again, one person may pursue some course of study, in order to qualify himself for some *profession* by which he may advance in life, and another, from having a *taste* for that study, and a desire for that branch of knowledge. This latter, though he may perhaps be, in fact, promoting his own welfare, is not acting from self-love. For as the object of thirst is not happiness, but drink, so the object of curiosity is not happiness, but knowledge. And so of the rest.

Self-love may, of course, like any of our other tendencies, be excessive, or improperly indulged, or ill-directed; but it is nothing evil in itself. And for one person who goes wrong through excess of self-love, there are ten who do so for the sake of gratifying some appetite or passion. A drunkard, for instance, or a gambler, or a quarrelsome man, etc., do not lead the life they do from *calculating* that this will conduce to their happiness; but the one from his craving for strong drink, another from covetousness, and another from pride and malice.

Selfishness, on the other hand, (which is a thing bad in itself,) consists not in the indulging of this or that particular propensity, but in disregarding, for the sake of *any* kind of personal gratification or advantage, the rights or the feelings of other men. It is therefore a *negative* quality; that is, it consists in *not* considering what is due to one's neighbors, through a *deficiency* of justice or of benevolence. And selfishness accordingly will show itself in as many different shapes as there are different dispositions in men.

You may see these differences even in very young children. One selfish child, who is greedy, will seek to keep all the cakes and sweetmeats to himself; another, who is idle, will not care what trouble he causes to others, so he can save his own; another, who is vain, will seek to obtain the credit which is due to others; one who is covetous, will seek to gain at another's expense, etc. In short, each person, you should remember, "has a *self* of his own." And, consequently, though you may be of a character very unlike that of some selfish person, you may yet be, in your own way, quite as selfish as he. And it is possible to be selfish in the highest degree, without being at all too much actuated by self-love, but unduly neglectful of others, when your own gratification, of whatever kind, is concerned.

Even the most amiable feelings require to be watched, with a view to this fault. A liberal and benevolent man, for instance, may be tempted to wish to keep entirely to himself some work of beneficence, in which others may desire, and reasonably desire, to have a share. And a brave and public-spirited man may be tempted to wish to be the *sole* performer of some great exploit, to the unfair exclusion of others.

The great safeguard against selfishness is to apply the "Golden Rule," and imagine yourself in another's place.

§ 4. — *Retiring from the World.*

You must guard against the mistake of imagining that there is anything virtuous in seeking to escape temptation by what some call "renouncing the World"; — that is, withdrawing from active life into a Hermitage, or a Monastery, or some such retreat. Those who thus fly from the World's dangers, generally fly from many of its duties also. And, after all, though they may thus escape some kinds of temptation, they will meet with others of some different kind instead. And we cannot have the same ground of hope for Divine support against temptations that are of our own creating, and which we have gone out of our way to encounter, as against those occurring in the ordinary course of life marked out for us by Providence.

Again, the prospect of being engaged in some great and important good work, must not be allowed to draw you off from definite duties that are especially appointed for you. A good soldier will not quit without orders the post where he has been stationed, to go and perform some exploit against the enemy elsewhere.

A man would be to blame, for instance, who should leave his children to the mercy of chance, while he went about attending public Meetings for some good object, or travelled as a Missionary in foreign lands.

As for our Lord's immediate followers, when some of them left homes and parents to act as his attendants, or his messengers, this was at the command of Him who knew perfectly all the particulars of each case, and who had an undoubted right to their services. But no one is justified in giving up his own definite duties on his own fallible judgment.

§ 5. — *Occasions for doing Good to be looked out for.*

On the other hand, be not satisfied with being able to say to yourself, "I am doing *no harm*," if there is any *good* left undone which you could do without deserting your own proper duties. Suppose it is something that is not *more* your particular business than that of several other persons; instead of saying, "Why does not one of *them* undertake this good work?" you should say, "If it be a thing right to be done, it must be right that *some*body should do it; is there any reason why I should not be that somebody?"

A man who is eager for gain is continually on the look-out for some profitable employment of the time or the capital he may have to spare, even though it may not exactly be in his own line of business. He will never willingly let his money or his hands remain idle. And if there be some scheme of profit which several other persons might engage in as well as he, this will only make him the more anxious that none of them should outstrip him in industrious enterprise. Now this conduct of "the children of this World" who are "wise in their generation," should serve as an example to "the children of light."

12

LESSON XVII.

MISCELLANEOUS CAUTIONS. — PART II.

§ 1. — *Veracity and Fidelity.*

All would agree that it is a duty to tell truth, and to keep promises; but there are several mistakes afloat respecting this branch of duty.

Remember, then, that we must look to the sense which the words spoken on any occasion *may be expected* to convey, and not to any other which they might grammatically bear. Hence, if you say something that is in the literal sense true, but which you know, or believe, will be otherwise understood, you are just as much morally guilty of falsehood as if the expression itself had been altogether false.

If, for instance, in some Mahometan country, you were to describe yourself as "*a true believer*," without giving any explanation of your meaning, this would be a deception; because it is well known that those words are (there) understood to mean a *Mahometan*. And it would be the same kind of deceit if you were to call yourself "a Catholic," when speaking to those who, you knew, would understand by that (however improperly) a member of "the Church of Rome."

So also, when our Lord said, "My kingdom is not

of this world," the expression might, indeed, be interpreted to mean "it *is* not so now; but I intend that it *shall* be such, hereafter." But if this had been his meaning, and He had designed that, as soon as ever his disciples should become powerful enough, they should rise in arms, and put down all idolatrous princes, and enforce the profession of Christianity, or at least secure to themselves a monopoly of all civil power, and civil rights, — in that case, He would have been guilty of a deception no less than if his declaration had been literally false. For He was vindicating himself before Pilate from the charge of "speaking against Cæsar"; and therefore must have known that He could not have been understood in the above sense; since that would have been to admit the charge.

And the same may be said of all the declarations of the Apostles, about "submitting to every ordinance of Man," etc. If they were honest men, they must have really meant what they could not but be certain they were *understood* at the time to mean; namely, a renunciation of all design, of themselves and their followers, to subvert by force any political institutions, or to enforce the profession of their own religion; or to monopolize for Christians civil rights.

§ 2. — *What constitutes Moral Truth and Falsehood.*

On the other hand, there is no moral falsehood in saying what is literally untrue, when we know that it will not be literally understood. Thus, Fables [or Parables] and, in short, all avowedly fictitious tales, are no violation of veracity. And when any one signs himself "your obedient servant," every one knows that this is merely the customary expression of civil courtesy.*

Again, when, in war, a General seeks to mislead the enemy as to the numbers or the position of his troops, — or when a ship of war is disguised as a merchantman, to entice a Pirate or a Slaver within reach, — or when a Policeman dresses in plain clothes, or some other disguise, in order to detect thieves, — in such cases there is no fraud, because the parties are aware that every kind of artifice will be resorted to against them; and no confidence is violated where none is placed. But when a *Flag of Truce* is displayed, or *Signals of Distress* hoisted, any deception is unjustifiable; because, according to the custom of all nations, these are understood as demands of confidence, and promises of good faith.

Every assertion, then, or promise, or declaration of whatever kind, is to be interpreted on the principle that the right meaning of any expression is that which may be *fairly presumed to be understood* by it. This may chance to be different from what the other party actually did understand; for you are not bound to be an-

---

* It is necessary, in each country, to be acquainted with the customary forms of expression of this kind; else you may be greatly perplexed yourself, and may perplex others. In Spain, for instance, the common form of civility to an acquaintance is to ask him to dinner, which he is expected civilly to decline; to accept such an invitation the first or the second time, would astonish and perplex a Spaniard as much as it would us if any one should understand literally the phrase "your obedient, humble servant," and should thereupon desire you to black his shoes. If a Spaniard really means to invite you to dinner, he repeats the invitation *a third time*, and then he is understood to mean it literally.

swerable for his mistakes. And again, it may be different from what you yourself inwardly meant, if you were designing to mislead the other by an equivocation, or if you expressed yourself carelessly and inaccurately. But in whatever sense it might reasonably be expected that a declaration of any kind will be understood, this is to be regarded as the true sense, and that to which you are bound.

§ 3. — *Implied Promises.*

And it is plain that the same rule applies to *acts* as well as to words. If, for instance, you asked any one the way to some place, and he *pointed* with his hand in a wrong direction, he would be acting a lie. And if any one should take some child into his family, and bring him up as a son of his own, he would be bound to provide for him. If he left him without any provision, he would be guilty of a breach of promise, though he might never have actually *said* anything on the subject. For the very reason why any promise is binding, is because he who knowingly excites expectations is bound to fulfil them.

So, also, if you should induce some laborers to come and settle on your land, and work for you, conforming to certain rules, with full permission to them to go to their own church or chapel on Sundays, then if you should afterwards withdraw this permission, and establish a new rule on the subject, you would be a deceiver, even though you had never said that the original rule was not to be changed, because you must have known what were the expectations you had raised, and which had induced them to accept your proposal.

Again, if some College, or School, or other such Institution, were established with a declaration that it was to be open to all, of whatever religious persuasion, and that none were to be excluded or expelled from it on account of their religion, this would of course be understood to mean that the pupils should not be obliged to learn or to practise anything against their religious conviction, however erroneous that conviction might be. For else some might be virtually excluded who might fairly claim, according to the original declaration, to be admitted.

Or again, if persons are invited to bestow their money and time and labor in establishing some Hospital or Dispensary, or some School, College, Public Library, etc., and are promised aid from a public fund on condition of keeping to a certain system, they have a fair claim to that aid as long as they conform to the system. If certain rules have been laid down as to the medicines to be administered, the books to be employed, or the plan to be followed, and then material alterations in these rules, etc. are afterwards introduced, and quite different ones enforced, this might be justly complained of as a fraud. Though no *express* promise had been made that the system should not be changed, both parties must have been fully aware that the invitation which was given, and accepted, would have been no invitation at all, but for the expectation that the system originally set forth was to remain the same.

Sometimes it is an *understood condition* of some promise that the fulfilment shall be *possible*, and that the promiser is only bound to do his very *utmost;* in which case he is not to be blamed for an unavoidable failure. But it is best that, whenever this is designed, the condition of "if possible" should be *distinctly expressed*, so as to make sure that both parties shall be fully aware of it. For whatever you promise unconditionally and *absolutely*, you are *absolutely* bound to make good; and you should not have made such an engagement, unless you were not only designing to use your best endeavors, but also absolutely certain of success; because it was you that induced the other party to rely upon it absolutely.*

---

* Dr. Paley lays it down as "evident" that a promise is not binding where performance is impossible; except only when the impossibility was known beforehand to the promiser. As, for instance, if you promise to procure a man a certain situation, knowing privately that it is already disposed of. And it is very common to hear people say, "Such a one is not to be blamed for not having made good what he promised, because he did his best, and it was found to be impossible." And yet every one knows that this rule does *not* hold good. For instance, if a merchant or manufacturer contracts to deliver such and such goods by a certain day, and fails, he is always held bound to make good the damage to the other party; though the failure may have been caused by the wreck of a ship, or by a strike among his workmen. He is never allowed to plead that it was *out of his power* to fulfil the contract, unless a condition to that effect was expressly inserted in it. The other party may choose to forego his claim, out of kindness and compassion, if he thinks the case one of peculiar hardship. But that he *has* the claim to compensation, just the same as if the failure had been wilful, no one doubts.

For he who makes an engagement unconditionally, is unconditionally bound to fulfil it.

If, therefore, a Minister of State, for instance, induces persons to vote for a certain measure, by the assurance that it will lead to such and such good results, he ought not to be allowed afterward to plead, that, on trial, he found it impossible to accomplish that object. Having led them to place full confidence in him, he must bear the whole blame of their disappointment.

§ 4.—*Cases in which a Promise is not binding.*

In any kind of assertion, then, or profession or promise, we are to look to what is *reasonably* to be understood; which may be something not distinctly stated in words. You are bound to nothing *less* than this, and to nothing *more.* For instance, if a man comes to you with a tale of distress, and you promise to relieve him; if you afterwards discover that he is an impostor, you are not bound by the promise: not merely because, if you had known this before, *you* would not have *made* the promise, for this is not enough; but because he *himself* must have understood your promise of relief to proceed on the supposition of his tale being true.

According to this rule, therefore, the Israelites, though they thought fit to spare the Gibeonites, were not bound to do so by their promise; because that was made, as the Gibeonites themselves well knew, on the supposition that they were a People of "a very far Country."*

---

* Afterwards, indeed, the Israelites *ratified* the promise they had been thus tricked into, and thus, in fact, entered into a *fresh* engagement with the Gibeonites, with a full knowledge of the circumstances. This new engagement, therefore, was binding. And it was for a violation of *this* engagement that Saul incurred guilt in slaying the Gibeonites.

Sometimes the unwary are tricked into a promise of *secrecy* by an art which they ought to be well on their guard against; since they may thus be brought into situations of much difficulty. A person gives you an account of some secret transaction or design, and then says, "Of course you will not mention this to any one." If you are inexperienced and incautious, you will be likely to answer hastily, "O certainly not"; and *then* you are pledged to secrecy; and thus, perhaps, made a party to some dishonorable transaction, or at least in-

In no case, in short, can any one be reproached with breach of a promise, who has been tricked into making it by a false representation of the matter it relates to. If, for instance, you were to be shown a pretended letter, or will, of your father, and were induced, by a regard for his supposed wishes, to make some promise, you would of course be freed from it as soon as you detected the forgery. So also if you had been induced to promise your assistance in arresting, and delivering over to death, a supposed heretic, or if you had been persuaded to make a vow of celibacy, or of implied obedience to the Superior of some Convent, from having been taught to believe that such is the will of God, then, if you were afterwards fully convinced that this is contrary to the truth, you would not be bound by any such engagement or vow.

As for such a case as that of King Herod, who had promised the daughter of Herodias to "give her whatsoever she should ask," a wise and upright counsellor would have advised him to answer her, "You understood — or *ought* to have understood — that the promise was, of anything *rightfully mine* to give, and did not extend to the commission of a crime."

---

volved in much perplexity. You ought to answer, "I shall act according to my own discretion; I shall conceal the matter, or divulge it, as I may see fit. If you had meant to secure my silence, you should have asked me for the promise *before* you made the communication; and I should probably have declined to pledge myself, in which case you might have told me nothing; but I will not have a confidence *forced* upon me without my own consent. As it is, you have thought fit to make this communication at your own risk, without previously exacting any promise. I have made none; and I decline to make any."

As for the *oath* in this, or indeed in any case, that, it is plain, has nothing to do with the question as to the fair *interpretation* of what is said. It only marks the promise or the assertion as a *deliberate and solemn* one. And a truly upright and pious man will consider himself to be *always* on his oath when he is speaking deliberately and solemnly. For such expressions as "calling God to witness," etc., can only mean, reminding *yourself* that He *is* a witness, and a judge, of all that you say or do: since it would be absurd to imagine that our acts are not known to Him unless we *invite* Him to notice them; or that He needs our *permission* to punish a wrong-doer.* But in all cases, a promise can be no excuse for doing anything that is in itself wrong; because you were *already bound to the contrary.* If, therefore, you have been drawn in to promise something unjustifiable, there was one sin in *making* the promise, and there would be another sin in keeping it.

§ 5. — *Falsehoods of Suppression.*

It follows from what has been above said, that there may be lies of *omission.* For if, when it is understood that you are giving a fair and full statement of any matter, you *suppress* some important circumstance, you are

---

* With respect to the "Coronation Oath," and the rest of what we call "oaths of office," it has been explained in the "Lessons on the British Constitution," that they bind no one to anything which he was not *already bound* to by the very act of accepting the office. Perhaps, therefore, it would be better if this were made more clearly understood, by omitting altogether all promissory oaths and declarations of this kind, and, instead of these, explaining to each person what are the duties of the office he is undertaking, and solemnly warning him that he is morally bound to fulfil those duties.

guilty of a deception, though all you do say may be quite true. Accordingly, witnesses in a Court of Justice swear to tell "the truth and the *whole* truth." For half the truth may amount to a falsehood.

If, for instance, an ignorant rustic is told that the Sun stands still, but is not informed, or cannot be made to understand, that the Earth turns round, he will be more at a loss than ever to understand the changes of day and night.

Again, an inscription, we learn, has been discovered at Nineveh, recording King Sennacherib's invasion of Judæa; stating that, after having taken several cities, he returned home. All which is true; but no mention is made of his having lost nearly two hundred thousand men before Jerusalem, which compelled him to make a hasty retreat. This, therefore, is a false record, according to the principle above laid down, that everything is to be understood as meaning what is fairly to be understood from it. For a professed narrative of any transaction is understood to give us *all* the essential parts of it.

So also, if one person sets forth all the moral precepts of the Gospel, and keeps back all mention of redemption by the sacrifice of our Saviour, and another preaches to his People justification through faith, and omits all notice of good works, each of these, though saying nothing that is not true, or that is not Scriptural truth, is falsifying the Gospel.

§ 6. — *Connivance at Deceit.*

It is to be observed also, that whoever connives at or takes advantage of a falsehood, makes himself a partner in the guilt of it. Suppose, for instance, you were a candidate, or a supporter of a candidate, for a seat in Parliament, or some other office, and that you found a report had been spread that the rival candidate had been guilty — which you knew he was not — of some atrocious crime; if you allowed this report to remain uncontradicted, so that men would vote against him from having been thus misled, you would be a partaker in the guilt of this falsehood, though you had not yourself invented it. Indeed, such conduct corresponds closely with the receiving of stolen goods; which is described by the Psalmist, saying, "When thou sawest a thief, thou consentedst unto him." For the like rule applies to both cases. He who says, "It was not I that invented and circulated this calumny," might equally well say, "It was not I that stole these goods; but they were offered me for sale, and I bought them."

One way in which some who are far from being quite indifferent about duty are apt to fail in that most important and difficult virtue, strict Justice, is, by *mistaking the question* to be decided, and fancying themselves right because they have judged rightly on some point that was not really the one in question. What we mean may be illustrated by the well-known story of Cyrus and the two coats. The famous King Cyrus was, as the tale goes, when a boy, punished by his master for giving an unjust decision. One of his schoolfellows, who was tall and stout, had a coat that was too small for him; and proposed to a smaller boy, whose coat was much too big for him, to make an exchange. But the other refused; whereupon the bigger boy took away the coat by force, and left his own in exchange; and Cyrus, on being appealed to, decided in favor of the exchange. He had judged rightly which coat best fitted each boy; but this was not the real question; which was, whether it was right to take away another's property without his consent.

So, in the case above alluded to, you may perhaps have judged rightly that the candidate against whom a false charge had been circulated was not the fittest person to be elected: but this does not justify you in suffering him to be injured by a false charge.

So also, if you compel a man to vote at an election for the candidate *you* think the best, or to spend his money in what appears to you the wisest manner, or to bring up his children in what you judge to be the truest religion, you are guilty of a wrong, even though your judgment on all these points should be right; because the real question is, not whether your opinions or his are the better, but whether he should be left to follow his own judgment and conscience, or be forced to follow yours.

So also, supposing you judged rightly in thinking that some falsehood which you propagate, or connive at, will lead to a good consequence, and that people may in such a case be deceived to their own advantage, still that is not the real question before you, but whether you have any *right* to deceive them at all. But by mistaking the real point to be decided on, men often justify to themselves the use of fraud (as well as of unjust force) for attaining what they consider a good end.

§ 7.—*Pious Frauds.*

There is accordingly no case in which men are oftener tempted to *connive* at falsehood, than where Religion and Virtue seem to be concerned. Some there are, indeed, who are directly guilty of what are called "pious frauds"; such as circulating false stories of miracles,—pretensions to inspiration, etc. The supposed goodness of the end blinds them to the sinfulness of the means; and they "do evil that good may come." But a truly pious as well as honest man will regard a "pious fraud" as the worst of all frauds, because, besides the sin of lying, it has also that of presumptuous profaneness. To suppose that the God of Truth can be served by falsehood, and can approve of it, is to attribute to Him the character of the Evil One, who is called in Scripture "the father of lies." What is called a *pious* fraud, therefore, is really an *impious* fraud.

Some, however, who would scruple distinctly to *assert* what they know to be untrue, will think it allowable and right to avoid undeceiving those who are under some (supposed) salutary delusion, for fear of what is called "unsettling their minds." * For instance, there are a good many readers of the Bible who are ignorant that the divisions into Chapters and Verses were not made

* It is a most important point of prudence, not to give *unnecessary* offence to any one, by expressing your opinions in a paradoxical and revolting form, or with an air of arrogant disdain; nor to agitate men's minds, for no object, by dragging in discussions of doubtful questions that have no necessary connection with the matter immediately in hand. Thus, if you were giving religious instruction to some persons who thought very differently from you on some points of politics, or medicine, or natural philosophy, not essential to the subject you were engaged on, it would be very unwise to go out of your way to alarm or disgust them, or agitate their minds with doubts by introducing, unnecessarily, disquisitions on those points. It is under the disguise of this kind of prudence that the disingenuous procedure we are speaking of has usually crept in.

by the Writers, but were introduced, long afterwards, for the sake of reference. Now there are some persons (of the character just described) who would indeed scruple to *tell* people that the Sacred Writers made those divisions, but wish that the ignorant should be *left* in that mistake ; and would even take care to suppress any correction of it, for fear of "unsettling their minds."

This particular mistake, many would regard as of very small importance ; though it is of much more than they suppose; since it causes many readers to misunderstand, or imperfectly understand, several parts of Scripture which would otherwise be quite clear.* But if you

* It should be remembered that the division into chapters and verses is not the work of the Sacred Writers themselves. They did not divide their writings into chapters and verses at all. Those divisions were made many hundred years afterwards, for the convenience of *reference;* because, as the *pages* of different Bibles do not correspond, we could not have found any passage we might want by looking to such and such a *page*, as we do in other books. But the chapters and verses have not always a reference (as some seem to suppose) to the *sense* of the Sacred Writers: on the contrary, they often interrupt and obscure the sense. In many parts of Scripture, for instance, a chapter will end, and a new one begin, just in the middle of a discourse. As, for instance,

At the end of the	19th	and beginning of	20th	Matt.
"	"	24th	"	"	25th "
"	"	2d	"	"	3d John.
"	"	18th	"	"	19th Acts.
"	"	7th	"	"	8th Rom.
"	"	10th	"	"	11th 1 Cor.
"	"	12th	"	"	13th "
"	"	3d	"	"	4th Coloss.

Note to p. 10, *Dublin edition, of a Tract on Self-Examination, for the Use of Persons who have been confirmed.*

And hence a person who reads the two chapters separately, at per-

once bring yourself to disregard truth in matters that seem to you of no great importance, you will gradually slide further and further into disingenuousness and double-dealing.*

§ 8. — *Consequences of Deception.*

And, moreover, any deception you may have propagated or connived at will be likely to lead to far greater evil effects than in what regards the particular point that is immediately concerned. For when it is detected — as deceptions generally are, sooner or later — men's confidence is shaken as to *every*thing that comes from the same quarter. "This man," they will say, "has led us, or left us, to believe something that he knew to be false; how can we trust him when he tells us that our Bible is faithfully translated from the Original? or indeed that there ever *was* any Original? How can we be sure that he is not deceiving us throughout?" And thus it often happens, according to the Proverbs, that "a liar is not believed even when he

---

haps several days' interval, will be very likely to understand but little of either; or perhaps even to make some dangerous mistake as to the Sacred Writer's meaning. Some of the plainest passages in Scripture have, I believe, been commonly misunderstood, merely through the mistaken attention paid to the division into chapters and verses.

* Accordingly, we have seen, of late years, persons venerated as "holy men" who have not only practised, but openly advocated, the system of what they call "reserve" or "economy"; that is, teaching something different from what they inwardly believe; and who have even acknowledged without shame that the strong censures uttered by them on some person or Church were what they did not themselves believe at the time to be just! — See No. XIII. of *Cautions for the Times.*

tells truth," and that "Frost and Fraud both end in foul."

Accordingly, pious frauds have (as Dr. Paley remarks) done more damage to Christianity than all other causes put together.

But to perceive the *expediency,* in the long run, of keeping scrupulously to truth, is a thing *not given* to those who do not venerate truth in itself, and adhere to it on moral grounds. The maxim that "honesty is the best policy," is one that you will find no one habitually *acting* on; for a truly honest man is always *before* it, and a knave is generally *behind* it. Those, that is, who merely look out for what is "the best policy," generally fail to find out, till too late, that honesty is really the best policy. And a really honest man, who does what is right, not on grounds of policy, but on moral principle, will usually be rewarded by finding that his course turns out to have been really the most politic.

LESSON XVIII.

MISCELLANEOUS CAUTIONS. — PART III.

§ 1. — *Coveting.*

THE sin of coveting, in the sense in which it is forbidden in the Tenth Commandment, is one concerning which some people fall into mistakes.

There is no sin in your wishing for a house, or a horse, or any other article, belonging to your neighbor, if you are willing to pay him a fair price for it; else indeed all buying and selling would be a sin. As it is, *each* party obtains an advantage, when there is fair dealing. For he who buys a horse shows that he *prefers* the horse to the money; and he who sells it, that he prefers the money to the horse.

But the sin of coveting consists in desiring to obtain another's property *without an equivalent*; — in short, to gain by his loss.* And this is what is done in *gam-*

---

* A man may indeed have such an excessive and absurd fancy for some article belonging to another, as to be willing to pay even *more* for it than it is really worth, or more than he can properly afford. This would be a piece of *extravagance* and folly; but no breach of the Tenth Commandment, if he did not wish to obtain it without an equivalent.

Again, a man may be said, in a certain sense, to gain by another's loss, if he sets up a shop in some place where there had before been

ing; including under that name all kinds of betting. Of course, any one who robs or (which comes to the same thing) cheats his neighbor, is also guilty of coveting: but then he is guilty of stealing too. He breaks both the Tenth Commandment and the Eighth. But in the case of gaming, where there is fair play, it is *only* the Tenth Commandment that is broken.

You may meet with treatises and tales directed against gaming, in which the writers speak all along not of fair play, but of *cheating*. And hence there is a danger of their leading the reader to think that where there is no cheating there is nothing wrong. Again, some of these writers draw lively pictures of the *ruinous losses* men have suffered in gaming; and this may mislead people into thinking that, as long as they proceed *prudently*, and do not stake more than they could afford to lose, they are doing nothing wrong. Sometimes again the *waste of time* is dwelt on; and hence the reader may be led to infer that he is merely required to game in *moderation*.

But all these admonitions and cautions have nothing to do with Gaming in particular, and as a thing evil in itself. For in buying and selling, and other such transactions, there may be cheating, or fair dealing. And there may be prudent or imprudent speculations in Mining, or Farming, and various other concerns. There may also be excess or moderation in every kind of

---

but one, and draws off a portion of the custom from him who had been enjoying a kind of monopoly. But there is evidently no sinful coveting in this; since what he desires to gain, and does gain, is the money of his customers in return for the goods they buy of him; not anything that was the *property* of the *other shopkeeper*.

recreation; as in Music, or in Field-sports, or the cultivation of a flower-garden, etc. All those admonitions, therefore, which are usually given, have no peculiar relation to Gaming. But what does especially belong to it is, that it is a breach of the Tenth Commandment, though not of the Eighth; being an attempt to obtain another's property without an equivalent, — to gain by his loss.*

Gamesters, it is true, do very often fall into the hands of sharpers, or become sharpers themselves; and many squander their time, or their fortunes, at the gaming-table or the race-course. But hardly any one *begins* with such a *design*. They begin by designing to play *fairly*, and to associate with none but fair players, and to game *moderately*, and *prudently*. And they have been taught to think that the *only* evils of gaming consist in a departure from these rules. Afterwards they are led on, step by step, into utter ruin. But they would not have taken the *first* step, if they had been taught from the first that gaming is *bad in itself*. There is reason to think, therefore, that those treatises and tales, etc. above alluded to are likely to do at least as much harm as good.

Those who attempt to defend Gaming say, "I do the other no wrong, for I have his *consent:* he agrees

---

* It is true the Ten Commandments, as indeed the rest of the Mosaic Law, were addressed to the Israelites alone, and that Law has not *in itself* any binding force on us. (See "Lessons on Religious Worship.") But all *moral* precepts — of which the Tenth Commandment is manifestly one — are (as was observed above) binding on every man from their own nature. Coveting — and the same may be said of theft, murder, etc. — is not wrong *because* it was *forbidden*, but was forbidden because it is wrong.

to risk his money for the chance of winning mine; and I do the same." Why, if this were not the case, it would be the same thing as *stealing;* and we do not charge you with a breach of the Eighth Commandment, but only of the Tenth. But it is plain that you are, each of you, wishing and seeking to profit by another's loss; and if this be not the sin of coveting, what is?

Of course, if the sum staked on some game or bet be so utterly insignificant to the players that it makes no perceptible difference whether they win or lose it, there is no sinful covetousness in the case. And accordingly, that might not be Gaming to one person which is so to another. For a few shillings would be, to a man of fortune, a mere nothing; though as many pence would be a serious loss or gain to a poor laborer. But if your *example* leads any one to play for a stake which is to him (though not to you) of some consequence, you will have been encouraging him in the sin of Gaming.*

§ 2.—*Personal Injuries.*

Generous forgiveness of injuries is a point of Christian duty respecting which some people fall into confusion of thought. They confound together personal *resentment* and *disapprobation* of what is morally wrong. A person who has cheated you, or slandered, or other-

---

* As for the scruple felt by some persons about games of *chance*, because they consider a *lot* as something *sacred*, that, it is plain, has nothing at all to do with the present subject. For people may, and often do, play at games of chance without any stake at all. And again, at billiards, which is altogether a game of skill, much gambling often takes place.

wise wronged *you*, is neither *more* nor *less* a cheat or a slanderer, than if he had done the same to a stranger. And in that light he ought to be viewed. Such a person is one on whom you should not indeed wish to inflict any suffering beyond what may be necessary to reform him, and to deter other wrong-doers; and you should seek to benefit him in the highest degree by bringing him to a sense of his sin. But you ought not to choose such a man as an associate, or to trust him, and in all respects treat him as if he had done nothing wrong. You should therefore take care, on the one hand, that the personal injury you may have suffered does not lead you to think worse of a man than he deserves, or to treat him worse; and, on the other hand, you should not allow a false generosity to destroy in your mind the distinctions of right and wrong. Nor, again, should the desire of gaining credit for great magnanimity, lead you to pretend to think favorably of wrong conduct, merely because it is you that have suffered from it. None but thoughtless or misjudging people will applaud you for this. The duty of Christian forgiveness does not require you, nor are you allowed, to look on injustice, or any other fault, with indifference, as if it were nothing wrong at all, merely because it is you that have been wronged.

And, universally, you should take care not to confound together tenderness and kindness towards the *persons* who are in error or in fault, and indifference about the *faults themselves*. A charitable disposition is chiefly shown in making due allowances for those whom we do think in the wrong; not in persuading ourselves that they are right, or that it is of little consequence whether a man thinks and acts rightly or wrongly. *Faults* and *errors*, you should be careful neither to overrate, nor to underrate; and the persons who may have fallen into them, you should be careful not to judge too harshly, yet without destroying in your own mind the distinctions of true and false, or of good and evil.

§ 3.— *Christian Humility.*

There are also mistakes afloat respecting the duty of Christian Humility. (1.) It is a mistake to suppose that it is a part of Christian Humility to renounce the use of your Reason, and give yourself up to be led by your feelings; or to follow blindly some human leader.

Of course, it would be a fault to be over-confident in your own judgment, or to employ your Reason on matters above human reason, or to refuse to listen attentively to those who are able to give you good advice and instruction. And young people especially ought to follow the guidance of those older and wiser than themselves. But they should endeavor also to learn to *understand* the instructions they receive; in order that as they grow up they may become capable of guiding *themselves*, and not remain children all their lives. "Be not," says the Apostle, "children in understanding: howbeit, in malice be ye children, but in understanding be men."

But to resolve to give yourself up, to follow, all your life, as a safe guide, some person or party who can show no miraculous proof of infallibility, is to humble yourself, not before God, but before Man.*

* You will observe that the Apostle Paul (1 Cor. chap. iii.) calls

And there is no Christian humbling of yourself — though debasement there is — in resigning yourself to your feelings, and following what some call "the dictates of the Heart," instead of what Reason shows to be true and right; because your Feelings are as much a part of your *self* as your Reason is; so that this is only humbling one portion of yourself before another portion.

The disciples, you should remember, were led by the sober decision of a sound understanding to say, "No man can do these miracles except God be with him"; and thence to trust and believe Jesus implicitly; but Peter was led by his "Heart" — that is, his inclinations and prejudices — to say, "Be it far from Thee, Lord! there shall no such thing happen unto Thee."

§ 4. — *Confessions of the Depravity of Man.*

(2.) There is no personal humility in confessing generally the weakness and ignorance and sinfulness of the whole *human race*. It is indeed quite right that we should be duly sensible of that weakness. And you should not listen to any one who attempts to explain the nature of the Most High as He is in Himself,

---

the Corinthians "*carnal* and walking as men," when they formed themselves into parties. And he is far from confining what he says to some few superior persons, leaving ordinary Christians to continue "carnal": but censures partisanships altogether. And as he condemns those who said, "I am of Paul, and I of Apollos, and I of Cephas," etc.; so he would, no doubt, if he had lived in later days, have censured those who say, "I am of Whitfield, or I of Wesley, or I am a Calvinist, or I an Arminian," etc.

and why, and how, the sufferings of Christ were necessary for Man's salvation, and why evil exists in the universe, and other mysterious points which are beyond human Reason, and which Scripture does not reveal.

And equally to blame are both those who profess to explain, where God has not given us revelation, the reasons of his dealings with Man, and those again who insist on it that in such and such a case He *had* no reason at all, but acted as He did "to declare his sovereignty," and "for his own glory"; as if He could literally desire glory! When the Most High has merely revealed to us his Will, we have no right to pronounce that He *had* no reasons for it except his will,* because he has not made them known to us. Even an earthly king, who is not responsible to any of his subjects for the reasons of his commands, may think fit sometimes to issue commands without explaining his reasons: and it would be very rash for any one to conclude that he had *no* reason at all, but acted from mere caprice.

So also, a dutiful child will often have to say, "I do

---

* "Many," says Calvin (Inst. 53, c. 23, § 7), "as if wishing to remove odium from God, while they admit *election*, yet deny *reprobation*; but in this they speak ignorantly and childishly; since election itself could not be maintained except as contrasted with reprobation. God is said to set apart those whom He adopts, as children for salvation. Those therefore whom He passes by, He condemns; and that *for no cause whatever except that He chooses* to exclude them from the inheritance which He predestinates for his children." And again, shortly after, he says, "Whence comes it that so many nations, with their infant children, should be sentenced irremediably to eternal death, by the fall of Adam, except that *such was God's will?* ..... The Decree is, I confess, a horrible one," etc.

so and so because my parents have commanded me; that is reason enough for me." But though this is — to the child — a very good reason for *obeying* the command, it would be a very bad reason with the *parents* for *giving* that command. And he would show his filial veneration and trust, not by taking for granted that his parents *had* no reason for their commands, but, on the contrary, by taking for granted that there *was* a good reason both for acting as they did, and for not giving him any explanation.

It is therefore no pious humility, but, on the contrary, great presumption, for Man to pronounce — where Scripture does not tell us — either what were the reasons of God's dealings with us, or that He had none at all. One who pretends to be so much wiser, or better informed, than the Apostles and Prophets, as to tell us what they knew not, or at least were not commissioned to make known, must greatly overrate the faculties of Man.

But though it is most important to think rightly and humbly of the Human Race generally, no one will feel *ashamed* and *personally* humbled at the thought that he is no wiser or better than the very wisest and best of mankind; nor will this, therefore, incite him to seek improvement. A child is not ashamed of not having the full structure and intellect of a man, but only if he fails in something that might fairly be expected of a child. And moreover, it is possible for you to think very lowly of the wisdom or the virtue of the *human species*, and yet to overrate your*self* as compared with other men. You may thus fancy yourself very eminent in the virtue of Christian Humility, while, in truth, you are puffed up with spiritual pride; trusting that you are exempt from this, because you do not think highly of Human Nature generally, and because you acknowledge with gratitude that whatever there is of good in you is a gift of God; even as the Pharisee in the parable was *thankful* for not being "as this Publican."

It may seem strange that there should be any need — but a need there certainly is — to admonish you that there is no humility in confessing the sins of other people. If, for instance, you believe that some act of our rulers, in which you had no hand, is very wrong, and amounts to a national sin, it is possible you may be right in thinking so, but you cannot be personally humbled by this thought. You are right in believing that our first Parents committed a grievous sin; but it would be absurd to imagine that you ought to be — or that you *can* be — penitent for the sin of Adam. All real penitence must be for the faults you are conscious of in yourself; and personal humility consists, not in forming a low estimate of some other persons, or of the whole human Race, but in not thinking too highly of yourself individually.

§ 5. — *Just Estimate of One's Self.*

(3.) On the other hand, it is a mistake to think that any one who does happen to be superior to the generality, intellectually or morally, is bound, as a point of modesty, to be ignorant of this, or to pretend to be so, and to think, or profess to think, himself inferior to what he really is. For, on the one hand, it cannot be a part of Duty to be under any kind of *mistake;* and, on the other hand, there cannot be any virtue in feigning or affectation of any kind.*

But if your belief is, that you do possess some superior endowments as to any point, take care — as far as regards yourself — to be thankful to the Giver of all such advantages, and to remember that, for every talent intrusted to you, you are accountable to Him. And, as far as regards others, take care to avoid *ostentation* and disdainful assumption of superiority. For this is offensive, even in such matters of fact as admit of no possible mistake or doubt. A person, for instance, who should have gained some great prize in a competition, or discovered a new Planet, or invented a new Telegraph, or performed some other notable exploit, must not boast, nor be always reminding people of what he has done.

And, on the other hand, even if he should be mistaken in his opinion of his own abilities, and think them greater than they are, a mere error of judgment will not be imputed to him as a sin, provided he keep clear of pride;

---

* Properly speaking, self-conceit and modesty have reference to a man's estimate of himself as *compared with the reality*. A conceited man *overrates* himself; and a modest man does not. But many people do not at all take this into account. They are apt to reckon a man conceited who has a *high* opinion (whether rightly or wrongly) of his own powers; and him modest who forms a *low* one. And yet it may so happen that this latter may be in reality overrating himself in thinking himself not below the average, or only a little below; and the other may possibly be even underrating himself in thinking himself only a little above it.

If you could imagine a mouse imagining itself just equal to such a *small* animal as a rabbit, and an elephant believing itself only equal to such a *large* animal as an ox, they would be making opposite mistakes.

nor will he be offensive to others, if he is but free from disdainful arrogance, and from ostentation.

§ 6. — *General Confessions, and Confession without Amendment.*

(4.) Again, there is no humility in a mere *general* confession that you are a "miserable sinner," if in each particular case you always stoutly justify yourself, and can never be brought to own a fault.

(5.) Lastly, there is no humility in confessing any faults which you do not strive to *correct.* It would indeed be a shocking presumption to think that you need not aim at improvement, but are quite good enough, being *without* faults; but it is still greater presumption to think that you are good enough *with* all your faults. "If we say that we *have no* sin, we deceive ourselves"; but if we say that we *have* sins, and yet do not earnestly seek God's promised help "to cleanse us from all unrighteousness," this would be even a more fatal self-deception.

Remember then that the virtue of Christian Humility is not to be considered as some bitter potion, which you can swallow in a large dose, once for all, and so have done with it; but rather as a kind of *alterative* medicine, to be taken daily, and drop by drop.

You must study, daily, to be open to conviction, — patient of opposition, — ready to listen to reproof, even when you are not convinced that it is deserved, — ready, when you *are* convinced, to confess an error, — and glad to receive hints, and suggestions, and corrections, even from your inferiors in ability, — and never overbearing or uncharitable towards those who differ from you, or ostentatious of superiority.

All this will be a more laborious and difficult task than to make fine speeches about your ignorance, and weakness, and sinfulness; but it is thus that true Humility is shown, and is exercised and cultivated.

§ 7. — *Moral Judgments of the Vulgar.*

You must remember, not only that we are not to act for the *sake* of human approbation, but also that we are not to measure our conduct by the prevailing opinions of men. For though men in general do, on the whole, (as has been formerly remarked,) approve of virtue and condemn vice, the moral judgment of a great part of mankind is, in several points, apt to be incorrect; and their standard of virtue is rather a low one. It is a true and wise remark of Lord Bacon, that "the lowest of the virtues the vulgar praise; the middle ones they admire; of the highest they have no perception." By "the vulgar" he means not merely the lowest in station, and the utterly illiterate, but the common run of mankind. And by "the virtues" he means those parts of virtue — or habits that commonly pass for virtues — of which we have formerly spoken. The humblest of these, — such as Hospitality, Liberality, Gratitude, good-natured Courtesy, etc., — he says are what the vulgar praise. Those which they admire, — such as daring Courage, and Fidelity to friends, and to the cause or the party one has espoused, are what he puts in the next highest place. But the loftiest virtues of all, — such as disinterested Public Spirit, thoroughgoing even-handed Justice, and disregard of general unpopularity when

Duty requires it, — of these, he says, the vulgar usually have no notion.

And he might have gone further: for it often happens that a large portion of mankind not only do not praise or admire, but even censure or despise, the highest qualities. Cases will sometimes occur in which, though you may obtain the high approbation of a very few persons of the most exalted and refined moral sentiments, you must be prepared to find the majority (even of such as are not altogether bad men) condemning you as "unnatural," "unkind," "faithless," and not to be depended on; or deriding you as "eccentric," "crotchety," "fanciful," and "absurdly scrupulous."

§ 8. — *Virtues that are not generally approved.*

If, for instance, you refuse to defend, or to deny, or to palliate, the faults of those engaged in what you consider a good cause, and if you are ready to bear testimony to whatever there may be that is right, on the opposite side, you will be regarded by many as treacherous, or lukewarm, or inconsistent. If you are an advocate for tolerating an erroneous faith, and protest against forcing, or entrapping, or bribing, any one into the profession of a true one, many will consider you as yourself tainted with error, or indifferent to true religion.

If, again, you consider a seat in Parliament, or any other place you may occupy, or the power of appointing another to such a place, as a sacred *trust* for the public service, and therefore requiring sometimes the sacrifice of private friendship, — if you do justice to an opponent against a friend, or to a worse man (when he happens to have right on his side) against a better,—if you refuse to support your friends, or those you have been accustomed to act with, or those to whom you have a personal obligation, when they are about doing something that is unjustifiable;—in these, and other such cases, you will be perhaps more blamed or despised by the generality, than commended or admired. For party men will usually pardon a zealous advocate of their party for many great *faults*, more readily than they will pardon the *virtue* of standing quite aloof from party, and doing strict justice to all.

And, again, it will often happen that when a man of very great real excellence does acquire great and general esteem, four fifths of this will have been bestowed on the minor virtues of his character; and four fifths of his admirers will have either quite overlooked the most truly admirable of his qualities, or else regarded them as pardonable weaknesses.

You should guard then against the opposite dangers, of either lowering *your own* moral standard to the level of some of your neighbors, or judging too hardly of *them*. Your general practical rule should be, to expect *more of yourself than of others*. We do not, of course, mean, that you should ever call wrong conduct right. But you should consider that that which would be a very great fault in *you*, may be much less inexcusable in some others who have not had the same advantages. You should be ready to make allowances for want of clearness of understanding, or for defective education, or for a want of the highest and best examples. Those may be really trying to do their duty according to the best lights they have, whose moral views are, on some points, as yet but dim and imperfect, and whose conduct on the whole falls far short of what may fairly be expected — and *will* be expected — of one whose moral judgment is more enlightened, and his standard of duty more elevated.

LESSON XIX.

SELF-EXAMINATION. — PART I.

§ 1. — *Stated Times for Self-Examination.*

EVERY prudent man who is engaged in business of any kind, besides paying careful attention to that business from day to day, will also set aside certain stated times for looking over his accounts, and examining the whole state of the concern he is carrying on. He will do this, probably, once a week; and again, more particularly and thoroughly, once a month, or once a quarter; and most fully of all, at the end of each year.

Now this is what you should do in reference to your moral character, if you are as much in earnest about the improvement of *that*, as every prudent man of business is about his worldly success. Besides examining your own heart, and your conduct, daily, you should also have fixed times for making a more complete review of your whole life and character. And suitable times for such self-examinations you can fix on, for yourself, according to your own convenience. The beginning of a new year, or the beginning of *your own* new year — that is, your Birthday — are very proper to be selected for this purpose. So also is the anniversary of your *Confirmation* (which may be called your religious *coming of age*), or of any other remarkable event connected with yourself. And so also is any of the great Festivals of the Church, such as Christmas-day, or Easter.

But whatever day you fix on for such a purpose, you should keep to it strictly, as a sort of private religious festival; and not allow yourself to be tempted to put off, without some strong necessity, your proposed self-examination, on the ground that one day will do as well as another. So it would, originally; but habits of regularity, and of adherence to a plan once fixed on, are of great importance. For if you learn the custom of lightly putting off till to-morrow what you had fixed on to-day for doing, you will at length find the truth of the proverb, that "To-morrow comes never."

§ 2. — *Candor in Self-Examination.*

Our Prayer-Book directs us (in one of the exhortations in the Communion Service) to "examine our consciences, and that not lightly" (negligently) "and after the manner of dissemblers with God." Now it may seem strange that there should be any need even to mention such a thing as "dissembling with God," — with Him who sees all hearts. But though it is impossible to deceive *Him*, it is possible, and easy, for us to deceive *ourselves*. And that is what you *will* do, if, in examining yourself, you proceed just as men do who are trying to deceive their fellow-mortals, by seeking to justify or excuse their faults; — by softening down, or passing over, some of the worst points, and seeking to put the best appearance on their own conduct, and to make out the best case they can for themselves. If you proceed thus, when you are examining yourself with respect to your duty, you will completely succeed in deceiving — not God indeed — but yourself. You will succeed, perhaps, in quieting your conscience; but not in correcting your faults, and purifying your heart, and amending your life.

But no one proceeds thus, in any matter in which he is thoroughly in earnest. A careful farmer does not try to persuade himself that his crops and his cattle are thriving, but to judge whether they really are. He does not try to overlook any weeds that may be in his fields, but to *find* them, in order to root them out. And a diligent shopkeeper does not try to falsify his accounts, so as to persuade himself that his trade is prospering more than it really is; but to learn exactly what is the real state of his affairs. And you will proceed in the same manner if you are as much in earnest about "laying up treasure in Heaven" as every prudent man is about the concerns of his worldly business.

You should observe, too, that no one who finds his business going on badly, takes comfort in the thought that some of his neighbors' concerns are in a still worse condition, and that they are farther on the road to ruin than himself. He knows that *their* imprudences and losses will not save *him*. Do not therefore satisfy yourself with finding, or fancying, that you are as good as many others, or perhaps better; but consider whether you are as good as you may be, and ought to be. For our course of duty is not like a race, which is won by him who runs however slowly, if the rest are still slower. Examine therefore your*self* rather than your neighbors; and remember that the greatest faults of theirs are, to you, of less consequence than a much smaller one in yourself; both because it is for this you will be accountable, and because it rests with *you* to correct it.

§ 3. — *Progress in Virtue to be marked.*

We have spoken of the importance of examining yourself fairly, and not seeking to conceal from yourself your faults, or to make out excuses for them. But do not suppose that by this we mean that you should look out for *faults* only. By a fair self-examination, we do not mean an inquiry after sins and defects *only*, without any notice being taken of improvements; — without looking out for, or hoping for, any "growth in grace." On the contrary, as you have been taught to *strive* and to *pray* for continual advancement, so you ought also to *watch* for it. And although, as was formerly observed, the performance of any *particular act of duty* does not, of itself, and as such, afford positive pleasure, but merely exemption from the pain of self-reproach, still, to observe an improvement in *virtuous character*, generally, does afford pleasure. And this is a kind of pleasure which tends to encourage our efforts towards improvement; and which was doubtless bestowed by our great Master for that very purpose. You ought therefore carefully to observe, with thankfulness to the Giver of all good, any progress you may have made in your Christian course. There is no benefit you ought so much to rejoice in, or to be so thankful for, as an increase in holiness of life and of heart, and in the knowledge and love of God. Every such increase, therefore, should be as carefully inquired for, as any sins you may have committed. And whatever improvement you may find in yourself should encourage you to fresh hopes, and fresh efforts after a still further advance.

You may perhaps meet with some well-meaning persons who will advise you to think of nothing but your sins and your unworthiness; and in all your self-examination to look out for nothing but what is wrong; without ever allowing yourself to think that you have made any improvement. "Every one is so much inclined," they say, "to think of his goodness and to overlook his sins, that we ought to draw men as far as possible the contrary way, and advise them to dwell on the thought of their own sinfulness, and on nothing else."

But you may easily see that this is quite a mistaken plan. For you will never find an instance of any one's continuing very long to labor for any object, when he was convinced that he was laboring in vain. If, for instance, any one sets himself to learn some science or art, and finds, after very attentive study for a considerable time, that he makes no progress at all, he will give it up. Some will persevere longer than others; but every one will abandon the pursuit as soon as he is fully convinced that it is hopeless. So also, a man engaged in some business, if he finds, after a long trial, that, instead of gaining by it, he is losing, and that there is no prospect of doing any better, will give over the business altogether. It is the same with a person taking a course of medicine with a view to the recovery of his health; or with one who is trying to bring a piece of land into a productive state; and with other such cases.

And so it is with respect to Christian Virtue, as well as everything else.

§ 4. — *Despair leads to Neglect.*

Persons may *begin* striving (as the Apostle Paul bids us) to "draw nigh unto God, that He may draw nigh unto them" (James iv.), and to "resist the Devil, that he may flee from them"; they may begin an endeavor to "work out their own salvation" (Philippians ii.), "casting off the sin that besets them" (Heb. xii.), and "giving all diligence, to add to their faith, virtue, and knowledge, and temperance, patience, godliness, brotherly-kindness, charity" (2 Peter i.). They may set about all this; but if they are convinced that they are making no progress in it, and must never think of making any, you may be sure that they will, before long, give over their efforts. They will either fall into gloomy despondency, or else (and more likely) sit down in a sort of careless security; fancying that there is much Christian humility in saying and thinking that there is no good in them, nor ever can be any. They will consider what the Apostle Paul says (Rom. vii.) of being "carnal and sold under sin," and living in habitual disobedience to God's laws, as meant to describe the Apostle's own condition, and, of course, that of all other the very best Christians. And hence they will conclude that it is vain and hopeless for them to strive against sin; and that there is nothing to be done but to throw themselves on God's mercy, without seeking to avail themselves of his promised help to "bring forth fruits meet for repentance."

§ 5. — *Virtuous Progress to be hoped for.*

Let no one therefore persuade you to distrust God's promise to "give his Holy Spirit to them that ask him." (Luke xi. 13.) Our great Master has said, "Blessed are they that hunger and thirst after righteousness, for *they shall be filled.*" (Matt. v. 6.) If you trust in Him, and really mean to accept his gracious offers, you will not only wish, and pray, but also strive, and hope, for continual Christian improvement. And of course you will also carefully examine yourself from time to time, to observe whether this improvement does take place or not. Try never to overlook either any fault, or any improvement; and never attempt to deceive yourself either way, by saying in your private confessions and prayers, either less, or more, than you sincerely believe to be the truth. And especially, you should observe whether each return of such an anniversary as you may have fixed on (such as New-Year's-day, or your Confirmation-day) finds you a better Christian than the last; — more full of the thoughts and hopes of Heaven, and more advanced on your way thither.

You will see, in the Epistles, that this is the way the Apostles proceeded; expressing joy and gratitude for all the progress their converts had made, and their hope that this would be an encouragement to them to "grow in grace" (2 Peter iii.), and to "abound more and more" (1 Thess. iv.).

And you should seek for, and watch for, improvement in your *motives*, as well as in your outward conduct. For we generally act from a mixture of motives; and some of these motives, even when not wrong in themselves, may be inferior to others. Some act, for instance, may be what you are convinced is morally right, and also such as will gain you the esteem of the best men, and also such as is commanded by your Divine Master, and well pleasing in his sight; and it may be also such as to benefit your country, and thus gratify your feelings of patriotism. There will then be several distinct feelings, all tending the same way. And it is a matter on which you should take great pains and care in self-examination, to observe what are the motives on which you act, and in what degree each of them operates, and to strive to act on the best and highest motives.

LESSON XX.

SELF-EXAMINATION. — PART II.

§ 1. — *Christian Knowledge.*

THE point in which you can the most easily *mark* your own improvement is Christian *knowledge.* This is indeed only the means, and not the end, of a Christian life. For the more you *know* of your duty, if you do not practise it, the greater is your sin. "The true knowledge and understanding of God's Word," if you do not, in your life, "set it forth and show it accordingly," * will profit you nothing. But still though Christian knowledge be the *least* part of the Christian's business, it must be the *first* part. For you cannot act on Christian principles without knowing something of what your religion is. And moreover, if you are very ignorant of it, and are *content* to *remain* so, this is a sign that your heart is not engaged in God's service. For if any one received a letter from his father, or some other friend whom he professed to love and revere, containing directions for his conduct, and yet never read that letter with any attention, you would at once conclude that his professed love and respect were not real.

If, therefore, you do feel a real love and reverence for

---

* Litany.

your Maker, Redeemer, and Sanctifier, you will study what he has thought fit to reveal to us. And you will study it, not as a task which you dare not entirely omit, but as a high honor and privilege. You will also not merely "read," but endeavor to "learn and inwardly digest, the Holy Scriptures"; not as if it were a virtuous act to go through a certain portion of Scripture; but with the same attention with which every one reads any book on some subject in which he takes great interest and delight; not for the sake of *saying* that he has been reading it, but for the sake of gaining valuable instruction and information from it.

§ 2. — *Scripture to be studied intelligently.*

If then you read with a view to improvement, you will not be satisfied with reading — or even learning by heart — detached passages, single verses, or single chapters, — taken one from one part of the Bible, and another from another. He who studies in that manner does not give himself a fair chance of taking in the true and full sense of what he reads; even if it be one *single work* of any one author that he is engaged on. But the volume which we call the Bible, you should remember, is not properly *one* book, but several; written at very distant times, and on different occasions. Even the New Testament alone consists of more than twenty distinct works, addressed by the Sacred Writers to different classes of people. And the Old Testament was written for the use, in the first instance, of a people living under a dispensation different from the Gospel, and preparatory to it.

To open the Bible, therefore, at random, and take the

first passage that happens to meet your eye, or to attract your notice, as applicable at once to ourselves now, and as a suitable guide for our belief and practice, would be such a procedure as every one would perceive to be absurd in any like case. For instance, suppose a person had received from a wise and good father a great number of instructive letters, from the time when he was a child, barely able to read, till he was a grown man, and long after; if he laid by these letters carefully, but in a promiscuous heap, and on any occasion when he needed counsel took up the first of them that came to hand, as containing directions for his conduct, he would be accounted a mere fool.

In order, then, to read profitably, you should, in your private studies, go through one entire work, continuously; one of the Gospels, for instance, or one of the Epistles; going on from time to time from the place where you had left off, till you have finished the book you had begun. And you should not make it your ordinary practice to begin and end at the beginning and end of a *chapter*, but wherever there is a convenient break in the sense. For the chapters and verses, which (as was remarked above) were not the work of the Sacred Writers, have no necessary reference to their sense, but often interrupt it; and thus often obscure the meaning, to those who consider these divisions as designed by the original writers.

§ 3. — *Practical Study.*

But of all the cautions to be observed in your study of Scripture, the most important is, to keep in view your own *practical* benefit, in the improvement of your character and life. For, as has been already said, the more knowledge you have of what is right, the worse you will be, if you do not strive to bring that knowledge into practice. It is not merely that the sin is greater of that "servant who knew his Lord's will, and did it not," but also, besides this, there is a danger of your becoming hardened against all religious impressions, by letting the most awful and awakening thoughts pass through your mind, without these thoughts being accompanied with an effort to form practical habits answering to those religious impressions. An early familiar *acquaintance* with Scripture, without reference to practice, leads to the danger (as was formerly remarked, Lesson XI.) pointed at by the proverb, that "Familiarity breeds contempt." The oftener any impression on the mind is repeated, the less forcible it becomes. The more frequently any thought comes before us, the less strongly does it excite us. So that the more you are accustomed to think and talk about Religion, and about Moral Duty, if you do not at the same time strive to acquire a practical habit of acting accordingly, the more insensible you will become to all good impressions. And, on the other hand, if you do strive to bring your principles into practice, you will find the practice become easier and easier.

It is so in all other matters, as well as in Religion and Morality. A mariner, for instance, who has been long at sea, is very little affected by the terrible appearance of a storm, compared with what you would be if you were in a storm at sea for the first time. And for the same reason, that is, from long custom, he goes about his duty in the ship actively and coolly; and in the midst of the tempest exerts his skill and strength in doing whatever is required, with that readiness which is the fruit of long habit. And in other cases also you may see the same effects produced by practice. In short, you have only to keep in mind the well-known maxim, that "Practice makes perfect."

But you should also take care to avoid the mistake, formerly noticed, of those who expect to learn one thing by practising another. Remember, therefore, what was there said (Lesson XI.) of the opposite habits that may be acquired by being accustomed to the same things; as, for instance, by two persons each accustomed to the sound of a certain bell; one of whom learns to sleep quietly through the ringing, and another to be instantly roused by it. By merely reading and hearing and talking about Virtue or Religion, you will acquire a habit of talking, etc., without doing; and by continued efforts to impress on your heart what you learn, and set it forth in your conduct and character, you will acquire a habit of "being a doer of God's Word, and not a hearer only, deceiving your own self." (James i.)

§ 4. — *Outward Acts not the only Virtuous Practice.*

You are not to suppose, however, that some *outward* act is always required in order to form a practical habit; and that you must wait for an opportunity of performing what are called "good works." Virtuous acts are acts of the *mind.* An earnest endeavor to fix on your heart the examples of Christ and his Apostles, and to form your character on that pattern, is, itself, virtuous practice. There is real active virtue in forming a hearty good resolution, with earnest prayer for divine help to keep it. Every effort to "set your affection on things above, not on things on the earth" (Col. iii. 2); every earnest struggle against ill-temper, pride, or envy, — against coveteousness, — against sensual desires, and every kind of evil thoughts; every inward effort to cultivate a kind and forbearing, a pure, and holy, and truly Christian disposition; — every such effort is virtuous practice. And thus, even when you are not performing any *outward* acts, (there being, at the moment, no opportunity,) you may be gaining practical habits, which will not fail to show themselves in action when opportunities do occur.

In fact, outward actions (as has been formerly observed in Lesson V.) are not properly virtuous or vicious at all, except as they are the signs of the inward dispositions. And accordingly, when the Apostle Paul is enumerating the "fruits of the Spirit," he makes mention of *nothing but the dispositions:* "The fruit of the Spirit is love, joy, peace, long-suffering, goodness, gentleness, faith, meekness, temperance, patience, and such like." (Gal. v. 22.) He well knew — as indeed every one must know — what kind of outward conduct such dispositions will lead to.

§ 5. — *Advice of Friends.*

What has been said as to the importance of reading and listening with a view to practical improvement will, of course, apply not merely to the Scriptures, but to any other useful books; and likewise to any good instruction you may receive from Christian ministers, or from other friends.

It was formerly remarked that the counsel of a worthy and judicious friend will often be of great service in guarding you against self-deception, and pointing out to you some things which you may yourself have overlooked. And such a friend may sometimes be able also to give useful advice for the correction of your faults. For this purpose it will sometimes be necessary that you should unbosom yourself to him, and confess some things which he could not otherwise know. But such confessions should be with a view to *consultation*. As for the forgiveness of sins against God, it is God alone that can grant that. And, therefore, a full and *complete* confession of all the sins you are conscious of should be made to Him, and not to any human being. The contrary practice does much more harm to the moral character than good.

Of course, if you are conscious of having *wronged* any one, you should confess your fault to him, and ask his pardon. And it may now and then happen, that, in *giving* advice to another, you may find it useful to tell him of some error you had yourself fallen into, in order that he may take warning from your example. But in seeking, through the aid of a friend, the improvement of your own character, you should confine yourself to these two cases: (1.) when you are conscious of some failing, and wish for advice as to the best way of *curing* it; and (2.) when you are *in doubt* whether something you have done be right or wrong, and wish for a judicious friend's opinion on the question. In all other matters, confessions of sin should be made to God only.

§ 6. — *Signs of Progress.*

If you persevere in such a course of practical study as has been recommended, it may be hoped that, through divine aid, you will find in your self-examinations, from time to time, a continual "growth in grace, and in the knowledge of your Lord and Saviour." And when you do find this, you should, with all thankfulness for it, draw fresh encouragement from it, for renewed efforts after a still further growth. "I count not myself," says the Apostle Paul, "to have apprehended; but this one thing I do; forgetting those things which are behind, and reaching forth unto those that are before, I press towards the mark, for the prize of the high calling of God in Christ Jesus." And if, in any of these examinations, you are struck with the consciousness of some faults or deficiencies which you had not perceived in yourself before, be not disheartened at this, unless you find that they really are faults *newly sprung up*. If indeed you do find, on a candid survey of your own conduct and character, that you have been led into some sin of which you had not been guilty before, and that you have been falling back instead of advancing, this, certainly, is a just cause of alarm. But if it be only that you are become *conscious* for the first time of deficiencies or sins which had *existed* before, but which you had overlooked, this (as has been above remarked, Lesson XI.) is a promising sign. It is a sign that your spiritual discernment is improved, — your moral standard raised, — your estimate of the Christian character become more just. For what you ought to seek for is, not the most *quiet* conscience, — the conscience that is the most *easily satisfied;* but a tender conscience, a *watchful* conscience, an upright and *well-regulated* conscience. And you must expect that, as your conscience improves in all this, it will show you defects that were before overlooked.

When the sun's rays (as was formerly observed) are admitted into a room that had been half darkened, and kept in a slovenly state, you will see clouds of dust floating in the air which before were unseen; and various stains of dirt will appear which were before unnoticed. The light which is let in does not increase the impurities, but only makes them manifest. And this excites and enables a person who has a regard for neatness to cleanse them away.

And so it is with spiritual and moral light. It enables us to see better and better what is impure and faulty in our own hearts, in order that, by the promised help of God's Spirit, we may proceed in the work of purifying them.

But though you must (as was above said) carefully watch for faults, and frankly confess to God all that you are conscious of, without seeking to soften them down, you should never confess *more* than you really are conscious of. There is no real humility in using language of very strong self-condemnation beyond what you feel to be just. Even if it really be in itself true, still it is not true for *you*, unless you feel it to be so. And you should above all things cultivate a habit of perfect *sincerity;* universally, and not least in your communings with God. A person would be in a less hopeful state who should have accustomed himself to say more than he really feels, (though it may, perhaps, be no more than the truth,) than one who has confessed but the half of his real sins, but has said neither more nor less than what he really thinks and feels. For this latter, if he prays for God's enlightening Spirit, will hereafter come to know himself better; while the other will have learnt the habit of saying what he does not really believe.

§ 7. — *Heads of Self-Examination.*

Several heads of self-examination you can draw out for yourself from the foregoing Lessons. But if we were to say everything that is to the purpose on the subject, we should have to go through the whole of a Christian's duties, and trials, and temptations; since on all of these it is needful for him to examine himself. But it has been thought best to offer only a few hints on some of the most important points; namely, (1.) on the importance of a *candid* inquiry after *faults;* (2.) on looking out for signs of *improvement;* (3.) on a right advancement in Christian *knowledge;* (4.) on the *practical application* of what you learn; (5.) an attention to *motives and dispositions* as well as to outward acts; (6.) on the use to be made of the advice of friends; and (7.) on that increased insight into your own defects, which you may expect to acquire as you advance.

CHRISTIAN EVIDENCES.

CHRISTIAN EVIDENCES.

LESSON I.

FIRST RISE OF CHRISTIANITY.

§ 1. SUPPOSING you were asked the question how you came to be a Christian, perhaps you would answer that it is because you were born and brought up in a Christian country, and that your parents were Christians, and had taught you to believe that the Christian religion is true. And if, again, your parents were asked the same question, perhaps they might give the same answer. They might say, that their parents had brought them up as Christians; and so on.

But you know that it cannot always have been so. You know that the Christian religion had a beginning. You know that the disciples of Jesus Christ, and their followers, went about among various nations, making converts to his religion, among people who had been worshippers of the Sun and Moon, and of various false gods. Our forefathers were among those nations. In former days, the people of these Islands were what we call Heathen, or Pagans; that is, worshippers of a number of supposed gods, whom they believed to govern the world, and to whom they offered sacrifices and prayers. We have among us a kind of monument of this, in the names of the days of the week; each day having been sacred to some one of their gods. Thus, the first day of the week, which we sometimes call the Lord's day, in honor of the resurrection of the Lord Jesus, still keeps also the name of Sunday, from its having been dedicated, in former times, to the worship of the Sun; as Monday was to the Moon; Tuesday to Tuesco, the god of war; Wednesday to Woden; Thursday to Thor; and so of the rest.

Now our forefathers, who were worshippers of these gods, would have told any one who might have questioned them on the subject, that this was the religion of their country, and what they had learned from their parents. And at the present day there are many nations still in the same condition with our forefathers; among others, great numbers of our fellow-subjects in the British dominions, in the East Indies, have been brought up as Pagans, and worship various false gods. And, again, there are many who are followers of Mohammed, whom they hold to be a prophet superior to Jesus Christ.

§ 2. Now what I want you to consider is this: Have you any better reason for believing in the truth of the Christian religion, than a Mohammedan has for believing in his religion, or the Pagans in theirs? And do you think you can learn, and ought to learn, to give some better reason? They believe what their parents have told them, merely for that reason, and because it is the religion of their country, and the wisest men of the nation have told them it is true. If you are content to do the same, then, though there may be a great difference between your religion and theirs, there is no difference at all in the grounds of your belief and of theirs. If ten persons, for example, all hear different accounts of some transaction, and each believes just what he happens to hear from his next neighbor, then, if nine of those accounts are false, and one true, he who chances to have heard the true one is right only by accident, and has no better grounds for his belief than the rest. In the same manner, if several different persons hold each the religion of their fathers, and have no other reason for doing so than because it is the religion of their fathers, then, though one of them may happen to believe a true religion and the rest false ones, it is plain he has no better grounds for his belief than they. What he believes may be in itself right; but we cannot say that he is more right in so believing it, than the others are in believing as they do.

§ 3. Now do you think it is the duty of each man to keep to the religion of his fathers, without seeking any proofs of its being true, but satisfied with merely taking it on trust, because his teachers have told him so? If so, our forefathers would have been wrong in renouncing their Pagan religion, and embracing Christianity. They had been brought up in the worship of the Sun, and Moon, and Woden, and their other gods; and so had the ancient Greeks, and Romans, to whom the Apostles preached. This had been the long-established religion of their country, handed down to them from their forefathers, many of whom were great statesmen, and wise and learned writers; and if this had been a sufficient reason for their keeping to it without inquiry, they would have been bound to reject the Gospel, and continue Pagans.

And this we know is what many of them did; refusing to listen to the Apostles and others, who offered them proof that the Christians had "not followed cunningly devised fables in making known to them the coming and power of the Lord Jesus Christ." (2 Peter i. 16.) Now we cannot think these men acted more wisely than those Pagans who set themselves to inquire what was true, and who did embrace Christianity.

§ 4. These last must have had strong reasons for doing as they did. It could not have been from love of change for its own sake, or mere idle whim; for we know that many of them had to face ridicule, and blame, and sometimes persecution, from their friends and countrymen. And, what is more, they had to change their mode of life, and to renounce, on becoming Christians, many evil habits which had been tolerated in the Pagan religions. For we find the Apostles — Paul especially — speaking often of the abominable vices in which the Pagans had been accustomed to indulge, and which the converts to Christianity were required to abstain from.

Now it must be a difficult thing for a man to bring himself to throw off (as the early converts to Christianity must have done) his early habits, and his veneration for the gods of his country, in whose worship he had been brought up, and his reverence for wise, and illustrious, and powerful men among his countrymen, and his regard for the good opinion of his neighbors, and also his care for his own peace and safety. Yet all this must have been done by many of those of our forefathers, and other Pagans, who first embraced the Christian religion. They must, therefore, have had a strong conviction of the truth of the religion; not from their having been brought up in it, as you were; for it was quite the contrary with them; but for some other reason. They must have had some convincing evidence of its truth; or else we may be sure they would not have received it.

And these men could not have been convinced of the truth of the Gospel by any such *experience* as many Christians have of that inward consolation and peace of mind, and enlightening of the understanding, produced by their religion: which affords them a satisfactory assurance of its coming from God. *For those who had not embraced Christianity could not have had this experience.* And yet some convincing proofs they must have had, to lead them to embrace it, in spite of so many prejudices, and so many difficulties.

§ 5. And it appears that they were taught by the Apostles not only to *have* a reason, but also to be able to *give* a reason to others, for the faith which they held. Be "ready always," says the Apostle Peter, "to give an answer [or defence] to every one that asketh a reason of the hope that is in you." And it does certainly seem very fair that they should be asked by their neighbors, and should be expected to answer the question, "*Why* do you renounce the gods of the country, and embrace the religion of this Jesus, and call on us to do the same?" This, I say, would appear a very fair question to be asked of persons living in the midst of Pagans, and educated as such.

But perhaps you may think this was not at all intended to apply to you who have had the happiness of being brought up in a Christian country. You should remember, however, that you may some time or other chance to meet with some of these Pagans, or Mohammedans, whom we have been speaking of; to some of whom we have sent missionaries to convert them. And besides this, you may hereafter meet with persons of our own nation, who doubt or disbelieve the truth of Christianity; and their doubt or disbelief is likely to be very much strengthened, if they find that you have no better reason for being Christians than the Turks have for being Mohammedans, the ancient Greeks and Romans for worshipping Jupiter, or our own forefathers for serving Thor and Woden; namely, that such is the religion of the country. They will be apt to say: "These religions cannot be all true; but they may be all equally false; they are, perhaps, only so many different forms of superstition in which the people of different countries have been brought up, and which they all believe in, each because they have been brought up in it, without seeking for any other reason."

§ 6. The Apostle's direction, therefore, you may be sure, applies to all Christians in every age and country. It is needful for all of them to be able to give a reason of the hope that is in them. And among others, you may give as one reason, what I have just put before you; that those who first embraced Christianity, renouncing for it, as they did, their early prejudices, and their habits, and often their friends, and their comfort and safety in this world, must have had some strong evidence to convince them that it was true. It is not merely from the Christian writers of the New Testament that we learn how much those persons had to bear and to do who embraced the Gospel; heathen writers record the persecutions under which they suffered. We may be sure, even from the very nature of the case, how great their difficulties must have been. And therefore we could feel no doubt, that when they did become Christians, it must have been on some strong reasons, even though we had no knowledge what these reasons were.

It is possible for us, however, to inquire, and to learn what the reasons were which satisfied them of the truth of the religion. And it must, therefore, be a duty, for all who have the opportunity, to learn what proofs it rests on; that they may be "ready to give an answer to those that ask them a reason of their hope." And you shall observe, also, that the Apostles not only required their converts to be ready to give a reason, but must themselves have *supplied* them with reasons; since they could not have made them converts, without offering proofs to satisfy them that the religion was true.

And this is one point which distinguishes the Christian religion from those of the Pagans; for *it does not appear that any of these religions ever made any appeal to proof*, or claimed to be received except from their being the ancient established belief of the country. *The Christian religion was brought in*, in opposition to all these, *by means of the reasons given,—the evidence, which convinced the early Christians* that the religion did truly come from God. It must therefore be the duty of Christians to learn what that evidence is.

LESSON II.

FAITH AND CREDULITY.

§ 1. OUR forefathers, and the other Pagans who embraced the Gospel, must have had some strong reasons to bring them to shake off their habits of life, their early prejudices, and their veneration for the gods they had been brought up to worship, for the sake of Christ and his religion, which were new to them. But perhaps you may suppose that their ancient religions also must have been embraced by their forefathers in the same manner; that the worship of the Sun, and Moon, and Jupiter, and the rest of their gods, must have been first brought in by strong proofs, — at least by what were thought to be strong proofs.

But this does not appear to have been the case. We have no accounts of the first origin of the Pagan religions; and it is likely that no one of them was ever brought in all at once, but that these various superstitions crept in little by little, and religion became gradually corrupted, as men lost more and more that knowledge of the one true God, which we suppose to have been originally revealed. This, at least, is certain, that it was not even pretended that these religions rested on any evidence worth listening to. A Pagan's reason for holding his religion is, and always was, that it had been handed down from his ancestors. They did, indeed, relate many miracles, said to have been wrought through their gods ; but almost all of these they spoke of as having been wrought among people who were *already* worshippers of those gods, not as having been the means of originally bringing in the religion. And all the Pagan miracles they believed merely because these were a part of the religion which they had learned from their fathers. They never even pretended to give any proof that these miracles had ever been performed.

§ 2. The pretended prophet Mohammed did indeed found a new religion, which spread very rapidly and widely under him and his followers. But his religion was propagated, not by evidence, but by the sword. At the head of a small number of valiant warriors, he gained victories, which enabled him and his successors to collect larger and larger armies, and with these they subdued extensive regions, forcing the conquered people everywhere to acknowledge the Mohammedan faith, on pain of death or bondage. But the Mohammedan religion never made way (as Christianity did) in any country in which its opponents had the chief power, and were disposed to resist. And Mohammed never pretended to perform any miracles as *signs* of his coming from God. His pretended visions, and ascent to heaven, and visits from angels, which he relates in the book called the Koran, were not even pretended to have been shown openly, as proofs to convince unbelievers, but were to be received by the believers in Mohammed, on his bare word. With the Mohammedans, in short, (as with the Pagans,) the religion did not rest on the miracles, but the miracles rested on the religion. Those who believed the religion, believed the miracles as a *part* of the religion, but not as a *proof* of it. In fact, no such proof was ever even attempted to be offered of these religions.

The Christian religion was distinguished from these by its resting on evidence,—by its offering a reason, and requiring Christians to be able to give a reason for believing it.

§ 3. Some persons, however, have a notion that it is presumptuous for a Christian—at least for an unlearned Christian—to seek any proof of the truth of his religion. They suppose that this would show a want of faith. They know that *faith* is often and highly commended in Scripture as the Christian's first duty; and they fancy that this faith consists in a person's readily and firmly believing what is told him, and trusting in every promise that is made to him; and that the less reason he has for believing and for trusting, and the less he doubts, and inquires, and seeks grounds for his belief and his confidence, the more faith he shows.

But this is quite a mistake. The faith which the Christian Scriptures speak of and commend, is the very contrary of that blind sort of belief and trust which does not rest on any good reason. This last is more properly called *credulity* than faith. When a man believes without evidence, or against evidence, he is what we rightly call credulous. But he is never commended for this: on the contrary, we often find in Scripture mention made of persons who are reproached for their unbelief or want of faith, precisely on account of their showing this kind of credulity; that is, not judging fairly according to the evidence, but resolving to believe only what was agreeable to their prejudices, and to trust any one who flattered those prejudices.

§ 4. This was the case with those of the ancient Heathen who refused to forsake the worship of the Sun and Moon, and of Jupiter and Diana, and their other gods. Many of the Ephesians (as you read in the Book of Acts) raised a tumult against Paul, in their zeal for their "goddess Diana, and the image which fell down from Jupiter." Now if a man's faith is to be reckoned the greater, the less evidence he has for believing, these men must have had greater faith than any one who received the Gospel; because they believed in their religion without any evidence at all.

But what our sacred writers mean by faith is quite different from this. When they commend a man's faith, it is because he listens fairly to evidence, and judges according to the reasons laid before him. The difficulty and the virtue of faith consists in a man's believing and trusting, not against *evidence*, but against his expectations and prejudices, against his inclinations, and passions, and interests. We read, accordingly, that Jesus offered sufficient proof of his coming from God; He said, the works (the miracles) that I do in my Father's name, (by my Father's authority,) they bear witness of me. If you believe not me, believe the works; that is, if you have not the heart to feel the purity and holiness of what I teach, at least you should allow, that "no man can do such miracles, except God be with him."

§ 5. But we are told, that "for all He had done so many miracles among them, yet did they not believe on Him." They acknowledged that he wrought miracles; as the unbelieving Jews acknowledge at the present day. But they had expected that the Christ [or Messiah] whom they looked for should come in great worldly power and splendor, as a conquering prince who should deliver them from the dominion of the Romans, and should make Jerusalem the capital of a magnificent empire. They were disappointed and disgusted ("offended" is the word used in our translations) at finding Jesus coming from Nazareth, a despised town in Galilee, and having no worldly pomp or pretensions about Him, and having only poor fishermen and peasants as his attendants. Accordingly they rejected Him, saying, "Shall [the] Christ come out of Nazareth?" "As for this man, we know not whence he is." "Out of Galilee ariseth no prophet." And they persuaded themselves, (as their descendants do to this day,) that Jesus was a skilful magician, and performed miracles, not by Divine power, but by the help of some evil spirits or demons, with whom He had allied himself. Though He went about doing good, healing the sick and afflicted, and teaching the purest morality, they reckoned him a "deceiver," who "cast out demons through Beelzebub, the prince of the demons."

But if He had come among them offering to fulfil their expectations, and undertaking to deliver their country from the Romans, then, even though He had shown no miraculous power, many of them would have received Him readily. And indeed it is recorded of

Him, that He declared this himself, and foretold to his disciples, "Many will come in my name," (that is, taking on them my character,) "saying, I am [the] Christ, and will deceive many." And again, "I am come in my Father's name," (that is, with my Father's authority and power,) "and you receive me not; if another shall come in his own name," (that is, requiring to be believed on his bare word, without any miraculous signs,) "him ye will receive."

§ 6. And so it came to pass; for in the last siege of Jerusalem many impostors came forward, each one claiming to be the Christ, and drawing multitudes to follow him, and leading them to make the most desperate resistance to the Romans; till at length the city was taken and the nation utterly overthrown.

Now the Jews who believed any one of these impostors were led to do so by their prejudices, and expectations, and wishes, not by any proof that was offered. They showed, therefore, more credulity than the Christians did. And these unbelieving Jews, as they are called, are the very persons who were reproached for their want of faith. You may plainly see from this, that the faith which the Christian writers speak of is not blind credulity, but fairness in listening to evidence, and judging accordingly, without being led away by prejudices and inclinations.

Moreover, we find in the Book of Acts that the Jews of Beræa were commended as being "more noble" (that is, more candid) than those of Thessalonica, "because they searched the Scriptures," (the books of the

Old Testament,) to see whether those things were so "which the Apostle taught."

It is plain, therefore, that Jesus and his Apostles did not mean by Christian faith a blind assent without any reason. And if we would be taught by them, we must be "prepared to answer every one that asketh us a reason of the hope that is in us."

LESSON III.

ANCIENT BOOKS.

§ 1. We have said that Christians, even those who have not received what is called a learned education, ought to have some good reason for being Christians; and not to believe in our religion, as the Pagans do in theirs, merely because their fathers did so before them. But some persons suppose that, however strong the evidences may be for the truth of Christianity, these must be evidences only to the *learned*, who are able to examine ancient books, and to read them in the original languages; and that an ordinary unlearned Christian must take their word for what they tell him.

You do, indeed, read in English the accounts of what Jesus and his Apostles said and did, and of what befell them. But the English book which we call the Bible professes to be a translation of what was originally written in Greek and Hebrew, which you do not understand. And some one may perhaps ask you, how you can know, except by taking the word of the learned for it, that there *are* these Greek and Hebrew originals which have been handed down from ancient times? or how you can be sure that our translations of them are faithful, except by trusting to the translators? So that an unlearned Christian must, after all, (some people will tell you,) be at the mercy of the learned, in what relates to the very foundations of his faith. He must take their word (it will be said) for the very existence of the Bible in the original languages, and for the meaning of what is written in it; and therefore he may as well at once take their word for everything, and believe in his religion on their assurance.

And this is what many persons do. But others will be apt to say, "How can we tell that the learned have not deceived us? The Mohammedans take the word of the learned men among them; and the Pagans do the same; and if the people have been imposed upon by their teachers in Mohammedan and Pagan countries, how can we tell that it is not the same in Christian countries? What ground have we for trusting with such perfect confidence in our Christian teachers, that they are men who would not deceive us?"

§ 2. The truth is, however, that an unlearned Christian may have very good grounds for being a believer, without placing this entire confidence in any man. He may have reason to believe that there are ancient Greek manuscripts of the New Testament, though he never saw one, nor could read it if he did. And he may be convinced that an English Bible gives the meaning of the original, though he must not trust completely to any one's word. In fact, he may have the same sort of evidence in this case, which every one trusts to in many other cases, where none but a madman would have any doubt at all.

For instance, there is no one tolerably educated, who does not know that there is such a country as France, though he may have never been there himself. Who is there that doubts whether there are such cities as London, and Paris, and Rome, though he may never have visited them? Most people are fully convinced that the world is round, though there are but few who have sailed round it. There are many persons living in the inland parts of these islands who never saw the sea; and yet none of them, even the most ignorant clowns, have any doubt that there is such a thing as the sea. We believe all these, and many other such things, because we have been told them.

§ 3. Now suppose any one should say, How do you know that travellers have not imposed upon you in all these matters; as it is well known travellers are apt to do? Is there any traveller you can so fully trust in, as to be quite sure he would not deceive you? What would you answer? I suppose you would say, *one* traveller might perhaps deceive us; or even two or three might possibly combine to propagate a false story, in some cases where hardly any one would have the opportunity to detect them; but in these matters there are hundreds and thousands who would be sure to contradict the accounts if they were not true; and travellers are often glad of an opportunity of detecting each other's mistakes. Many of them disagree with each other in several particulars respecting the cities of Paris and Rome; and if it had been false that there are any such cities at all, it is impossible but that the falsehood should have been speedily contradicted. And it is the same with the existence of the sea, — the roundness of the world, — and the other things that were mentioned.

§ 4. It is in the same manner that we believe, on the word of astronomers, that the earth turns round every twenty-four hours, though we are insensible of the motion; and that the sun, which seems as if you could cover it with your hat, is immensely larger than the earth we inhabit; though there is not one person in ten thousand that has ever gone through the mathematical proof of this. And yet we have very good reason for believing it; not from any strong confidence in the honesty of any particular astronomer, but because the same things are attested by many different astronomers, who are so far from combining together in a false account, that many of them rejoice in any opportunity of detecting each other's mistakes.

Now an unlearned man has just the same sort of reason for believing that there are ancient copies, in Hebrew and Greek, of the Christian sacred books, and of the works of other ancient authors, who mention some things connected with the origin of Christianity. There is no need for him to place full confidence in any particular man's honesty. For if any book were forged by some learned man in these days, and put forth as a translation from an ancient book, there are many other learned men, of this and of various other countries, and of different religions, who would be eager to make an inquiry, and examine the question, and would be sure to detect any forgery, especially on an important subject.

And it is the same with translators. Many of these are at variance with each other as to the precise sense of some particular passage; and many of them are very much opposed to each other, as to the doctrines which they believe to be taught in Scripture. But all the different versions of the Bible agree as to the main outline of the history, and of the discourses recorded: and therefore an unlearned Christian may be as sure of the general sense of the original as if he understood the language of it, and could examine it for himself; because he is sure that unbelievers, who are opposed to all Christians, or different sects of Christians, who are opposed to each other, would not fail to point out any errors in the translations made by their opponents. Scholars have an opportunity to examine and inquire into the meaning of the original works; and therefore *the very bitterness with which they dispute against each other, proves that where they all agree they must be right.*

§ 5. All these ancient books, in short, and all the translations of them, are in the condition of witnesses placed in a witness-box, in a court of justice; examined and cross-examined by friends and enemies, and brought face to face with each other, so as to make it certain that any falsehood or mistake will be brought to light.

No one need doubt, therefore, that the books of our English New Testament are really translated from ancient originals in Greek, and are, at least, not forgeries of the present day; because unbelievers in Christianity would not have failed to expose such a forgery.

But in the case of the books of the Old Testament, we have a remarkable proof that they could never have been forged *by Christians* at all; because they are preserved and highly reverenced by the unbelieving *Jews* in various parts of the world at this day. These are the Scriptures which the *Jews* at Beræa were commended for searching with diligent care. In these they found the prophecies to which the Apostles were accustomed to refer, as proving that Jesus was the promised Christ, or Messiah. And the history goes on to relate, that the consequence of their searching those Scriptures was, that "many of them believed."

LESSON IV.

PROPHECIES.

§ 1. BUT these Old Testament Scriptures are, in some respects, more instructive to *us*, even than to the persons who lived in the Apostles' time; on account of the more complete fulfilment of some of the prophecies that have since taken place.

In the times of the Apostles, the religion of Jesus Christ was, indeed, spreading very rapidly, both among Jews and Gentiles; but still it was but a small and obscure portion of either that had embraced it compared with those who either knew nothing of it, or rejected it with scorn and hatred. *Now*, Jesus is, and has been for many ages, acknowledged as Lord, in all the most civilized portions of the world. His disciples overthrew the religions of all the most powerful and enlightened nations, and produced, without conquest, and without the help of wealth, or of human power, or learning, the most wonderful change that ever was produced in men's opinions, and on the most important point. The number of those who profess Christianity is computed at about two hundred and fifty millions; comprehending all the most civilized nations of the world. And to estimate properly the greatness of the effect produced, we should take into account that there are about one hundred and twenty millions of persons whose religion is so far founded on Christ's, that it could never have existed such as it is, if Christ had never appeared, — I mean the Mohammedans ; for though these have departed widely from the religion which Jesus taught, and regard Mohammed as a greater prophet than He, yet they acknowledge Jesus as a true prophet, and as the Messiah, or Christ; and profess that their religion is founded on his.

§ 2. This should be taken into account; because what we are now speaking of is the great and wonderful *effect* produced, — the extraordinary *change* brought about in the world, — by Christ and his Apostles. So great is this effect, that every man, whether believer or unbeliever, if not totally ignorant of history, must allow that Jesus Christ was by far THE MOST IMPORTANT AND EXTRAORDINARY PERSON that ever appeared on earth; and that he effected the most wonderful revolution that ever was effected in the religion of mankind. Yet this wonderful change was made by a person of the Jewish nation, — a nation which was never one of the greatest and most powerful, — never at all equal in the fame of wisdom, and knowledge, and skill in the arts of life, to the Greeks, and several other of the ancient nations. And all this was done by a person who was despised, and persecuted, and put to a shameful death, by the Jews themselves, his own countrymen. If, therefore, you were to ask any unbeliever in Christianity, " Who was the most wonderful person that ever existed? and *who* brought about the most extraordinary effect, in the strangest and most wonderful manner?" he could hardly help answering that Jesus of Nazareth was the person.

And then you might ask him to explain how it happened, (supposing our religion to be an invention of man,) that all this had been foretold in the ancient prophecies of the Old Testament; in books which are carefully preserved, and held in high reverence, by the unbelieving Jews at this day.

§ 3. You may find such prophecies as I am speaking of, in various parts of the Old Testament. As, for instance, it was prophesied that a great blessing to all nations of the earth should spring from the nation that was to descend from Abraham. (Gen. xxii. 18.)

Now, when the descendants of Abraham did actually become a nation, and did receive, through Moses, a religion which they held in the highest veneration, they would naturally expect the above prophecy to refer to the extension of that very religion. And any one of them professing to be a prophet, but speaking really as a mere man, would have been sure to confirm that expectation. Yet it was foretold, that the religion which the Israelites had received from Moses was to give place to a *new* one: as in Jer. xxxi. 31: "Behold the days come [are coming], saith the Lord, that I will make a new covenant with the house of Israel, and with the house of Judah: not according to the covenant that I made with their fathers," &c.

See also, for prophecies of the Messiah, Micah iv. 1–3; v. 2–4; Isaiah ix. 6; xi. 1; Ezekiel xxxiv. 23; Jer. xxiii. 5; Zech. vi. 12; ix. 9, &c.; Mal. iii. 1.

Now many of these prophecies were delivered (as the unbelieving Jews of this day bear witness) six hundred years before the birth of Jesus; at which time, and also at the time when the Gospel was first preached, the Jews were so far from being a great and powerful people, that they had been conquered and brought into subjection by other nations. So that, according to all human conjecture, nothing could have been more strange than the delivery of the prophecies and their fulfilment.

§ 4. This fulfilment, by the wide spread of Christ's religion among various nations, though it was *expected* by the early Christians, had not been *seen* by them, as it is by *us*. They saw, however, that what Jesus had done and suffered did agree with the prophecies of the Old Testament; that He was born at the time when it had been foretold that Christ was to come, and when the whole Jewish nation were in expectation of his coming; that He was acknowledged by his enemies to have wrought those miracles which had been prophesied of: "Then the eyes of the blind shall be opened, and the ears of the deaf shall be unstopped: then shall the lame man leap as an hart, and the tongue of the dumb sing" (Isaiah xxxv. 5; Luke vii. 22); that, notwithstanding this, He had been rejected and put to death, as had been foretold; and that his disciples bore witness to his having risen from the dead, agreeably to other prophecies: "Thou wilt not leave my soul in hell (*i. e.* the grave); neither wilt thou suffer thine Holy One to see corruption." (Psalm xvi. 10; Acts ii. 27.)

All this led them to conclude, when they examined candidly, that the miracles which they saw were not the work of evil spirits, but that the Gospel did come from God. On the other hand, we, who have not actually seen the miracles which *they* saw, have an advantage over them in seeing such an extraordinary fulfilment of prophecy, in what has happened since their time.

LESSON V.

MIRACLES. — PART I.

§ 1. The people who lived in the times of the Apostles, though they had not seen so much as we have of the fulfilment of the ancient prophecies, yet had seen them so far fulfilled in Jesus, as to afford good reasons for receiving Him.

But you may, perhaps, be inclined to wonder how they should need to search the Old Testament Scriptures for a confirmation of what the Apostles taught, if those Apostles really performed such miracles as we read of. It may seem strange to you, that men who healed the sick with a touch, and displayed so many other signs, far beyond human power, should not have been at once believed, when they called themselves God's messengers.

§ 2. I have said that the works performed by Jesus and his disciples were beyond the unassisted powers of man. And this, I think, is the best description of what is meant by a miracle. *Superhuman* would perhaps be a better word to apply to a miracle than *supernatural;* for if we believe that "nature" is merely another word to signify that state of things, and course of events, which God has appointed, nothing that occurs can be strictly called "supernatural." Jesus himself accordingly describes his works, not as violations of the laws of nature, but as "works which *none other man* did." But what is in general meant by "supernatural," is something out of the *ordinary* course of nature; something at variance with those laws of nature which *we* have been *accustomed to.*

But then it might be objected, that we cannot decide what does violate the ordinary laws of nature, unless we can be sure that we are *acquainted* with all those laws. For instance, an inhabitant of the tropical climates might think it contrary to the laws of nature that water should never become hard; since he had never seen ice. And when electricity was first discovered, many of its effects were contrary to the laws of nature which had been hitherto known. But any one who visits colder regions may see with his own eyes that water does become solid. And any one who will procure an electrical machine, or who attends lectures on the subject, may see for himself the effects of electricity.

Now suppose Jesus had been a person who had discovered some new natural agent, through which any man might be enabled to cure diseases by a touch, and perform the other wonderful works which He did, and through which any one else might have done the like, this would soon have become known and practised by all; just like the use of electricity, or of any newly discovered medicine; and from his time down to this day every one would have commonly performed just the same works that he did. He might indeed have kept it to himself as a secret, and thus have induced some to believe that He wrought miracles. But so far from acting thus, He imparted his power first to the twelve

Apostles, and afterwards to seventy others: and after his departure, his Apostles received the power of not only performing mighty works themselves, but also of bestowing these gifts on all the disciples on whom they laid their hands; as you may see from Acts viii. 14–23; Acts xix. 6; Rom. i. 11; 1 Cor. xii. 7–11, &c. There must have been, therefore, in the early Church many hundreds, and probably many thousands, performing the same sort of works as Jesus and his Apostles. And if, therefore, these had been performed by means of any natural agent, such as any one else might use as well as they, the art would soon have been universally known; and the works performed by the disciples of Jesus would have been commonly performed by all men ever after, down to this day.

But the Jews were convinced, with good reason, that the works of Jesus were beyond the powers of unassisted man. And it may seem strange to us, that they did not all come at once to the same conclusion with Nicodemus, when he said, "No man can do these miracles which thou doest, except God be with him."

But you must remember how much the people of those days were accustomed to believe in magic. Indeed, in much later times, long after Christianity prevailed, it was a very common notion that there were magicians who were able, through the help of evil demons, to work various miracles. And in the days of the Apostles this belief in the power of magic was very general, both among the Jews and the Heathen. Those Jews among whom Jesus lived, and who rejected him, maintained that He was a magician who did mighty works through the prince of demons. This is not only related by the Christian writers in the New Testament, but is a *common tradition among the unbelieving Jews at this very day*, who have among them an ancient book giving this account of the origin of Christianity. And there can be no doubt that this must have been (as our sacred writers tell us it was) what the adversaries of Jesus maintained from the first. For if those who lived on the spot in his time had denied or doubted the facts of the miracles, and had declared that the accounts of them were false tales, and that no miracles had ever really been wrought, we may be sure that the same would have been said ever after by their descendants. They would never have thought of rejecting the accounts given by their own ancestors, and preferring that of the Christian writers. If, therefore, any of the Jews among whom Jesus lived had denied the fact of his miraculous powers, it is inconceivable that another generation of Jews should have betaken themselves to the pretence of magic to account for miracles which had never been acknowledged at the time, but had been reckoned impostures by the very people among whom they were said to have been performed.

The Pagan adversaries of Christianity also seem to have had the same persuasion on this subject as the Jews, and to have attributed the Christian miracles to magical art. We learn this from all the remains that have come down to us of the ancient writings against Christianity, and of the answers to them written by Christians.

§ 3. Now suppose that in the present day any one should appear professing to be sent from God, and to work miracles as a sign of his being so sent, you would naturally think that the only question would be as to the reality of the miracles; and that all men would at once believe him as soon as ever they were satisfied that he had performed something clearly beyond human power. But men certainly did not judge so in ancient times. It was not then only one question, but two, that had to be settled: first, whether any sign had really been displayed which showed a power beyond that of man; and secondly, whether this supernatural power came from God, or from an evil demon.

Now, after the former of these questions was decided, that is, after the fact of the miracles was admitted, the Jews were inclined still to doubt or disbelieve the religion which Jesus taught, because it was so different from what they had been used to expect; and hence it was that the greater part of them attributed his miracles to magic. But others were of a more candid mind, (" more noble," as it is in our translation,) such as the people of Beræa. These, by carefully searching the Scriptures, satisfied themselves that the ancient prophecies respecting the Christ did really agree with all that Jesus had done and suffered. And this it was that convinced them that his miracles were wrought, not by evil spirits, but by the Divine power; and thus they were brought to the conclusion that the "kingdom of Heaven was at hand."

§ 4. If, then, any one should say to you, "How great an advantage the people who lived in those days, and saw miracles performed before their eyes, must have had over us, who only read of them in ancient books; and how can men in these days be expected to believe as firmly as *they* did?" you may answer, that different men's trials and advantages are pretty nearly balanced. The people who lived in those times were not (any more than ourselves) forced into belief, whether they would or no, but were left to exercise candor in judging fairly from the evidence before them. Those of them who were resolved to yield to their prejudices against Jesus, and to reject him, found a ready excuse (an excuse which would not be listened to now) by attributing his miracles to the magical arts which in those days were commonly believed in. And again, though they saw many miracles which we only read of, they did not see that great miracle (as it may be called) which is before our eyes, in the fulfilment of prophecy since their time. They could see, indeed, many prophecies fulfilled in Jesus; but we have an advantage over them, in witnessing the more complete fulfilment of the prophecies respecting the wonderful spread of his religion.

LESSON VI.

MIRACLES. — PART II.

§ 1. "BUT can we of these days really find sufficient proof," some one may say, "and such proof as is within the reach of ordinary Christians, for believing that miracles really were performed which we never saw, but which are recorded in books as having happened nearly eighteen hundred years ago?" Is it not expecting a great deal of us, to require us to believe that there were persons who used to cure blindness and other diseases by a touch or a word, and raise the dead, and still the raging of the sea, and feed a multitude with a few loaves?

Certainly these things are in themselves hard to be believed; and if we were to find in some ancient book accounts of some great wonders which led to no *effects that exist at this day*, and had nothing to do with the present state of things among us, we might well be excused for doubting or disbelieving such accounts; or at least none but learned men, who had the ability and the opportunity to make full inquiry into the evidence of such a book, could fairly be expected to trouble themselves about the question. But the case of the Christian miracles is not one of this kind. They are closely connected with something which we do see before us at this day; namely, with the existence of the Christian religion in so great a part of the world. A man cannot, indeed, be fairly required to believe anything very strange and unlikely, except when there is something still *more* strange and unlikely on the opposite side. Now that is just the case with respect to the Christian miracles; for, wonderful as the whole Gospel history is, the most wonderful thing of all is, that a Jewish peasant should have succeeded in changing the religion of the world. That *he should have succeeded in doing this without displaying any miracles, would have been more wonderful than all the miracles that are recorded;* and that he should have accomplished all this by means of *pretended* miracles when none were really performed, would be the most incredible of all. So that those who are unwilling to believe anything that is strange, cannot escape doing so by disbelieving the Gospel, but will have to believe something still more strange if they reject the Gospel.

§ 2. And it is the same in many other cases as well as in what relates to religion. We are often obliged to believe, at any rate, in something that is very wonderful, in order to avoid believing something else that is still more wonderful. For instance, it is well known that in these islands, and in several other parts of the world, there are great beds of sea-shells found near the tops of hills, sometimes several thousand feet above the sea. Now it is certainly very hard to believe that the sea should ever have covered those places which now lie so far above it. And yet we are compelled to believe this, because we cannot think of any other way that is not far more incredible by which those shells have been deposited there.

And so it is with the Gospel history. We are sure that the Christian religion does now exist, and has overspread most of the civilized world; and we know that it was not first introduced and propagated (like that of Mohammed) by force of arms. To believe that it was received, and made its way, without miracles, would be to believe something more miraculous (if one may so speak) than all the miracles that our books record.

§ 3. But some people may say that the ancient Jews and Pagans, who so readily believed in magical arts and the power of demons, must have been very weak and credulous men; and that therefore they may have given credit to tales of miracles without making any careful inquiry. Now there is, indeed, no doubt that they were weak and credulous; but this weakness and credulity would never have led them to believe what was against their early prejudices, and expectations, and wishes: quite the contrary. *The more weak and credulous any man is, the harder it is to convince him of anything that is opposite to his habits of thought and inclinations.* He will readily receive without proof anything that falls in with his prejudices, and will be disposed to hold out against any evidence that goes against them.

Now all the prejudices of the Jews and Pagans were against the religion that Jesus and his Apostles taught; and, accordingly, we might have expected that the most credulous of them should have done just what our histories tell us they did; that is, resolved to reject the religion at any rate, and readily satisfy themselves with some weak and absurd way of accounting for the miracles. But credulous as they were about magic, the enemies of Jesus would never have resorted to that pretence, if they could have denied the facts. They would certainly have been more ready to maintain, if possible, that no miracles had taken place, than to explain them as performed by magic; because this pretence only went to make out that Jesus, notwithstanding his miracles, *might possibly* not come from God; whereas, if they could have shown that He or his Apostles had attempted to deceive people by pretended miracles, this would at once have held them up to scorn as impostors.

§ 4. We read in the Gospel of John (chap. ix.), that the Jewish rulers narrowly examined into the reality of a miracle performed by Jesus, on a man that was born blind. This is exactly what we may be sure must have been done in the case of other miracles also; and if the enemies of Jesus could have succeeded in detecting and exposing any falsehood or trick, they would have been eager to do so; because they would have been thus sure to overthrow his pretensions at once.

It is plain, therefore, that the weakness and credulity of the people of those days would be very far from disposing them readily to give credit to miracles in favor of a religion that was opposed to their prejudices; and that, on the contrary, such persons would be likely, some of them obstinately, to reject the religion, and others only gradually and slowly to receive it, after having carefully searched the ancient prophecies, and found that these went to confirm it. Now this is just the account that our histories give.

It appears certain, then, that the unbelieving Jews and Pagans of those days did find it impossible to throw any doubt on the fact of the miracles having really been performed; because *that* would have enabled them easily to expose Jesus to contempt as an impostor. *Their acknowledging the miracles, and attributing them to magic, as the unbelieving Jews do to this day, shows that the evidence for them, after the strictest scrutiny by the most bitter enemies, was perfectly undeniable, at the time and place when they were said to be performed.*

LESSON VII.

MIRACLES. — PART III.

§ 1. THERE are persons, some of whom you may, perhaps, meet with, who, though they are believers in Christianity, yet will not allow that the miracles recorded in Scripture are any ground for their belief. They are convinced (they will tell you) that Jesus Christ came from God, because "never man spake like this man." They find the religion so pure and admirable in itself, and they feel it so well suited to their wants, and to the wants of all mankind, and so full of heavenly wisdom and goodness, that they need no other proof of its being from heaven; but as for miracles, these (they will tell you) are among the difficulties to be got over: they believe them as a *part* of the religion, from finding them recorded in the Bible; but they would have believed the Gospel as easily, or more easily, without them. The miracles (they will say) were indeed a proof to those who lived at the time, and *saw* them; but to us of the present day, who only *read* of them, they are a part of our faith, and not a part of the *evidence* of our faith. For it is a greater trial of faith, they say, to believe in such wonderful works as Jesus is said to have performed, than to believe that such wise and excellent doctrine as He delivered was truly from heaven.

Now there is indeed much truth in a part of what these persons say; but they do not take a clear view of the whole subject of evidence. It is indeed true, that there is, as they observe, great weight in the internal evidence (as it is called) of Christianity; that is, the reasons for believing it from the character of the religion itself. The more you study it, the more strongly you will perceive that it is such a religion as no *man* would have been likely to invent; and of all men, a Jew most unlikely. But there are many different kinds of evidence for the same truth; and one kind of evidence may the most impress one man's mind, and another another's. And, among the rest, the Christian miracles certainly are a very decisive proof of the truth of Christ's religion to any one who is convinced (as you have seen there is reason to be) that they really were wrought. Of course, there is more difficulty for us in making out this point, than there was for men who lived at the same times and places with Jesus and his Apostles; but when this point *has* been made out, and we do believe the miracles, they are no less a proof of the religion to us than to those early Christians.

§ 2. It is quite a mistake to suppose that the difficulty of proving any fact makes that fact, when it is proved, a less convincing proof of something else. For example, — to take an instance formerly given, — those who live in the neighborhood of the places where great beds of sea-shells are found near the tops of hills, and have seen them there themselves, are convinced by this that at some time or other those beds must have been under the sea. Now a person who lives at a distance from such places has more difficulty than those on the spot, in making out whether there *are* any such beds of shells. He has to inquire of travellers, or of those who have conversed with them; and to consult books, and perhaps examine pieces of the rock containing some of the shells; but when once he is fully satisfied that there are such beds of sea-shells, this is just as good a proof to him as to the others, that the sea must have formerly covered them.

And so also, in respect of the Christian miracles. The difficulty we may have in deciding whether they were really wrought, does not make them (when we *are* convinced that they were wrought) a less decisive proof that the Christian religion is from God.

But as for the difficulty of believing in anything so strange and wonderful as those miracles, you should remember, that every difficulty (as was observed before) should be weighed against that on the opposite side. Now, the difficulty of believing the miracles recorded in our sacred books is much less than the opposite difficulty of believing that the Christian religion was established without miracles. That a Jewish peasant should have overthrown the religion of the civilized world, without the aid of any miracles, is far more miraculous, — at least, more incredible, — than anything that our books relate; and it will appear still more incredible, if you remember that this wonderful change was brought about *by means of an appeal* to miracles. Jesus and his Apostles did certainly *profess* to display miraculous powers in proof of their being sent from God; and this would have been the greatest hinderance to their propagating a new religion, if they had really possessed no such powers; because this pretence would have laid them open to detection and ridicule.

§ 3. But there is a distinction between our religion and all others, which is often overlooked. Almost all religions have some miraculous pretensions connected with them ; that is, miracles are recorded to have been wrought in support of some Pagan religion, among people who *already* believed it. But you will not find that any religion except ours was ever *introduced* — and introduced among enemies — by miraculous pretensions. Ours is the only faith that ever was FOUNDED on an appeal to the evidence of miracles. And we have every reason to believe that no such attempt ever did or could succeed, if the miracles were not really performed. The difficulty, therefore, of believing that the Christian religion was propagated by means of miracles, is nothing in comparison of the difficulty of believing that it could have been propagated without any.

Indeed, we have every reason to believe, that many *more* miracles must have been performed than are particularly related. Several particular cases, indeed, of our Lord's miracles were described; but, besides these, we are told, in various places, of great multitudes of sick people being brought to him, and that " He healed them all." (Matt. xii. 15 ; xix. 2.) So also, besides particular miracles related as done by the Apostles, (Acts ii. 33 ; iii. 7 ; ix. 33 ; xiii. 11 ; xiv. 8 ; xxviii. 5,) we are told, generally, of their not only performing many miracles, (Acts viii. 6 ; xix. 11,) but also bestowing miraculous powers on great numbers of disciples. (Acts vi. 5, 8 ; x. 44 ; xix. 6.) And we find St. Paul, in one of his Epistles, speaking of it as a thing familiarly known, that miracles were "the sign of an Apostle." (2 Cor. xii. 12.) And in all these books we find miracles not boastfully dwelt on, or described as something unusual, but *alluded* to as familiarly known to the persons to whom the books were familiarly addressed; that is, to the Christians of those days.

§ 4. But besides the accounts given in the Christian Scriptures, we might be sure, from the very nature of the case, that the Apostles could never have even *gained a hearing*, at least among the Gentiles, if they had not displayed some extraordinary and supernatural power. Fancy a few poor Jewish fishermen, tent-makers, and peasants going into one of the great Roman or Grecian cities, whose inhabitants were proud of the splendid temples, and beautiful images of their gods, which had been worshipped time out of mind by their ancestors; they were proud, too, of their schools of philosophy, where those reputed the wisest men among them discoursed on the most curious and sublime subjects, to the youth of the noblest families; and then fancy these Jewish strangers telling them to cast away their images as an abominable folly, — to renounce the religion of their ancestors, — to reject with scorn the instructions of their philosophers, — and to receive instead, as a messenger from heaven, a Jew, of humble station, who had been put to the most shameful death. How do you think men would have been received who should have made such an attempt as this, with merely such weak human means as preaching? You cannot doubt that all men would have scorned them, and ridiculed or pitied them as madmen.

§ 5. As for the wisdom and purity and sublimity of

the religion of the Gospel, this might have gained them some attention, — not, indeed, among the mass of the people, who were too gross to relish or perceive this purity and wisdom, — but among a very few of the better sort, if once they could be brought to listen to the description of the religion. And this, perhaps, they might have done if it had been taught by some Greek or Roman philosophers, famous for knowledge and wisdom. But the Gospel was preached by men of a nation which the Greeks and Romans looked down upon as barbarian; and whose religion, especially, they scorned and detested for being so different from their own. And not only did the Apostles belong to this despised nation, but they were the outcasts of that very nation, being rejected and abhorred by the chief part of their Jewish brethren.

If, therefore, they had come among the Gentiles teaching the most sublime religious doctrine, and trusting merely to the excellence of what they taught, it is impossible they should have even had a hearing. It is not enough to say that no one would have *believed* them; but no one would even have *listened* to them, if they had not first roused men's serious attention by working (as we are told they did) "remarkable [special] miracles." (Acts xix. 11.)

§ 6. Afterwards, indeed, when the Gospel had spread, so as to excite general attention, many men would be likely to listen to the preaching of it even by persons who did not pretend to miraculous power, but who merely bore witness to the miracles they had seen; giving proof, at the same time, that they were not false witnesses by their firmness in facing persecution. And this was certainly a good ground for believing their testimony. For though men may be mistaken as to the *opinions* which they sincerely hold, they could not be mistaken as to such *facts* as the Christian miracles, of which they professed themselves eyewitnesses; as the Apostles, for instance, were of their Master's resurrection. And it is not to be conceived that men would expose themselves to dangers and tortures and death in attesting false stories, which they must have known to be false. If there had been any well-contrived imposture in respect of pretended miracles, it is impossible but that some persons at least, out of the many hundreds brought forward as eyewitnesses, would have been induced by threats, tortures, or bribes to betray the imposture.

There were many, therefore, who received the Gospel — and with good reason — on such testimony as this, as soon as they could be brought to listen to and examine it. But, in the first instance, the Apostles could not have brought any of the Gentiles, at least, to listen to them, if they had not begun by working evident miracles themselves. A handful of Jewish strangers, of humble rank, would never have obtained a hearing among the most powerful and most civilized and proudest nations of the world, if they had not at first roused their attention by the display of some extraordinary powers.

LESSON VIII.

WONDERS AND SIGNS.

§ 1. It is plain, for the reasons which have been put before you, that the Apostles must have roused men's attention, and gained themselves a hearing, by performing — as our books tell us they did — many wonderful works. And these works, as well as those of Jesus, which they related, must have been such as to admit of no mistake either about the facts or about their being really superhuman. Else, surrounded as they were by enemies, and with men's prejudices opposed to them, it seems impossible they could have been believed, or even attended to. If, for instance, there were a report of some sick men having been miraculously cured by them, but such a report as to leave a doubt either as to the *fact* of the cure having taken place, or as to the *manner* of the cure, — that is, whether the man might not have recovered by natural means, — any such doubt would have been enough to have shut men's ears against them.

And besides this, it was necessary that the miracles should be both so numerous and so various in kind as to exceed the powers generally supposed to belong to magicians. For most persons seem to have thought that a magician might, through the aid of demons, be enabled to perform *some* miracles, and not others of a different kind. We find it related, accordingly, that Jesus not only healed the lame and blind and sick, some present and some absent, grown persons and children, but also raised the dead, fed a multitude with a few loaves, stilled the waves and winds at his bidding, blasted a tree at his word, changed water into wine, &c. And this seems to have been no more than a necessary condescension to the weakness of men's minds in those days. They did not at once conclude that he must be a true prophet from his working *one* miracle; but said, "When [the] Christ cometh, will he do more miracles than these which this man doeth?" (John vii. 31.) So also Nicodemus says, not "No man can do *any* miracles," but "No man can do *these* miracles which thou doest, except God be with him." (John iii. 2.) And the disciples, who had witnessed so many miraculous cures, were astonished, we are told, at finding that Jesus had a command over the storm. "What manner of man is this, that even the winds and the sea obey him?" (Matt. viii. 27.)

And we find the same variety also in the miraculous gifts possessed by the Apostles, and bestowed by them on other Christians (as you may see in 1 Cor. xii. and elsewhere).

§ 2. You should observe, too, that it would not have satisfied men's minds merely to see some extraordinary occurrence, unless it were also something plainly *done* by the Apostles, as a *sign*, testifying that they were divine messengers. It would have been impossible for them, in the midst of adversaries, to take advantage of some remarkable event, calling it a miracle, and to explain it so as to favor their own pretensions.

This has often been done, indeed, in support of some religion, or some doctrine, which men already believe, or are inclined to believe. The Pagans were, many of them, ready enough to attribute anything wonderful to a miraculous interference of Jupiter or some of their other gods. And so, also, Mohammed easily persuaded his followers that some of his victories were miraculous, and that God sent angels to fight for him. He was a great warrior, and his followers, being full of enthusiasm, and eager for conquest, glory, and plunder, often defeated a very superior force of their enemies, and gained victories, which may be rightly called wonderful, though not more wonderful than several which have been gained by others. It is not strange, therefore, that Mohammed should easily have persuaded them that their victories were miraculous, and were a proof that God was on their side.

§ 3. In all times, indeed, men are to be found who call any extraordinary event miraculous, and interpret it so as to favor their own views and prejudices. If a man's life is preserved from shipwreck, or any other danger, in a remarkable manner, many people speak of it as a miraculous escape. Or if a man loses his life in a remarkable manner, or a plot is discovered by some curious train of circumstances, or, in short, if any extraordinary event takes place, there are persons who at once will call it a miraculous interference, and a *sign* of the Divine favor or displeasure towards some of the parties concerned.

§ 4. But it is very rash to pronounce in this manner as to any remarkable event that occurs. A mere *wonderful occurrence*, of itself, *proves* nothing; but when a man *does* something that is beyond human power to do, or *foretells* something beyond human foresight, and makes this a testimony of his coming from God, it is then, and then only, that he is properly said to offer a miraculous proof. And accordingly the works performed by Jesus and his Apostles are called in Scripture, not merely (as they really were) *Miracles* (that is, *wonders*), but *Signs;* that is, miraculous *evidence.* (Mark xvi. 20.)

For instance, that a violent storm should suddenly cease, and be succeeded by a complete calm, is something extraordinary; but of itself proves nothing. But when the disciples heard Jesus give his command, and rebuke the wind and waves, which immediately became still, they justly regarded this as a *sign* that God was with him. (Matt. viii. 26.) So also, that a person seemingly dead should suddenly revive and rise up, is indeed a wonderful event; but, of itself, is merely a wonder. But when Jesus told the child of Jairus, (Luke viii. 54,) and the widow's son of Nain, (Luke vii. 14,) to rise up, and each of them did so at his word, these became proofs of his divine mission. These were among the "works which," as he said, "bore *witness* of Him." Again, if any one who is opposing some particular religious sect or system, should suddenly lose his eyesight, it would be very presumptuous to pronounce at once that he was struck blind as a divine judgment. But when St. Paul rebuked Elymas, and declared that the hand of the Lord was upon him, and that he should become blind, and immediately a darkness did fall upon him, (Acts xiii. 10, 11,) the Roman governor justly regarded this as a *sign;* and believed accordingly in what Paul was teaching.

§ 5. Anything wonderful, in short, is then (and then only) a miraculous sign, when some one *performs* or *foretells* it, in a manner surpassing human power, so as to make it *attest* the truth of what he says. And this may fairly be required of any one professing to be a messenger from Heaven. For if a stranger were to come to you professing to bring a message from some friend of yours, you would naturally expect him to show you that friend's handwriting, or some other such *token*, to prove that he really was so sent. And so also, when a man comes to this country as an ambassador from some other country, he is required first to produce his "*credentials*," as they are called; that is, papers which prove that he is no impostor, but is really commissioned as an ambassador. And it is equally right, that men professing to bring a message immediately from God should be required to show what may be called their "*credentials*"; that is, such miraculous powers as God alone could have bestowed, as a sign or token, to prove the reality of their divine commission.

§ 6. But credulous and superstitious people often overlook this rule; and are ready to interpret as a miraculous sign any remarkable occurrence, — such as a victory, or a famine, or a thunder-storm, or a sudden recovery from sickness, or the like, — when these are so explained as to favor, or at least not oppose, their prejudices, and the religious belief they are already inclined to. The Apostles, however, found no such prejudices in their favor. They would never have been allowed to explain in their own way anything strange that might happen. On the contrary, all the superstitious credulity of the people was *opposed* to them. And instead of

20*

men's being ready to cry "Miracle!" when anything extraordinary occurred, and to interpret it in favor of Christianity, the Apostles found the most credulous men disposed rather to attribute the Christian miracles to magic.

In order to gain converts, therefore, or even to obtain a hearing, they must have shown (as our books tell us they did) many mighty works, evidently performed by them, as "the Signs of an Apostle."

LESSON IX.

SUMMARY OF EVIDENCES.

§ 1. How comes it that some persons pretend that an ordinary Christian cannot be taught to understand the evidence for their religion, but must be content to take it for granted, as the Pagans do theirs, because they have been brought up to it? It is because, when they speak of "the evidences of Christianity," they mean *all* the evidences. And certainly, to be well acquainted with all of these, would be enough to occupy the whole life of a studious man, even though he should devote himself entirely to that study. Indeed, to go through all the books that have been written on the subject, and to examine and thoroughly master all the arguments on both sides that have ever been brought forward, would be more than any one man could accomplish, even if he had nothing else to do. But there are things which you may have very good reasons for believing, though you may not know a tenth part of the proofs of them that have been, or might be, produced. For instance, you may have good grounds for believing that there is such a city as Rome, and that it was formerly the capital of a mighty empire, of which Britain was one of the provinces. But *all* the evidence that might be brought forward in proof of this would be enough to occupy a learned man for many years, if he were to examine it thoroughly. It is sufficient in any case, if we have *enough* evidence to warrant our belief; even though there should be much more evidence of the same thing besides, which we have not examined. Although, therefore, the generality of Christians cannot be expected to know the whole, or nearly the whole, of the proofs of their religion, that is no reason against their seeking, and obtaining, proofs enough to convince a reasonable mind.

Even that small portion of the evidences you have now been learning, is perhaps more than sufficient for this purpose; though it is but a part even of what any man is able to understand.

§ 2. It is certain that Christianity now exists; and that Jesus Christ is acknowledged as Lord and Master, (in words, at least,) among all the most civilized people of the world. It is certain, too, that this cannot have been always the case; but that Christianity must have been introduced, by some means or other, among the Jews and Pagans; who must have had some reasons that appeared to them very strong, to induce them to change the religions they had been brought up in.

You know, also, that this great revolution in the religion of the world was begun by a person of humble rank, in one of the least powerful and least esteemed of the ancient nations. It was not a mighty warrior, or a rich and powerful prince, or a learned philosopher, but a Jewish peasant, that brought about this wonderful change. And you are sure, accordingly, that no one, whether friend or enemy, can reasonably doubt that Jesus of Nazareth is at any rate the most extraordinary and most important personage that ever appeared in the world.

§ 3. Again, you have seen that there is good reason to be certain that Jesus and his Apostles propagated their religion by an appeal to miracles; that is, that they professed to perform works beyond human power, as a sign of their being messengers from God. And no one has ever been able to point out any other way in which they did, or could, introduce the religion. Nor can we conceive how a few Jewish peasants, without power, or wealth, or learning, or popular prejudice on their side, could have been, at first, either believed or listened to, if they had not begun by appealing to the testimony of miraculous signs. Now this would have been no help, but a hinderance to their preaching, if their pretensions to superhuman powers had not been true; because, surrounded as they were by adversaries, and men prejudiced against them, any attempt at imposture would have been detected, and would have exposed them to general scorn. And, accordingly, it does not appear that any of the Pagan religions — in short, any religion except ours — ever was first introduced and established among adversaries by an appeal to the evidence of miracles.

We have good grounds for believing, therefore, that the people of those times, even the enemies of Christianity, found it impossible to deny the fact of the miracles being wrought (see Acts iv. 16); and thence were driven to account for them as the work of evil spirits. And this we find recorded, not only in the writings of Christian authors, but also in those of Jewish and Pagan adversaries.

§ 4. We find accounts, too, in the works of Pagan writers, as well as in the New Testament, of the severe persecutions which great numbers of the early Christians had to encounter. And this furnishes a proof of their sincerely believing not only the truth of their religion, but also the miracles which many of them professed to have seen, and in which they could not have been mistaken. For, if these miracles had been impostures, it is incredible that such numbers of men should have exposed themselves to dangers and hardships to attest the truth of them, without any one being induced by suffering (and this though some of them *were* driven to renounce Christianity) to betray the imposture.

§ 5. That the works of these writers have really come down to us, and that the general sense of them is given in our translations, you have good reason to be convinced, even without understanding the original languages, or examining ancient manuscripts. You need not take the word of a scholar for this, or feel such full confidence in the honesty of any two or three learned men, as to trust that they would not deceive you in anything, and to believe on their authority. There is, and has been, so great a number of learned men, in various countries and ages, some opposed to Christianity, and others, Christians of different sects, opposed to each other, that they never could have agreed in forging a book, or putting forth a false translation. On the contrary, any supposed mistake or fraud of any one of them, the rest are ready to expose. So that there is no reasonable doubt as to anything in which they all agree.

And this, you have seen, is the same sort of evidence on which most men believe that the earth is round,—that there is such a city as Rome,—and many other things which they have not themselves seen, but which rest on the *uncontradicted* testimony of many independent witnesses.

§ 6. You have seen also, that, in respect of the books of the Old Testament, there is this very remarkable circumstance, that they are preserved with the utmost care and reverence by the Jews, who reject Jesus Christ, although these books contain what appear to Christians most remarkable prophecies of Him.

And it was pointed out to you, that there are many parts of these prophecies of which we see the fulfilment before us, though the early Christians did not; namely, that a religion should arise among the Jews, which would have a wide spread among the Gentiles, but yet that it should be a *new* religion, not the same as taught by Moses; and that this religion should spring, not from the whole nation, but from one individual of that nation, and He a person despised, rejected, and persecuted even to death by his own people.

All this, which is so unlike what any one would have foretold from mere guess, but which we see has actually come to pass, is prophesied in books which enemies of Christianity (the unbelieving Jews of this day) reverence as divinely inspired.

Now if you reflect attentively on all these heads of evidence which you have been learning, and of which this short summary has just been put before you, you will perceive that even a portion of it might be fairly considered as a strong reason to be given of the hope that is in you; but that, when you take *the whole of it together*, it is sufficient to satisfy any reasonable mind. For to believe that so many marks of truth should be brought together by chance, or by *man's* contrivance, in favor of a false story,—to believe this, I say, would be much greater credulity than to believe that the Gospel really was from God.

§ 7. These marks of truth, you should observe, are (as has been said) a vast deal stronger when *taken together*, and confirming each other. For each of the separate proofs may be regarded as a distinct *witness*. And when several independent witnesses give the same evidence, their agreement may prove the matter completely, even when no one of those witnesses is, by himself, deserving of confidence. Suppose, for instance, that one out of several men—none of them much to be relied on—gives a particular account of some transaction which he professes to have seen: you may think it not unlikely that he may have invented the story, or have dreamed it: but then, if his account is confirmed by another, and another, of these men, who, you are sure, could have had no communication with the first, you then conclude that it must be true; because they could not have chanced, all of them, to invent the same story, or to have the same dream. And so it is, when you have a number of different marks of truth meeting together, as they do, in the Gospel History. Even if each of these, taken separately, had much less force than it actually has, it would be infinitely unlikely that they should all happeen to be found united in a false story.

§ 8. These arguments, however, have been laid before you very briefly; and hereafter, if you will study them at leisure, and dwell upon them more fully, in your own mind, and in conversation with others, you will see the force of them still more and more.

But though these arguments are enough to satisfy you that an ordinary Christian, who does not pretend to be a learned man, may yet believe in his religion on better grounds than the Pagans have for believing theirs, there are many other arguments besides; some of which are quite within the reach of the unlearned. In particular, what is called the *internal* evidence of Christianity, that is, the proof drawn from the character of the religion itself, and of the Christian Scriptures, — is a kind of evidence which you will find more and more satisfactory the more you reflect on and study the subject, if you endeavor at the same time sincerely to act up to the knowledge you acquire, and to be the better for it in your life.

LESSON X.

INTERNAL EVIDENCES.—PART I.

§ 1. If the Christian Religion was not from God, it must have been from Man. It must have been a "cunningly devised fable" of artful impostors, or else a dream of crazy enthusiasts, or some mixture of these two, if it was not really, what it professed to be, a divine revelation.

To examine then the *internal evidence*, is to inquire which of these is the most likely supposition, looking to the *character of the Gospel itself;* to consider whether the religion itself, and the Christian Scriptures, seem more likely to have proceeded from the God of truth, or from mere men, who were either designing impostors, or wild enthusiasts.

Now, it may be said, that we are very imperfect judges of the question *what* is likely to have come from God, since we have such a faint and imperfect knowledge of Him; so that we cannot decide with any confidence what we ought to *expect* in a divine revelation. This is very true. But you should remember that the question is not whether Christianity seems to us likely, *in itself*, to have come from God, and is just such as we should have expected a divine revelation to be; but whether it is *more* likely to have come from God, or from Man? For we know that the religion does exist; and therefore we have to consider not merely whether it is like what might be looked for in a true revelation from God, but also whether it is *unlike* what might be looked for in the work of human impostors or enthusiasts?

§ 2. Now, this is a question of which we *are* able to judge; because we have, or may acquire, such a knowledge of *human* nature as to decide, on good grounds, what is likely to have proceeded from man's device. And the more you learn of mankind, and of the works of various writers, and, again, the more you study the Christian religion, the more you will see how different it is from any religion that mere men (and particularly Jews) would have been likely to contrive.

A great part of this internal evidence is such, as to require some experience and knowledge of the world, and reflection, as well as acquaintance with the Scriptures, to enable any one to take it in properly. But still there are several internal marks of truth that may be pointed out; which, though but a small part of what you may hereafter find, are yet of great importance.

§ 3. For example, if the Christian religion had been contrived and propagated by a number of designing men, in such a way as would have seemed to them the best suited for gaining converts, you may be sure that they would naturally have put forth some book purporting to be written by Jesus himself, laying down the principles and precepts of his religion, and answering to the books of the Law written by Moses. All men who were at all disposed to listen to the preaching of the

Gospel, and to examine the Christian Scriptures, would have been likely to inquire, in the first place, (as, no doubt, many persons did,) for something written by the very Founder of the new religion. If, therefore, there had been any forgery, the forged books, or at least the principal of them, would certainly have been attributed to Jesus Christ as their author. And all that were not attributed to Him would naturally have been published with the names of the most distinguished and eminent of his Apostles.

Now, the fact is, as you know, that, of all the Christian Scriptures, there is no one book professing to be written by Christ himself; and of the four Gospels, there are only two that are attributed even to any of the Apostles as the writers, St. Matthew's and St. John's; and, again, of these two, St. John alone is much distinguished among the Apostles, very little being recorded of St. Matthew in particular. The other two Gospels, and also the book of Acts, which records the first propagation of Christianity, have come down to us as the work of two men, who appear, indeed, to have been companions of some of the most eminent of the Apostles, but who did not claim to be Apostles themselves.

All this is just the reverse of what might have been expected from crafty and designing men, seeking to impose on the credulous for the purpose of gaining converts.

§ 4. You should remember, too, that if the books of the New Testament, which contain accounts of so many wonderful occurrences, were really published near *the very time* when these occurrences were said to have taken place, the accounts in these books must be, substantially, true; because any material falsity would have been immediately exposed by the adversaries of Christianity. And if, on the other hand, these books had been forged a hundred or two hundred years later, and had been falsely attributed to the authors whose names they bear, we cannot doubt that some at least of those books would have been attributed to the great Founder of the religion himself.

And moreover, on that supposition, — that is, supposing the books to have been composed at a later period than that of the Apostles, — we should undoubtedly have found in them the title of CHRISTIANS applied to the believers in Jesus by themselves. For that title has been so applied, in every age down to this day, by all Christian writers *since* the times of the Apostles. And therefore there can be no doubt that any writer in the second or third or fourth century, who was composing pretended gospels and epistles, would have continually called Christians by that very name which he and all his neighbors had been accustomed so to employ.

But in all the books of the New Testament we do not once find the title of Christians *applied by themselves to one another*. The word occurs but three times in the New Testament; in the 11th chapter of Acts, in the 26th chapter of Acts, and in the 1st Epistle of Peter, chapter 4; and in no one of these places is it thus employed. It is mentioned as a name first given to the disciples at Antioch in Syria; doubtless by the Romans, as the word is of Latin formation. King Agrippa, again, uses the word in speaking to Paul; and the Apostle Peter introduces the word as denoting what was accounted a *crime* by the heathen rulers. "If any man," says he, "suffer for being a Christian, let him not be ashamed."

But addressing the Christians themselves, the Apostles never call them by that name, but "*believers*" [or "*faithful*"], "*elect*" [or "*chosen*"], "*saints*" [or "*holy*," that is, set apart and *dedicated* to God's service], "*brethren*," &c.

The reason why the Apostles always used these names in preference to the new name of *Christians* probably was in order to point out that Christianity was not so much a *new* religion, as a continuation and fulfilment of the old, and a completion of God's *original design;* and that all believers, whether Jews or Gentiles, were admitted to the same privileges — only much enlarged — which had belonged to God's people Israel. Now the Israelites are continually called in the Old Testament "Brethren," "a Holy People" [or "Saints"], God's "Chosen" [or "Elect"] People, &c. And hence it was, no doubt, that the Apostles chose to confine themselves to those titles.

After their time, when Jerusalem and its temple had been destroyed, and the admission of Gentiles into the number of God's people ceased to appear anything strange, — the Church consisting chiefly of Gentiles, — then Christians naturally adopted among themselves the title which had long been in common use among the rest of the world.

But whatever was the cause of the earliest Christians abstaining from the use of that title, the *fact* that they did so abstain is clear.

Here, therefore, you have a decisive INTERNAL PROOF

of the *antiquity* of our sacred books. Had they been composed at a later period than that of the Apostles, we should have found in them the disciples continually addressed by the name of Christians; which is, in fact, never once so used.

§ 5. Again, it is certain that, at the time when Jesus appeared, the Jews were earnestly expecting a Christ or Messiah (that is, an anointed Deliverer), who should be a mighty prince, and free them from subjection to the Romans, and make them a powerful nation, ruling over all the Gentiles. And this is what is still expected by the Jews at this day. Now, if Jesus and his Apostles had been enthusiasts or impostors, or a mixture of the two, they would most likely have conformed to the prevailing expectations of the people. They would have been likely to give out that the "kingdom of heaven" which was "at hand" was a glorious worldly empire, such as the Jews had fixed their hopes on, instead of a "kingdom not of this world," which was what they did preach.

And we know that the several pretended Christs who appeared a little before the destruction of Jerusalem, and even after it, did profess, each, to come as a temporal deliverer and conqueror, agreeably to the prevailing notions.

Jesus and his disciples, on the contrary, not only proclaimed no temporal kingdom, but did not even promise any worldly success and prosperity to their followers; but told them that "in the world they should have tribulation." (John xvi. 33.) And this is the more remarkable, because the Jews had been always brought up in the notion that worldly prosperity was a sign of

God's favor; such being the rewards promised in the Mosaic law. The hardships and afflictions in this life, which men were told they must make up their minds to if they became Christians, were not only disheartening, but also likely to raise a prejudice in their minds against Jesus and his disciples, as if they could not be really favored by God; according to the prophecy of Isaiah, "We did esteem Him stricken, *smitten of God*, and afflicted" (liii. 4).

All this, therefore, is what either impostors or enthusiasts of any nation, but especially of the Jewish nation, would have been very unlikely to teach.

§ 6. Again, if the Apostles had been designing men, willing to flatter the prejudices of the Jews for the sake of making converts, but yet afraid of proclaiming Christ as a *temporal* king and deliverer for fear of provoking the Romans, they would at least have taught that the Jews were to have a *spiritual* superiority; that is, that they were to be still God's peculiar people in a religious point of view. They would have taught that Jerusalem was still to be the Holy City, and that all men were to come thither to worship and offer sacrifices in the Temple, and were to observe all the laws of Moses, in order to obtain God's favor. This would have been the most acceptable doctrine to the Jews; and what the Apostles, being themselves Jews, would hardly have failed to teach if the Gospel had been a scheme of their devising. And accordingly we learn from the Acts, and from several of St. Paul's Epistles (especially that to the Galatians), that many of the Jewish converts did labor to bring the Gentile Christians to the observance of the Mosaic law. But the Apostles never would admit this doctrine; but taught that the Gentile Christians were not to take upon them the yoke of the Jewish law, and were perfectly on a level with their Jewish brethren; and that under the Gospel, Jerusalem and its temple had no particular sanctity.

Now all this is just the opposite of what might have been expected of impostors or enthusiasts preaching a religion of their own fancy or contrivance.

§ 7. It is true, indeed, that to have given this pre-eminence to the Jews, and their city and temple, though it would have been flattering to the *Jewish* prejudices, and might have been likely to allure converts of *that* nation, would not have been so acceptable to the Gentiles as a religion which should have put them on an equal footing with the Jews. But if the Gospel had been artfully framed to gratify and allure the Gentiles, it would at least have *one* ordinance which would have been acceptable to the Jews and Gentiles alike; namely, the *slaying of beasts in sacrifice.* In this point, the Jewish and all the different Pagan religions agreed. Sheep and oxen were slain as burnt-offerings, on the altars both of Jehovah and the heathen gods. Indeed, it is a kind of worship so suitable to men's notions, that it was revived, several ages after, by the Mohammedans, who have a sacrifice of a camel on certain festivals, as an ordinance of their religion. But at the time when Christianity first arose, neither Jew nor Pagan had ever heard of or conceived such a thing as a religion in which no animals were sacrificed. They had always been so accustomed to these offerings, that they most likely regarded them as essential to every religion, and were astonished and shocked at finding that the Christian religion was without them. And it is incredible that Christianity *should* have been without them, if it had been a religion invented by men. It would never have entered into the minds of its authors to make it an exception to all the religions that existed, or that they had ever heard of; and that, too, in a point which would be likely to shock all men's feelings and prejudices.

The whole character, indeed, of the Christian religion differs so widely, in many particulars, both from the Jewish and from all the other religions which had ever existed in the world, that one cannot conceive how any men could, of themselves, have thought of any such system, much less thought of it as likely to be well received.

And the same may be said of the character of Jesus himself, as drawn by the Evangelists. It is quite unlike all that had ever before appeared, or been described or imagined.

§ 8. Another point to be observed is this: that mere men, seeking to propagate their religion in whatever way they might think best, would naturally have been so eager to make converts that they would not have insisted very much on a strict moral life in those who did not show great zeal in their Master's cause; but would have allowed active services to their party to make amends for some neglect of other duties. Mohammed accordingly declared that the highest place in the Divine favor belonged to those who fought bravely in his cause. And in almost all sects and parties you may see the same disposition in men to reckon zeal in their cause as a virtue so great that it will excuse many and considerable faults in private life.

This mode of judging, which is so natural to man, is just the opposite of what we find in Jesus Christ and his Apostles. They not only taught their followers to be pure and upright [righteous], and kind and humble, but taught them also that nothing they could say or do in the cause of the Christian faith could make up for the want of these Christian virtues, or would be at all accepted by their Master. He not only compares a man who should hear his precepts without acting upon them to one who "built a house on the sand," and reproaches those who called him "Lord! Lord!" and "did not the things which he said" (Matt. vii. 26, Luke vi. 46); but He also declares that those who had "preached in his name," and in his name even "done many wonderful works," should be disowned and rejected by him if they were "workers of iniquity." (Matt. vii. 22, 23.) And the Apostles, in like manner, taught their converts that their professing the Christian faith was a reason for requiring not the less, but the more, strictness of morals from them (1 Cor. v. 11, 12); and that even the miraculous powers bestowed on them were worthless if they had not that charity which is humble, gentle, patient, and self-denying. (1 Cor. xiii.)

All this is what we might have expected from teachers sent from God. And experience shows how different it is from what might have been expected of mere human teachers, acting according to their own judgment and their natural feelings.

LESSON XI.

INTERNAL EVIDENCES. — PART II.

§ 1. You may observe, again, that the *kind* of moral duty which Jesus and his Apostles taught was not what was the most likely to gain them popularity with their hearers. The Jews had a great deal of national pride in being God's holy and peculiar people; they looked on the Gentiles as unclean and outcasts, and had a particular hatred and contempt for the Samaritans. The Romans, again, were no less proud of their military glory and political power; and the Greeks, of their superior wisdom and refinement. And all were zealous for the glory, and greatness, and superiority, each, of his own country. It was not acceptable to any of these to be taught to "love their enemies," — to return good for evil, — to be humble and forgiving, — patient under persecution, — gentle and kind to all men; and, lastly, to consider men of every race and every station as on a level in respect to the Gospel promises; and that, in God's sight, there was to be "neither Greek nor Jew, Barbarian, Scythian, bond nor free." (Coloss. iii. 11.)

Moreover, party spirit ran very high among the Jews, especially between the sects of the Pharisees and Sadducees. Now, an enthusiast would have most likely been a zealous partisan of one of these sects;

and a scheming impostor, if he did not join one of them, would have been likely to aim at the favor of both, by flattering each in turn, and gratifying each by exposing the faults of their opponents. Jesus, on the contrary, in his discourses to each party, sets before them their own errors (Luke xi. 42, &c.; xx. 27); and he does the same in respect of the Jews and Samaritans. (Luke x. 33; John iv. 22.)

All this is worthy of a "Teacher sent from God," and is quite different from what we might expect of mere human teachers.

§ 2. Many men, it is true, would be ready to praise and to recommend a life of *greater* purity and uprightness than their neighbors, or they themselves, are accustomed to practise. Several of the ancient heathen philosophers wrote moral treatises containing some excellent precepts, and describing a much higher degree of virtue than was commonly found in the lives of the Heathen generally, or even in the lives of those very philosophers themselves. And if the New Testament writers had been men of the higher and more educated classes, accustomed to converse with the learned, and to study philosophical works, instead of being mostly poor and ignorant Jewish fishermen and artisans, it would not have been wonderful that they should have taught a higher degree of morality than what men in general practised.

But the Gospel went beyond, not merely what men *practised*, but what they *approved*. It was not merely *better* than men's *conduct;* but, in several points, *contrary* to their *principles*. For instance, "to love one's enemies," — to return "good for evil," — to be "meek and lowly in spirit, — "not easily provoked," but forbearing, submissive, and long-suffering, — all this was not merely not *practised* by the ancient Heathen and Jews, but it was not even *admired;* on the contrary, it was regarded with scorn, as base and mean-spirited.

§ 3. And what is more, even now we may often find professed Christians, while they hold in reverence the very books which teach such lessons, yet not only practising, but approving, the very opposite. We may find some who value themselves on a quick resentment of affronts (calling it "indignation"), and in using what they call "strong language" towards opponents; that is, reviling and insult. And even fierce strife and bitter persecution will often be admired as "manly and spirited conduct," and as a noble Christian zeal. And you will find all this even in men who venerate the very Gospel, which relates how Jesus rebuked his Apostles for offering to call down fire from heaven on his enemies, and told them that they "knew not what manner of spirit they were of."

Since, then, Christianity is opposed, not only to men's natural *inclinations*, but also, in some points, to their *ideas* of what is dignified and praiseworthy, you may see how incredible it is that scheming or ambitious men should have contrived a religion which condemns, not only men's *conduct*, but their *principles.*

§ 4. Then, again, if you look to the style of writing in the historical books (the four Gospels and the Acts), you will observe that neither the miracles nor the sufferings of Christ or his Apostles are boastfully set forth, and eloquently described and remarked upon; as would have been natural for writers desirous of making a strong impression on the reader. There is no endeavor to excite wonder, or admiration, or compassion, or indignation. There is nothing, in short, such as we should have expected in writers who were making up a marvellous story to produce an effect on men's feelings and imaginations. The miracles performed, and the instances of heroic fortitude displayed, are all related, briefly, calmly, and dryly, and almost with an air of indifference, as if they were matters of every-day occurrence, and which the readers were familiar with. And this is, indeed, one strong proof that the readers to whom these books were addressed — the early Christians — really were (as the books themselves give us to understand they were) *familiar* with these things; in short, that the persecutions endured, and the signs displayed, by the Apostles, really were, in those times and countries, common and notorious.

You should observe, also, the candid and frank simplicity with which the New Testament writers describe the weakness and faults of the disciples; not excepting some of the most eminent among the Apostles. Their "slowness of heart" [that is, dulness of understanding], their want of faith [trust] in their Master, and their worldly ambition and jealousy among themselves, are spoken of without reserve, and as freely as the faults of their adversaries.

§ 5. This, and some of the other points in the New Testament that have been noticed, would be very remarkable if met with in any *one* book; but it is still more so, when you consider that the same character runs through *all* the books of the New Testament; which are no less than twenty-seven distinct compositions, of several different kinds, written apparently at considerable intervals of time from each other, and which have come down to us as the works of no less than eight different authors. You might safely ask an unbeliever to point out the same number — or half the number — of writers in behalf of any Sect, Party, or System, all of them, without a single exception, writing with the same modest simplicity, and without any attempt to excuse, or to extol and set off themselves.

In this respect, and in many others, both the Christian religion itself, and the Christian Scriptures, are totally unlike what they might have been expected to be, if they had been from Man. *They appear too simple, candid, and artless, to have come from impostors; and too calm, sober, and wise for enthusiasts.* And yet, if Christianity were the device of men, these men must have been either the most deliberate, artful, and wicked of impostors, or else by far the wildest and maddest set of enthusiasts that were ever combined together; since they did not (as many crazy enthusiasts have done) appeal merely to their own inward feelings and their dreams or visions, but to matters of fact coming under the evidence of the senses; in which none but a complete madman could be mistaken, and most of which their adversaries were free to judge of as well as themselves.

LESSON XII.

INTERNAL EVIDENCES. — PART III.

§ 1. These few heads, then, of internal evidence, which have been here briefly sketched out, would even alone furnish good reason for believing that the Gospel did not, and could not, have come from Man; and that, therefore, it must have come from God. And yet these internal marks of truth, which have been here pointed out by way of specimens, are but a very small part of what you may hereafter make out for yourself; and are not even selected as being the principal and the most conclusive, but only as those which could the most easily be put before you in a small compass. At some future time, when your power of judging is improved, you will feel the very character of our Saviour, as described in the Gospels, to be (as I have hinted to you) one of the strongest proofs, and the most satisfactory and delightful proof, of the truth of his religion.

But the moral excellence of his character, as drawn by the Evangelists, is what could not be set forth, so as to do justice to the argument founded on it, within a small space. For it would be necessary to dwell at some length on each of his sayings and acts, so as to point out the kindness and tenderness of heart, — the persevering benevolence, — the gentleness combined with dignity and firmness, — the active and unwearied, yet calm zeal, with which He labored for the good of mankind, — and the other great and amiable qualities which He displayed on so many occasions. And to do this properly, would require a volume nearly as large as the whole of this.

But you may, in a great measure, supply to yourself such a work, by attentively reading and reflecting on, with a view to the present argument, the Gospels themselves; and, especially, such passages as those referred to below.*

§ 2. In conducting for yourself such a study as we have been suggesting, these three points should be attended to, and steadily kept before the mind.

First, — The picture drawn by the Evangelists is, evidently, an *unstudied* one. There is nothing in it of the nature of *eulogium* and *panegyric*. They do not seem laboring to set forth and call attention to the excellence of their Master's character. They do not break out into any exclamations of admiration of it; and, indeed, make hardly any remarks on it at all; but simply relate what He said and did.

Secondly, — If they had had the inclination, they do not seem to have had the *ability*, to draw a fictitious character of great moral beauty, devised by their own imagination. They write like (what they were) plain, unpractised authors, without learning, or eloquence, or skill in composition.

Now let any one try the experiment of setting some person, of great ability as a writer, to draw up a ficti-

---

* See Note A, at the end of this Lesson.

tious narrative concerning some imaginary personage. Let him enter into *particular details* as fully as the Evangelists have done; and let him do his best to paint a character as consistent, and as morally beautiful, as that of Jesus. You would see how imperfectly he would succeed; and how far he would fall short of the picture drawn (and which must, therefore, be a *real* picture) by untaught Jewish fishermen and peasants.

And what we have been saying is confirmed by certain works commonly called the "Spurious Gospels"; of which some considerable portions have come down to us. They seem to have been composed (some of them as early as the fourth century) partly from invention, and partly from some vague traditions that were afloat. But they were never, as far as we can learn, received by any Church as Scripture. These narratives profess to give several particulars of the life of Jesus, — especially of his childhood, — which are not to be found in the genuine Gospels.

Now it is remarkable, that, though the writers evidently designed to raise admiration of our Lord, and manifest that design very strongly, yet the picture they draw of Him is, in many points, contemptible or odious; for instance, they represent Him as exercising, when a child, miraculous powers, not for any purpose connected with his ministry, but merely for his own amusement; as any ordinary child would be likely to do, if gifted with such powers.

And He is also represented as so passionate and mischievous a child, that he miraculously struck dead another boy for accidentally running against him.

In short, his character as given in these "spurious

Gospels" is quite a contrast to that given by each of our four Evangelists. And the whole tone of the narratives themselves — the spurious and the genuine — is no less contrasted.

§ 3. Thirdly, — You are to keep in mind that the private moral character of Jesus is *unimpeached* even by the opponents of his Gospel. None of them have ever imputed to Him avarice, or cruelty, or any kind of profligate sensuality. Now there is hardly any other very eminent man of whom this can be said, however groundless may be the charges brought against any of them. Certainly, no man was ever so unimpeached in character who had so many and such bitter enemies; — enemies who would have been glad to get hold of any story, however false, or even any suspicion, that could raise a prejudice against Him.

But even the Jews, in that book already mentioned (Lesson V. § 2), though they lavish on Him all the most abusive epithets, yet do not charge Him with any one immoral act, in his private life.

And you should keep in mind, among other things, that this man, whose extraordinary purity of moral character is thus strongly attested, did certainly *profess* to be a heaven-sent messenger, and to possess miraculous powers. Now any one who can believe that one whom he considers *a good man* would *falsely* put forth such pretensions, deceiving his disciples, or suffering them to deceive themselves, as to his miraculous powers, and thus practising what is called a "pious fraud" (in reality, an impious fraud) for the sake of spreading his doctrines, — any one who can believe this of one whom he accounts a virtuous man, must be himself a person of exceedingly low moral notions.

But all that relates to our Lord's moral character is a thing rather to be felt than described: and you will feel it the more, and the better estimate the force of the arguments drawn from it, in proportion to your sincere desire and endeavor to conform your own character to the purest and best pattern you can find.

The more, indeed, you learn of mankind, and of the Gospel, and the more you study (with a sincere desire to know what is true, and to do what is right) both other books, ancient and modern, and also the Christian Scriptures, the more you will perceive (as has been above said) how unlikely the Christian religion is to have been devised by man, and how well suited it is to meet the wants of man, and to improve his nature.

§ 4. But when you do come to perceive the force of the internal evidence for the truth of Christianity, you will find that, though it may be one of the reasons to *have*, it will often not be the best to *give*. A great part of this kind of evidence is better fitted to furnish a consoling satisfaction to the mind of a believer, than to convince an unbeliever. For there is much of the excellence of the Christian religion that can only be learned fully from experience. Sincere believers perceive in it a wisdom and purity and nobleness of character, which are not completely understood, nor thoroughly liked and relished by any one, till he has *become*, in a great degree, what the Christian religion is designed to *make* him, — till he has something of such a character as the Gospel does not *find* in man, but *forms* in him.

And this seems to be that *Christian experience* which the Apostles, especially St. John and St. Paul, often appeal to as an evidence (not indeed to unbelievers, who could not have had this experience, but) in addressing their converts. "The Spirit itself" (says St. Paul, Rom. viii. 16) "beareth witness with our spirit, that we are the children of God," &c.

It seems, indeed, to have been designed that man's conscience should bear witness, not only *against* what is *wrong*, but also in *favor* of what is right. And hence a Christian who has for some time been laboring to conform himself to the Gospel, and who finds his religious notions becoming clearer, and that he is growing better, and holier, and happier, gains by this an unexperimental proof, which confirms the other proofs, of the truth of his religion. His conscience testifies that he is practically influenced and "led by the Spirit of Christ"; and thus he is "filled" (as St. Paul says, Rom. xv. 13) "with all joy and peace in believing."

And this is a kind of evidence which will become, to such a Christian, stronger and stronger, the more he "grows in grace and in the knowledge of our Lord and Saviour." But this proof, from personal experience, is fitted (as has been said), not so much for the first conversion of an unbeliever, as for the confirmation of a practical Christian; because no one else can feel, or fully understand and value it.

§ 5. A life of genuine Christian virtue does, indeed, meet with some degree of approbation from most men, even though unbelievers; and it appears, accordingly, to have been, in the earliest times, a help towards the conversion of some of them. (1 Peter ii. 12.) And it is for you to bring before the minds of those you live with, this kind of testimony to Christianity from its moral excellence; not so much by talking of it, as by setting it forth in your life, and "letting your light so shine before men, that they may see your good works, and glorify your Father which is in heaven." (Matt. v. 16.) But you must not expect that any one will completely feel all the force of this kind of internal evidence of Christianity, till he shall have become himself a believer, and a sincerely practical believer. It is not easy to give a clear description of the inside of a well-built and commodious house, to one who is on the outside, and has never been in such a house, but always lived in a tent, like the wild Arabs, or in a smoky, slovenly hovel. But you may be able to point out to him enough of what is on the outside to induce him to come in; and when he *has* done this, he will gradually be able to judge for himself; and by the habits of neatness, order, cleanliness, and decency which he will be likely to acquire by living in such a house, will gain more and more the power of perceiving the commodiousness of it. And so it is with the evidences of Christianity. As soon as a man has seen enough, as he easily may do, of good evidence, to convince him that it is from God, if he will then be induced to *come in*, and heartily embrace it, and endeavor to understand it, and to apply it to himself, so as to be the better for it in his life, he will then be rewarded by a fuller and clearer view of many other evidences which he could not at first take in. And such a person will thus obtain the fulfilment of that promise of our Master: "If any man is willing to do [will do] the will of God, he shall know of the doctrine whether it be of God." (John vii. 17.)

§ 6. Great care should be taken not to misunderstand

what has just been said; because you may hear from some persons what appears, at the first glance, very like it, though in reality quite different. I mean, that you may meet with persons who profess to despise and dislike all that is commonly called "evidences for the truth of Christianity"; and who say, "Let a man but feel the *want* of it, — let him feel how suitable Christianity is to the needs of such a being as man, — how it supplies such motives, and such guidance, and hopes, and consolations, as human nature requires; and then he will want no evidence to convince him of its truth"; — with a great deal more to the same purpose.

Now, all this may seem at the first glance very plausible; but, on reflection, you will perceive that it is setting up Man — each man for himself — to be the standard of Divine truth. On this principle, each one is to receive as a revelation whatever religion suits his own judgment of what is good, and his own wants, and wishes, and tastes. Now, we know how widely men differ from one another on these points, and what various and erroneous systems they are, accordingly, disposed to embrace. For instance, the Jews, at the time when Jesus appeared, felt a *want* of a victorious and mighty earthly deliverer, who should exalt their nation, and reign in great worldly splendor. The kingdom of Jesus, which was a "kingdom not of this world," and which admitted "Gentiles to be fellow-heirs," was precisely what they did *not* want. It did not at all suit their hopes, and wishes, and habits of thought. And, accordingly the greater part of them rejected Jesus, and followed those false Christs who promised to lead them to victory over the Romans. Jesus, indeed, appealed to the evidence of his mighty works, while those false Christs produced no evidence at all, except the suitableness of what they taught to the judgment, and to the feelings and wants of the Jews. But most of the Jews, acting on the very principle I have been speaking of, disregarded evidence altogether, and gave themselves up to their own feelings, resolving to believe what suited them best.

In like manner, when Mohammed proclaimed himself a prophet, though he produced no miraculous evidence, he was joined by a multitude of followers. His religion suited a sensual, and gross-minded, and warlike, and ambitious people. He promised them victory and plunder in this world, and after death a paradise of sensual enjoyments. And finding that such a religion suited their tastes and wants, they embraced it without seeking for any further evidence of its truth. The Hindoos, again, and other Pagans, adhere to their own religion without any evidence, and find it suitable to their own wants and tastes.

And the same must be the case with all the most extravagant corruptions of Christianity that have arisen from time to time; such as that of the ancient Gnostics, who thought to obtain immortal life without practising moral virtue, and who had a taste for idle speculations concerning the nature of God. No one of these corrupt religions could ever have arisen at all, or have been received, if those who introduced it, and their followers, had not felt a "want" of some such system.

It is plain, therefore, that the principle I have been speaking of tends to lead men into an endless variety of errors.

§ 7. But the course I have been recommending is, in reality, exactly the reverse of all this. Jesus tells us, that if any man is willing and desirous to do the will of his Heavenly Father, he shall know the truth of the doctrine. You must begin, therefore, by a readiness to follow — not *your own* will, but — the will of God ; and to receive whatever shall appear to come from Him, however contrary to your expectations or wishes. And if in this temper of mind you proceed to examine those evidences which Jesus and his Apostles appeal to, you will see good reason for believing in the Gospel. And then, if you embrace the Gospel, and labor to conform your heart and your life to it, you will perceive that it does suit the nature and the real wants of man. For you will perceive that it tends to enlighten his judgment, and to improve his moral taste, and to lead him to live according to the best principles of his nature, and to secure him the truest peace and comfort. And in proportion as you come to perceive all this, you will thus obtain a strong additional *confirmation* of the truth of Christianity.

But you will have obtained this, not by rejecting evidence, and resolving to conform your religious belief to your own tastes and inclinations, but, on the contrary, by striving to conform your own tastes and inclinations to your religious belief.

§ 8. Observe, then, that this last is a kind of evidence which *all* Christians ought to have, and will have, more and more, in proportion as they fairly try the experiment of conforming themselves to the Gospel. Different persons may have been led by different kinds of proof to embrace the Gospel ; but when they *have* embraced it, they may all hope for this *confirmation* of their faith, by this further proof from experience. Suppose, for instance, some one should offer to several persons, suffering under a painful and dangerous disease, some medicine, which he declared would relieve their sufferings, and restore them to health; it would be natural and reasonable for them to ask for some testimony, or other proof, to assure them of this, before they made trial of the medicine: then suppose them all to be so far convinced, — some by one proof, and some by another, — as to make trial of the medicine; and that they found themselves daily getting better as they took it; they would then have — all of them — an evidence from experience, confirming the former proofs that had originally brought them to make the trial.

But these persons, if they were wise, would be convinced of the virtues of the medicine, not from its being immediately pleasant to the taste, or from its suddenly exciting and cheering them up like a strong cordial; but from its gradually restoring their strength, and removing the symptoms of the disease, and advancing them daily towards perfect health. So also Christian experience, you should remember, does not consist in violent transports, or any kind of sudden and overpowering impression on the feelings; but in a steady, habitual, and continued improvement of the heart and the conduct.

§ 9. We do not say, you will observe, that you, or other Christians, may not experience such sudden transporting impressions as those just alluded to. But it is a settled habit, an improved and improving character, that constitutes the Christian experience which we find described and alluded to in the New Testament Scriptures; which thus affords an additional internal evidence of their having been written by sober-minded men.* For the Apostles, if they had been wild enthusiasts, would have felt, and have taught their converts to expect, the sudden excitement of vehement emotions; and would have referred to some immediate, single, and momentary impression of that kind, as Christian experience. But what they do teach, and perpetually impress on us, is, "He that is Christ's hath crucified the flesh, with the affections and lusts";—the test they refer to is a "growth in grace and knowledge,"—a calm, gradual, and steady advancement in "bringing forth fruit with *Patience*." (Luke viii. 15.) For "PATIENCE" (says St. Paul, Rom. v. 4) "worketh EXPERIENCE; and Experience, Hope; and Hope maketh not ashamed; because the love of God is shed abroad in our hearts, by the Holy Ghost which is given unto us."

NOTE A.

WITH regard to the passages here referred to, (and to which many more might have been added,) you should observe that the picture they form of our Lord's character cannot but be a correct one; because, if He had really been at all a different kind of man from what He is represented, his enemies would not have failed to notice and to take advantage of this. Now, not only do they never charge Him with anything immoral, but He and his Apostles continually appeal to all men's testimony as to the moral excellence of his character, as a matter undeniable and notorious.

---

* See 2 Pet. i. 5; and 1 Thess. iv. 1; and Galat. vi. 9, &c.

See John vii. 46 – 51, viii. 46, and x. 32; Matt. xxvi. 59, xxvii. 23, 24; Luke xxiii. 13 – 15; Acts iii. 13, 14; 1 Peter ii. 21 – 23.

And it should be observed that this moral *teaching* is to be regarded as an appeal of this kind; since, if He had been guilty of any such moral wrong as He censured and rebuked, or had not been himself a model of the virtues He taught, his enemies would have been sure to detect, and to reproach, his inconsistency.

His extensive BENEVOLENCE and Compassionateness are shown in the following (and many other) passages: John iv.; Luke ix. 55, and x. 30 – 37; Mark vii. 26, &c., and x 13 – 21 and 45 – 52; Matt. ix. 36, &c.; Luke xiii. 16, xiv. 12, &c., xxii. 50, 51, xxiv. 34; Matt. xviii. 11, &c.

In reference to his *kind and affectionate* character, see John xi., xix. 25 – 27, &c.; Luke xix. 41, xxii. 61; Matt. xiv. 27 – 31.

For indications of MEEKNESS and Humility, see Matt. ix. 28, xviii., xxvi. 50; John xiii. 4, &c.; Matt. v. 1 – 12; Luke xxii. 24, &c.

For indications of MORAL COURAGE, firmness, and resignation, Luke iv. 23, &c., xiii. 31, &c., xviii. 29, &c.; John xi. 7, &c.; Mark x. 32, &c.; Matt. xxvi. 39 – 46; John xviii. 4, &c.

For indications of SINCERITY, and rebukes of the hypocrite and the seeker after popularity, Matt. vi. 1 – 18, x. 16 – 39, xxii. 18, &c.; Mark xii. 38 – 40; Luke xi. 44, &c.; John xvi. 1 – 6.

For indications of MODERATION, and absence of all enthusiasm and all affected austerity, Matt. xi. 19, xxiii. 23; Luke v. 29 – 35; John ii. 1, &c.; Mark xii. 17.

The passages above referred to contain a few out of many of the indications of a part — and only a part — of the virtues of our Lord's character. Many others will strike you in your perusal of the Gospels with this view.

But this study will affect different persons very unequally, according to *their own* character. Those of a low tone of moral sentiment will be but little struck with the character of Jesus. Those of a somewhat higher and purer mind will feel it more; especially if they have also a considerable knowledge of mankind in general. And one who is, like Nathanael, "an Israelite indeed, in whom is no guile," will (mentally) exclaim, like him, "Rabbi, thou art the Son of God! thou art the King of Israel!"

LESSON XIII.

OBJECTIONS. — PART I.

§ 1. As there are persons who reject the Christian religion, you may perhaps suppose that they have undertaken to refute the proofs of it; and that they have found answers, such as satisfy themselves, to the evidences and reasons on which it is believed; or at least to some of the principal of the reasons, such as have been just put before you.

But you are not likely to meet with any one who will undertake this. At least, no such attempt has been made in any book that has been hitherto published. Unbelievers, though they have had nearly eighteen centuries to try, have never yet been able to show, nor have they even attempted to show, how it could be that so many marks of truth should be found in the Gospel history, supposing it false. Of these marks of truth, even that portion (though far short of the whole) which have been just laid before you are such as certainly never met together, at least in any *known* false story; and how it is that they are found in the Gospel history, if that be not true, has never been explained. No one has ever explained in what way the first disciples of Jesus, circumstanced as they were, succeeded, or could have succeeded, in propagating, as we know they did, such a religion as theirs, supposing it to be, not from God, but from Man.

§ 2. And yet many persons have written and spoken against Christianity How, then, have they proceeded? Instead of accounting for the introduction of Christianity by natural causes, and on the supposition of its being a mere human device, they are accustomed to put forward various difficulties, and start *objections* against several points in the religion. And unlearned Christians often find themselves hard pressed with these objections; and suppose that they are called upon either to find answers to everything that can be urged against the Christian religion, and give a satisfactory solution of every difficulty that is pointed out, or else to abandon their faith, or at least confess that they cannot defend it.

Now you have, indeed, been taught that it is a Christian's duty to be "ready to give an answer to every one that asks a reason of the hope that is in you." But this is a very different thing from being prepared to answer every *objection*. If a person asks you why you are a Christian, or on what grounds you may call on a Pagan to embrace Christianity, this is quite a different thing from his asking you, "How can you explain this?" "and how do you reconcile that?" "and how do you remove such and such difficulties?"

§ 3. I am not saying, you will observe, that no such questions as these ought ever to be asked; or that there is no occasion to seek any answers to them; but only that they are not at all the *same thing* as the other question, — the inquiry for a reason of our Christian hope. And it should also be observed, that it is not the most natural and reasonable way of examining any question to *begin* with looking to the objections against any system, or plan, or history, before we inquire into the reasons in its favor. And yet it is thus that some people are apt to proceed in the case of the Christian religion. Having been brought up in it from childhood, and received it merely as the religion of their fathers, they perhaps meet with some one who starts objections against several points; and then they think themselves obliged to find an answer to each objection, and to explain every difficulty in the Gospel system, without having begun by learning anything of the positive evidence on which it is founded. And the end of this sometimes is, that their minds are disturbed, and perhaps their faith overthrown, before they have even begun to inquire into the subject in the right way.

Some persons will advise you, for fear of having your mind thus unsettled, to resolve at once never to listen to any objections against Christianity, or to make any inquiries, or converse at all on the subject with any one who speaks of any doubts or difficulties; but to make up your mind, once for all, to hold fast the faith you have been brought up in, on the authority of wiser men than yourself, and never to attend to any reasoning on the subject.

§ 4. You have already seen, that if our forefathers had gone upon this plan, we should at this day have been Pagans like them; and that if all the world had proceeded thus when the Apostles first appeared, all men would have kept to the religion of their fathers, (as the chief part of the most learned and most powerful among them did, see 1 Cor. i. 23,) and Christianity would not have existed at all. And you ought to observe, also, that when a learned man says that ordinary Christians had better shut their ears against all doubts and arguments, and be satisfied to take the word of the learned for the truth of the religion, a suspicion is often raised, that he does not really believe it himself, but wishes to support it for the sake of the lower classes; and considers that the less they think, and reason, and inquire, the less danger there is of their being undeceived. Such appears to have been, generally, the state of mind of the educated classes among the ancient Heathen in respect to their religion. They thought it useful for the vulgar to believe in the fables about their gods; and being aware that these would not stand the test of examination, they did not approve of any inquiry on the subject.

§ 5. But it is likely that many of those who discourage ordinary Christians from using their reason on the subject of Christian evidences, are not themselves unbelievers, but are merely timorous and distrustful, and see the dangers on one side, while they overlook those on the other. They see that there is a danger of men making an ill use of their reason, which there certainly is, as well as of any other gift. The servant in the parable (Matt. xxv. 25, Luke xix. 20), who was intrusted with one talent, might have employed it ill, and lost it; but it was not therefore the safe course to lay it by in a napkin. There is danger of the misuse of money, or of food. We know that many shorten their lives by intemperance. Yet food was bestowed for the support of life, and not for its destruction. And so, also, God has provided evidence to prove the truth of Christianity, and has given us the faculty of reason, by which we can understand that evidence; and what is more, He has expressly directed us (1 Peter iii. 15) to make that use of the faculty. But in the use of all his gifts there is danger; which we cannot escape without diligent caution. And those who would guard men against the danger of doubt and disbelief by discouraging the use of reason, are creating a much greater danger of the same kind, by the distrust which they manifest, — by appearing to suspect that their religion will not stand inquiry.

§ 6. But is it, then, to be expected, that you should be prepared to answer every objection that may be brought against your religion? By no means. You may have very good reason for believing something against which there are many objections; and objections which you cannot answer, for want of sufficient knowledge of the subject. In many other cases, besides that of religion, there will be difficulties on both sides of the question, which even the wisest man cannot clear up; though he may, perhaps, plainly see on which side the *greater* difficulties lie; and may even see good reasons for being fully satisfied *which* ought to be believed. Thus, in the case before mentioned of the bed of sea-shells found far above the present level of the sea, there are strong objections against supposing either that the sea was formerly so much higher than now, or that those beds were so much lower, and were heaved up, many hundred feet, to the height where they now lie. And yet no one who has examined and inquired into the subject has any doubt that those beds of shells do exist, and must, at some former time, have been the bottom of a sea.

To take another instance: the astronomer Copernicus first taught, about three hundred years ago, that the earth (which had formerly been supposed to be at rest in the midst of the universe, with all the heavenly bodies moving round it) travels round the sun in the course of a year, and is, at the same time, turning also on its own axis — that is, rolling over like a ball — every twenty-four hours. This theory of his (which has long since been universally admitted) was at first met by many objections; several of which, neither he, nor any one else in those days, was able to answer. Many years afterwards, when astronomy was better understood, some objections were answered, and difficulties explained. But there were others of which no explanation could be found till a very short time ago, in the memory of many persons now living. Yet, long before that time, notwithstanding the objections, there was no one at all acquainted with the subject who had any doubt of the earth's motion.

§ 7. Again, it is perfectly well established, that aerolites — that is, stones from the sky — have fallen in various countries, and at different times, to a considerable number. They are composed of iron, or a peculiar kind of iron-stone, and are of all sizes, from a few ounces to several hundred-weight. No explanation has been given of them that is at all satisfactory. There are strong objections against supposing them either to have been thrown out by volcanoes in the moon, or to be fragments torn off from some other planets, or to be formed in the air. In future generations, perhaps, when chemistry and astronomy are much improved, more may be known about these wonderful stones.

But, in the mean time, the fact of their having fallen is so well attested by numerous witnesses, that, in spite of all the difficulties, no one who has inquired into the subject has any doubt the thing has really occurred, however incredible it might have appeared.

Then, again, if we look to human transactions, we shall find several portions of history, even those which no one has any doubt of, full of such strange events, that difficulties might be pointed out in the accounts of them, and strong objections raised against the history, even when it rests on such satisfactory evidence as to be believed in spite of those objections. In the history, for instance, of Europe, for the last forty years, there are many events so improbable in themselves, — especially all that relate to the wonderful rise, and greatness, and overthrow, of the empire of Napoleon Bonaparte, — that it would be easy to find objections sufficient to convince many persons that the history could not be true, were it not that it is so well attested as to be believed notwithstanding all the difficulties.

Numberless other examples might be brought, to show how many things there are which men believe, and believe on very good grounds, in spite of strong and real objections, which they cannot satisfactorily answer; these being outweighed by more and greater difficulties on the opposite side.

§ 8. As for the particular objections which have been brought against the Christian religion, and the Christian Scriptures, it would of course be impossible to put before you, in a short compass, even the chief part of them, together with the answers that have been given. But what is of the most importance is, to lay down, generally, the right way of viewing objections, either against our religion or against anything else; namely, first, that you should not *begin* by considering the objections to any statement or system, before you are acquainted with the evidence in favor of it; and, secondly, that you should not think yourself bound to renounce your faith, if you cannot answer every objection, and clear up every difficulty that may be raised; but should remember that many things are believed, and must be believed, against which there are strong objections that have never been completely answered, when there are stronger objections against the opposite belief.

LESSON XIV.

OBJECTIONS. — PART II.

§ 1. Of the objections that have been brought against Christianity, there are some which ordinary Christians may learn enough to be able to refute for themselves. There are others, again, to which learned and able men have found answers, but which the generality of Christians cannot be expected to answer, or even to understand; and, again, there are other objections which no man, however learned, and however intelligent, can expect to answer fully, on account of the imperfect knowledge which belongs to man in this present life. For you are to observe, that, when we speak of any one as having much knowledge and intelligence, we mean that he is so *comparatively* with *other men;* since the best-informed man knows but few things, compared with those of which he is ignorant; and the wisest man cannot expect to understand all the works and all the plans of his Creator. Now this is particularly important to be kept in mind in the present case; because Christianity, we should remember, is a scheme imperfectly understood. What is revealed to us must be (supposing the religion to be true) but a part, and perhaps but a small part, of the whole truth. There are many things of which, at present, we can know little or nothing, which have, or may have, a close connection with the Christian religion. For instance, we are very little acquainted with more than a very *small part* of the *universe;* of the *whole* history, past and future, of the *world* we inhabit; and of the whole of *man's existence.*

This earth is but a speck compared with the rest of the planets which move round the sun, together with the enormous mass of the sun itself; to say nothing of the other heavenly bodies. It is likely that all these are inhabited; and it may be, that the Gospel which has been declared to us may be but one small portion of some vast scheme which concerns the inhabitants of numerous other worlds.

Then, again, we have no knowledge how long this our world is to continue. For aught we know, the Christian religion may not have existed a fifth part, or a fiftieth part, of its whole time; and it may, perhaps, have not produced yet one fiftieth of the effects it is destined to produce.

And we know that, as it holds out the hope of immortality beyond the grave, it is connected with man's condition, not merely during his short life on earth, but for eternity.

§ 2. Seeing, then, that Christianity, if true, must be a scheme so partially and imperfectly revealed to us, and so much connected with things of which man can have little or no knowledge, we might have expected that difficulties should be found in it which the wisest of men are unable to explain. And men truly wise are not surprised or disheartened at meeting with such difficulties, but are prepared to expect them from the nature of the case.

The view which we have of any portion of a system of which the whole is not before us, has been aptly compared to a map of an *inland country ;* in which we see rivers without source or mouth, and roads that seem to lead to nothing. A person who knows anything of geography understands at once, on looking at such a map, that the sources and mouths of the rivers, and the towns which the roads lead to, are somewhere beyond the boundaries of the district, though he may not know where they lie. But any one who was very ill-informed might be inclined presumptuously to find fault with the map, which showed him only a part of the course of the rivers and roads. And it is the same with anything else of which we see only a part, unless we recollect that it is but a part, and make allowance accordingly for our imperfect view of it.

There is much truth, therefore, in the Scotch proverb, that "children and fools should never see half-finished works." They not only cannot guess what the whole will be when complete, but are apt to presume to form a judgment without being aware of their own ignorance. If you were to see for the first time the beginning of the manufacture of some of the commonest articles, such as, for instance, the paper that is before you, you would be at a loss, if you had never heard the process described, to guess what the workman was going to make. You would see a great trough full of a liquid like pap, and would never think of such a thing as a sheet of paper being made from it. And if you were to see the first beginning of the building of a house or a ship, you would be very unfit to judge what sort of a work it would be when completed.

And the same holds good, only in a greater degree, in respect to the plans of Divine wisdom. So small a portion of them is made known to us, that it would be strange if we did not find many difficulties — such as Man cannot expect to explain — in that portion which we do see.

§ 3. Although, however, you must not expect to be able to answer all objections that may be brought, you will be able, in proportion as you improve in knowledge, and in the habit of reflecting and reasoning on the subject, to find satisfactory answers to many which at first sight may have appeared very perplexing. And in particular, you will find that some difficulties in the Christian religion which have been brought forward as objections to it, will appear to be, on the contrary, evidences in support of it. They may, indeed, still continue to be *difficulties* which you cannot fully explain, and yet may be so far from being *objections* against your faith, that they will even go to confirm it.

For instance, the bad lives of many Christians, who profess to expect that Jesus Christ will judge them, and yet act in opposition to what He taught and to the example He gave, is an objection which has often been brought forward by unbelievers, and which probably influences their minds more than any other. Here is a religion, they say, which professes to have been designed to work a great reformation in Man's character, and yet we find the believers in this religion living as if there were no world but the present, and giving themselves up to all the base and evil passions of human nature, just as the Heathen did. And besides those who are altogether careless and thoughtless about their religion, we find (they say) many who talk and think much of it, and profess great Christian zeal, and who yet live in hatred against their fellow-Christians, indulging in envy, slander, strife, and persecution of one another; and all the time professing to be devoted followers of One who taught them to love even their enemies, to return blessing for cursing, and to be known as his disciples by their love towards each other.*

§ 4. Now it is certainly most mortifying and disheartening to a sincere Christian, to find that his religion has produced hitherto so much less improvement among mankind than he might have been disposed to expect from it. And you should consider deeply what a double guilt Christians will have to answer for, whose life is such as to bring an ill name on their religion; and who thus not only rebel against their Master, but lead others to reject Him. But when the evil lives of so many Christians are brought as an objection against the Christian religion, you may reply by asking whether this does not show how unlikely such a religion is to have been devised by Man. If you saw in any country the fields carefully ploughed and cleared, and sown with wheat, and yet continually sending up a growth of grass and thistles, which choked the wheat wherever they were not weeded out again and again, you would not suppose wheat to be indigenous (that is, to grow wild) in that country; but would conclude that, if the land had been left to itself, it would have produced grass and thistles, and no wheat at all. So also, when you see men's natural character so opposite to the pure, and

* John xiii. 34.

generous, and benevolent, and forgiving character of the Gospel, that, even after they have received the Gospel, their lives are apt to be quite a contrast to Gospel virtue, you cannot think it likely that such a being as Man should have been the inventor of such a religion as the Christian.

§ 5. It is, indeed, strange that we should see men seeking to make amends for the want of Christian virtue by outward religious observances, and by active zeal — often, bitter and persecuting zeal — in the cause of Christianity, when the very Founder of our faith has declared that He abhors such conduct; so that such Christians, in professing to be followers of him, pronounce their own condemnation. This is certainly very strange; but it shows, at least, how strong Man's natural tendency is to that error; and it shows, therefore, how much more incredible it is that men should themselves have devised a religion which thus condemns their principles. All men, in short, and especially Christians, when they are leading an unchristian life (I mean a life on unchristian *principles*), are so far bearing witness that Christianity could not have come from men.

And the same may be said of the absurd extravagances into which some fanatical enthusiasts have fallen, and which have given occasion to unbelievers to throw ridicule on Christianity. There is nothing of this wild and extravagant character in our sacred books. On the contrary, their sobriety and calmness of tone present a striking contrast to what we see in some enthusiasts. So that their absurdities, instead of being an objection against the Gospel, are a proof, on the contrary, what a different thing the Gospel would have been if it had been the work of enthusiasts.

§ 6. To take another instance: it has been brought as an objection against Christianity, that it has not spread over the whole world. It professes to be designed to enlighten and to improve all mankind; and yet, after nearly eighteen centuries, there still remains a very large portion of mankind who have not embraced it. All the most civilized nations, indeed, profess the Christian religion; but there are many millions unconverted; and the progress of the religion among these appears to be very slow. This may be thought very strange and unaccountable; but at least it shows that the religion could not have been originally founded and propagated by mere human means. The nations professing Christianity are now far more powerful and intelligent, and skilful in all the arts of life, than the rest of mankind; and yet, though they send forth many active and zealous missionaries, the religion makes less progress in a century than it did in a few years when it was preached by a handful of Jewish peasants and fishermen, with almost all the wealthy and powerful and learned opposed to them. We cannot come near them in the work of conversion, though we have every advantage over them except in respect of miraculous powers. And therefore we have an additional proof, *that, if they had not had such powers, they could not have accomplished what they did.*

§ 7. Again, there are objections against our sacred books occasioned by the mistake of some injudicious Christians, who have taken a wrong view of the *object* proposed in the Bible.

These persons imagine, and teach others to imagine, that we are bound to take our notions of astronomy, and of all other physical sciences, from the Bible. And accordingly, when astronomers discovered, and proved, that the earth turns round on its axis, and that the sun does not move round the earth, some cried out against this as profane, because Scripture speaks of the sun's rising and setting. And this probably led some astronomers to reject the Bible, because they were taught that, if they received *that* as a divine revelation, they must disbelieve truths which they had demonstrated.

So also, some have thought themselves bound to believe, if they receive Scripture at all, that the earth, and all the plants and animals that ever existed on it, must have been created within six days of exactly the same length as our present days. And this, even before the sun, by which we measure our days, is recorded to have been created. Hence, the discoveries made by geologists, which seem to prove that the earth and various races of animals must have existed a very long time before Man existed, have been represented as completely inconsistent with any belief in Scripture.

It would be unsuitable to such a work as this to discuss the various objections (some of them more or less plausible, and others very weak) that have been brought — on grounds of science, or supposed science — against the Mosaic accounts of the creation, of the state of the early world, and of the flood, and to bring forward the several answers that have been given to those objections. But it is important to lay down the PRINCIPLE on which either the Bible or any other writing or speech ought to be studied and understood; namely, with a reference to *the object proposed* by the writer or speaker.

For example: suppose you bid any one proceed in a straight line from one place to another, and to take care to arrive before the sun goes down. He will rightly and fully understand you, in reference to the practical object which alone you had in view. Now *you* perhaps know very well that there cannot really be a *straight line* on the surface of the earth, since its surface is curved; and that the sun does not really *go down*, only our portion of the earth is turned away from it. But whether the other person knows all this or not, matters nothing at all with reference to your present object; which was, not to teach him mathematics or astronomy, but to make him conform to your directions, which are equally intelligible to the learned and the unlearned.

Now the object of the Scripture revelation is to teach men, not astrology or geology, or any other physical science, but *Religion.* Its design was to inform men, not *in what manner* the world was made, but WHO made it; and to lead them to worship Him, the Creator of the heavens and the earth, instead of worshipping his creatures, the heavens and earth themselves, as gods, which is what the ancient Heathen actually did.

Although, therefore, Scripture gives very scanty and imperfect information respecting the earth and the heavenly bodies, and speaks of them in the language and according to the notions of the people of a rude age, still it fully effects the object for which it was given, when it teaches that the heavens and the earth are not gods to be worshipped, but that "*God created the heavens and the earth,*" and that it is He who made the various tribes of animals, and also man.

But as for astronomy and geology and other sciences, men were left — when once sufficiently civilized to be capable of improving themselves — to make discoveries in them by the exercise of their own faculties.

§ 8. But it is also sometimes objected, that our sacred books do not give any full and clear revelation of several very interesting particulars, which men would naturally wish and expect to find in them. For example, there is not only a very short and scanty account of the creation of the world, and of its condition before the flood, but there is little said about angels, and, what is more remarkable, there is no full and particular description given of a future state, and of the kind of life which the blest are to lead in Heaven. All these, and especially the last, are very curious and interesting matters; and being beyond the reach of Man to discover, it appears very strange to some persons that books professing to contain a divine revelation should give so very brief and scanty an account of them, and leave such a natural curiosity unsatisfied.

Now this is a difficulty which you may *hereafter*, on attentive reflection, be able completely to explain. You may find good reasons for deciding that this absence of all that goes to gratify mere curiosity is just what might be expected in a revelation really coming from God. But you may perceive *at once* that it is *not* to be expected in a pretended revelation devised by *Men*. An impostor seeking to gain converts by pretending to have received a divine revelation, would have been sure to tempt the curiosity of the credulous by giving them a full description of matters interesting to human minds. He would have sought to excite their feelings, and amuse their imaginations, by dwelling with all his eloquence on all the particulars of a future state, and on the nature and history of good and evil angels, and all those other things which are so scantily revealed in our Scriptures. And a wild enthusiast, again, who should have mistaken his dreams and fancies for a revelation from Heaven, would have been sure to have his dreams and fancies filled with things relating to the invisible world, on which a diseased imagination is particularly apt to run wild.

Even though you should be unable, therefore, to understand why the Scriptures should be such as they are in this respect, supposing them to come from God, you may, at least, perceive that they are not such as would have come from Man. In this, as well as in many other points, they are just the reverse of what might have been expected from impostors or enthusiasts.

§ 9. Lastly, it is worth while to remember, that all the difficulties of Christianity, which have been brought forward as objections against it, are so far evidences in its favor, that the religion was introduced and established in *spite of them all.* Most of the objections which are brought forward in these days had equal force — and some of them much greater force — at the time when the religion was first preached. And there were many others besides, which do not exist now; especially what is called "the reproach of the cross," — the scorn felt towards a religion, whose founder suffered a kind of death reckoned in those days the most disgraceful, and whose followers were almost all of them men of obscure station, of low birth, poor, unlearned, and without worldly power.

Yet, in spite of all this, the religion prevailed. And that it should have made its way as it did, against so many obstacles, and difficulties, and objections, is one of the strongest proofs that it must have had some supernatural means of overcoming them, and that therefore it must have come from God.

LESSON XV.

MODERN JEWS.—PART I.

§ 1. ONE of the difficulties with which the minds of some Christians are perplexed is, that Jesus Christ should have been rejected by the greater part of his countrymen, the Jews; and that they who had been, according to our Scriptures, for so many ages, God's favored and peculiar people, should be, now, and for about seventeen centuries, without a country, and scattered as outcast strangers through the world.

Their present condition and past history are indeed something very extraordinary, and quite unlike what has befallen any other nation. But though we may not be able to explain all the circumstances relative to this wonderful people, it will be found on reflection, that they furnish one of the strongest evidences for the truth of the very religion which they reject.

You know that when the Jews received the law through Moses, they were promised success and prosperity as long as they should obey the Lord; and that heavy judgments were denounced against them in case of disobedience. It was foretold that they should be defeated by their enemies, driven from their country, scattered abroad, and continually harassed and oppressed. These threats are set forth in various parts of the books of Moses, and most particularly in the twenty-eighth chapter of Deuteronomy. "Thou shalt become an astonishment, a proverb, and a byword among all the nations whither the Lord shall lead thee. . . . . The Lord will make thy plagues wonderful, and the plagues of thy seed, even great plagues of long continuance. . . . . And the Lord shall scatter thee among all people, from one end of the earth even unto the other." (ver. 37, 59, 64.)

And the same is to be found in various parts of the writings of several of the prophets who lived some ages after. In particular, there is one in Ezekiel, which agrees most remarkably in one very curious particular with the state of the Jews at this day; namely, where he declares that they should, in the midst of their sufferings, remain a distinct people, unmixed with and unlike other nations; although it appears that, in his time, they were very much disposed to unite themselves with the rest of mankind, so as to become one of the Gentile nations, and to lay aside all the distinctions of their own race. "That which cometh into your mind shall not be at all, that ye say, We will be as the heathen, as the families of the countries, to serve wood and stone." (Ezekiel xx. 32.)

§ 2. Now we find in the Old Testament, that, in several instances, these judgments did fall on the Jews; and especially when they were carried away captive to Babylon. And some person may suppose that these instances were all that Moses and the prophets had in view. But whatever any one's *opinion* may be, it is a *fact* of which there can be no doubt, that the Jewish nation are actually suffering, at this day, such things as

Moses and the prophets predicted. Whether Moses and Ezekiel had in view what is now taking place, or not, may be a matter of opinion; but it is a matter of fact, that what is now taking place does agree with their predictions. Jerusalem and its Temple were taken and burnt by the Romans, about forty years after the crucifixion of Jesus Christ. The Jews were driven from their country, and never allowed to settle in it again. Hundreds of thousands were sold as slaves; and the whole people were cast forth as wanderers among the Gentiles; and they have ever since remained a nation of exiles, unsettled, harassed, and oppressed, in many instances most cruelly, not only by Pagans and Mohammedans, but also (to our shame be it spoken) by Christian nations; and still remaining a distinct people, though without a home.

§ 3. One of the most remarkable points relative to these predictions respecting the Jews, and their present condition, is this: that the judgments spoken of by Moses were threatened in case of their departing from the law which he delivered, and especially in case of their worshipping false gods; and yet, though in former times they were so apt to fall into idolatry, they have always, since the destruction of Jerusalem, steadily kept clear of that sin; and have professed to be most scrupulous observers of the law of Moses. And what is more, all the indignities and persecutions that any of them are exposed to, appear to be the *consequence* of their keeping to their religion, and not of their forsaking it. For a Jew has only to give up his religion, and conform to that of the country he lives in, whether Christian, Mohammedan, or Pagan, and lay aside the observances of the law of Moses, and he immediately ceases to be reproached as a Jew and an alien, and is mingled with the people around him. So that the Jews of the present day seem to be suffering, for their *observance* of the law, just the penalties threatened for their *departure* from it.

At first sight, this seems very hard to explain; but, on reflection, you will find the difficulty cleared up, in such a way as to afford a strong confirmation of your faith. First, you should observe, that the Jews themselves admit that a Christ or Messiah was promised them; and that to reject Him on his coming would be an act of rebellion against the Lord their God. Moses foretold that the Lord should raise up from among them a Prophet like Moses himself; and "whosoever should not hear that Prophet," God "would require it of him"; and "that he should be destroyed from among the people." (Deut. xviii. 15 – 19; Acts iii. 22, 23.) This is generally understood (as it is applied in the Acts) to relate to the Messiah or Christ; whom the other prophetical writers of the Old Testament (as both Christians and Jews are agreed) more particularly foretold and described. Now *we* hold that the Jews have been guilty of this very act of disobedience in rejecting the Christ. And though they, of course, do not confess themselves thus guilty, because they deny that Jesus of Nazareth was the true Christ, yet they so far agree with us as to acknowledge, that the rejecting of the true Christ on his coming would be such a sin as would expose them to the judgments which Moses threatened.

To us, therefore, who do believe in Jesus, this affords an explanation of their suffering these judgments.

§ 4. But, secondly, besides this, you will perceive, on looking more closely, that the Jews of these days do *not* really observe the law of Moses, though they profess and intend to do so. They have, indeed, kept to the *faith* of their forefathers; but not to their religious *observances.* For the chief part of the Jewish worship consisted in offering sacrifices distinctly appointed by the Lord himself, in the law delivered by Moses. There was a sacrifice appointed to be offered up every day, and two on the Sabbath; besides several other sacrifices on particular occasions. Now, the modern Jews, though they abstain from certain meats forbidden in their law, and observe strictly the Sabbath and several other ordinances, yet do not offer any sacrifices at all; though sacrifices were appointed as the chief part of their worship.

The reason of this is, that they were strictly forbidden to offer sacrifices except in the *one place* which should be appointed by the Lord for that purpose. And the place last fixed on for these offerings having been the Temple at Jerusalem, which was destroyed about seventeen hundred years ago, and has never been restored, the Jews are now left without any place in which they can lawfully offer the sacrifices which their law enjoins.

§ 5. The Jews, accordingly, of the present day, plead that it is not from wilful disobedience that they neglect these ordinances, but because they cannot help it. But to say that it is not their own fault that they do *not* observe the ordinances of their religion, is quite a different thing from saying that they do observe them. They may explain *why* they cannot keep the law of Moses; but they cannot say that they do keep it.

Now Christians hold that the ceremonies of that law were not originally designed to be observed by all nations, and for ever; that "the law had only a shadow of good things to come" (Heb. x. 1), that is, of the Gospel; and that it was designed that the sacrificing of lambs and bullocks should cease at the coming of the Christ. A Jew, on the contrary, will not allow that these were designed ever to cease; but he cannot deny that they *have* ceased, and that for above seventeen centuries. Let a Jew explain, if he can, how it is that for so long a time Providence has put it out of the power of the Jews to observe the principal part of their religion, which they maintain was intended to be observed for ever.

§ 6. And this also is very remarkable, that the religion of the Jews is almost the only one that *could* have been abolished *against the will* of the people themselves, and while they resolved firmly to maintain it. *Their* religion, and theirs only, could be, and has been, thus abolished in spite of their firm attachment to it, on account of its being dependent on a particular *place*,— the Temple at Jerusalem. The Christian religion, or, again, any of the Pagan religions, could not be abolished by any force of enemies, if the persons professing the religion were sincere and resolute in keeping to it. To destroy a Christian place of worship, or to turn it into a Mohammedan mosque (as was done in many instances by the Turks), would not prevent the exercise of the Christian religion. And even if Christianity were forbidden by law, and Christians persecuted, (as has in times past been actually done,) still, if they were sincere and resolute, they might assemble secretly in woods or caves, or they might fly to foreign countries, to worship God according to their own faith; and Christianity, though it might be driven out of one country, would still exist in others.

§ 7. And the same may be said of the Pagan religions. If it happened that any temple of Jupiter, or Diana, or Woden, were destroyed, this would not hinder the worshippers of those gods from continuing to worship them as before, and from offering sacrifices to them elsewhere.

But it was not so with the Jews. Their religion was so framed as to make the observance of its ordinances impossible when their Temple was finally destroyed. It seems to have been designed and contrived by Divine Providence, that, as their *law* was to be brought to an end by the Gospel (for which it was a preparation), so all men were to *perceive* that it did come to an end, notwithstanding the obstinate rejection of the Gospel by the greater part of the Jews. It was not left to be a question, and a matter of *opinion*, whether the sacrifices instituted by Moses were to be continued or not; but things were so ordered as to put it out of Man's power to continue them.

LESSON XVI.

MODERN JEWS.—PART II.

§ 1. It is likely that, when Jerusalem and its Temple were destroyed, several of the Jews who had till then rejected the Gospel may have been at length converted, by the strong additional evidence which was thus afforded. They saw the heavy judgment that fell on their nation, and that it was such as to make the observance of their law impossible. They saw also, that the event agreed with what Jesus had predicted forty years before. And they saw too that those of his followers who had been living in Jerusalem had been enabled to escape destruction by following his directions, and fleeing to the mountains as soon as they saw Jerusalem encompassed by an army. It is therefore likely that several may have been led by this additional evidence to embrace the Christian faith. But of this we have no records, as the book of Acts takes in only an earlier period. And in that book we have no particulars of the numbers of those Jews who were converted; though it appears they must have amounted to many thousands,—indeed, many *myriads*, that is, tens of thousands, as is said in the original Greek of Acts xxi. 20. But still these made but a small portion only of that great nation. And as the Jewish Christians would soon become mingled with the Gentile Christians, and cease to be a separate people, hence all those who are known as Jews at this day are the descendants of those who rejected the Gospel.

These are computed to amount, at the present time, notwithstanding the prodigious slaughter of them at the taking of their city, and on several other occasions, to no less a number than 4,800,000, scattered through various parts of the world; everywhere mixing and trading with other nations, but everywhere kept distinct from them by their peculiar faith and religious observances. And everywhere they preserve and read with the utmost reverence their sacred books, which foretell the coming of the Messiah or Christ at a time which (by their own computations) is long since past; namely, about the time when Jesus did appear. Their books foretell also such judgments as their nation is suffering; and foretell too, what is most remarkable, that notwithstanding all this they shall still remain a separate people, unmixed with the other nations.

§ 2. You should observe, too, that these prophecies are such as no one would ever have made by *guess.* Nothing could have been more unlikely than the events which have befallen the Jewish nation. Nothing like them has ever been foretold of any other nation, or has ever happened to any other. There are, indeed, many cases recorded in history of one nation conquering another, and either driving them out of the country or keeping them in subjection. But in all these cases the conquered people who have lost their country either settle themselves in some other land, or, if they are wholly dispersed, generally become gradually mixed and blended with other nations; as, for example, the

Britons and Saxons, and Danes and Normans, have been mixed up into one people in England.

The only people who at all resemble the Jews, in having been widely dispersed and yet remaining distinct, are those commonly called Gypsies, and whose proper name is Zinganies, or Jinganies. It has been made out that they are an East Indian nation, speaking a Hindoo dialect. And they are widely scattered through the world, keeping up their language, and some customs of their own, in all the countries through which they wander. They are certainly a very remarkable people; and if there had been any prophecy (which there was not) of their being thus dispersed, we might well have believed that such a prophecy must have come from inspiration.

But in some remarkable points their condition differs from that of the Jews, and is less unaccountable.

First, they do not (like the Jews) live in towns among other men, and in houses; but dwell in tents, by the road-sides, and on commons, leading the life of strolling tinkers, pedlers, and fortune-tellers. This roaming life, of course, tends to keep them separate from the people of the countries in which they are found.

§ 3. But, secondly, the chief difference is, that the Gypsies are always ready, when required, to profess the religion of the country, whether Christian or Mohammedan, or any other; seeming to have no religion of their own, and to be quite indifferent on the subject. The Jews, on the contrary, always, when they are allowed, settle in towns along with other men; and are kept distinct from them by their religion, and by nothing else. They are the only people who are everywhere separated from the people of the country in which they live, entirely by their peculiar faith and religious observances; and *that* too though their religion is such (which is the strongest point of all) that the most important part of its ordinances — the sacrifices ordained in their law — *cannot* be observed by them.

The Jews, therefore, in their present condition, are a kind of standing miracle; being a monument of the wonderful fulfilment of the most extraordinary prophecies that were ever delivered; which prophecies they themselves preserve and bear witness to, though they shut their eyes to the fulfilment of them. No other account than this of the present state and past history of the Jews ever has been or can be given, that is not open to objections greater than all the objections put together that have ever been brought against Christianity.

§ 4. This, then, as well as several other difficulties in our religion, such as have been formerly mentioned, will be found, on examination, to be, — even when you cannot fully explain them, — not so much objections against the truth of your religion, as confirmations of it.

And when you do meet with any objection which you are at a loss to answer, you should remember (as has been above said) that there are many things which all men must believe, in spite of real difficulties which they cannot explain, when there are much greater difficulties on the opposite side, and when sufficient proof has been offered.

And in the present case you have seen that it is not only difficult, but impossible, to account for the rise and prevalence of the Christian religion, supposing it not to have come from God.

1. It certainly was introduced and propagated (which no other religion ever was, for the religion taught by Moses we acknowledge as *part* of our *own*) by an appeal to the evidence of miracles. Nothing but the display of superhuman powers could have gained even a hearing for the Apostles; surrounded as they were by adversaries prejudiced against their religion by their early education and habits of thought and inclinations and hopes. And these superhuman powers were, as you have seen, acknowledged at the time by those adversaries, who were driven to attribute the Christian miracles to magic arts.

2. And you have seen, too, that the religion itself, and the character of Jesus Christ as drawn in the Christian Scriptures, and the whole of the narrative of those books, are quite different, and indeed opposite to what might have been expected from impostors or enthusiasts.

3. And, lastly, you have seen that many of the difficulties that have been brought as objections against Christianity turn out, on careful inquiry, to be an additional evidence of its truth.

Among others, this is remarkably the case with the difficulties relating to the history and condition of the Jewish nation. Though you may not be able fully to explain all the circumstances relating to that wonderful people, you may learn from them, what they refuse to learn from themselves, a strong proof of the truth both of their Scriptures and of the Gospel which they obstinately reject. It is so ordered by Providence, that even that very obstinacy is made to furnish an additional proof of Christianity, by setting *them* forth before all the world as a monument of fulfilled prophecy.

§ 5. There are several other instructions, and warnings also, which you may learn from attentively reflecting on the case of the Jews; and I will conclude by shortly mentioning a few of these.

First, — You should remember that when you see the Jews, both formerly and now, obstinately keeping to the faith of their forefathers, merely because it is what they were brought up in, and refusing to listen to any reasoning on the subject of religion, a Christian has no right to wonder at, or to blame them, if he does the same thing himself; that is, if he is satisfied to take upon trust whatever he may have been told, and is resolved neither to seek nor to listen to any arguments that may enable him "to give a reason of the hope that is in him." And the same may be said of Mohammedans and Pagans, as well as of Jews. Though the Christian happens to have a *religion* that is right, *he* is not more right than they, if he goes on the same plan that they do. At least, he is right only by chance, if he holds a faith that is true, and holds it not because it is true, but merely because it is that of his forefathers.

§ 6. Secondly, — You should remember that we are apt to make much less allowance for the unbelieving Jew, than for Christians who lead an unchristian life; and that we *ought* to do just the contrary.

It is difficult for us, of these days, to understand and fully enter into the great difficulty which the Jews had (and still have) in overcoming all the prejudices they had been brought up in, and which were so flattering to their own nation as God's favored people. It was a hard task for them to wean themselves from all the hopes and expectations of temporal glory and distinction to that nation; hopes which they and their ancestors had cherished for so many ages. No doubt it was a grievous sin in them to give way to those prejudices, and to reject the Christ as they did. But it is a greater sin to acknowledge Him, as some Christians do, as their Lord and Master, and to "believe that He shall come to be our judge," and at the same time to take no care to obey his precepts, and copy the pattern of his life. This is more truly impiety than that with which an infidel is chargeable. For, suppose two men each received a letter from his father giving directions for his children's conduct; and that one of these sons, hastily, and without any good grounds, pronounced the letter a forgery, and refused to take any notice of it; while the other acknowledged it to be genuine, and laid it up with great reverence, and then acted without the least regard to the advice and commands contained in the letter; you would say that both of these men indeed were very wrong, but the latter was much the more undutiful son of the two.

Now this is the case of a disobedient Christian, as compared with infidels. He does not, like them, pronounce his father's letter a forgery, that is, deny the truth of the Christian revelation; but he sets at defiance in his life that which he acknowledges to be the Divine command.

§ 7. Lastly, you should remember that no argument

you can bring against unbelievers will have greater weight with most of them than a Christian life; and nothing, again, will be more likely to increase and confirm their unbelief, than to see Christians living in opposition to the precepts and spirit of the Gospel, and especially to see them indulging bitter and unkind and hostile and uncharitable feelings towards their fellow-creatures, and even their fellow-Christians.

The objection thence raised against the Christian religion is indeed (as has been above said) not a real and sound one; but still it *will* be raised, and therefore you cannot too carefully consider how much you will have to answer for if you contribute to bring an ill name on your Christian faith; and if you do not, on the contrary, endeavor to the utmost "to adorn the doctrine of God our Saviour in all things."

QUESTIONS FOR EXAMINATION.

QUESTIONS FOR EXAMINATION.

LESSONS ON MORALS.

Lesson I.

Ought the Law of the Land to be made the standard of moral right and wrong? § 1.

Give a reason from the nature and extent of moral duty? § 1.

The essential character of moral conduct precludes the law's being made the standard? § 2.

Twofold insufficiency of this standard, as respects moral requirements? § 2.

Notions of right and wrong not dependent on human laws? § 3.

What has led some to doubt the existence of any moral sense or faculty? § 3.

How might this objection be answered? § 3.

Illustration of this? § 3.

What inference has been drawn from a prevailing mistake as to the character of Scripture? § 4.

This inference disproved by the real character of Scripture? § 6.

By its omissions? § 4.

By its appeals? § 4.

Man's supposed natural destitution of a moral faculty inconsistent with the rule of judgment laid down by our Lord? § 5.

With the exhortations of the Apostles? § 5.

With the writings of Heathens? § 5.

So also with the character of God as given in Scripture? § 6.

In what sense may all notions of morality be said to be derived from the will of God? § 6.

Admitted ground of obedience to the Divine command inconsistent with the contrary sense? §§ 6, 7.

Distinction between the possible grounds of obedience to the will of another? § 7.

Illustrations of this distinction? § 7.

Lesson II.

One circumstance contributes to confusion of thoughts as to the origin of the notion of duty? § 1.

Conduct of a pious man in such a case? § 1.

Ground of this implicit obedience to a Divine command on a particular point? § 1.

The possibility of such a creation of a new duty implies a moral sense? § 1.

Illustration? § 1.

Distinction between Moral and Positive Precepts? § 2.

Illustration of this distinction from commands to children? § 2.

From legislative enactments? § 2.

From private contracts? § 2.

Instances from the Jewish Law of similar distinction? § 2.

Important distinction with regard to the observance of these two kinds of precepts? § 3.

This distinction exemplified in some precepts of our Lord? § 3.

And in some injunctions to the Israelites? § 3.

The implicit obedience to any particular Divine command is in conformity with our feelings and conduct towards our fellow-men? § 4.

The imputation of sin implies a Moral Faculty? § 5.

This evident from the nature of sin? § 5.

Admission of this in the limited application of the term sin? § 5.

Effect of an express command? § 5.

This effect, how spoken of by Paul? § 5.

Lesson III.

Summary of the last two Lessons? § 1.

What is our next inquiry? § 1.

What does Scripture teach in the first place in reference to duty? § 2.

Opinions of the ancient philosophers on this point? § 2.

Of the vulgar among the ancient heathen? § 2.

Character of their worship? § 2.

Contrast presented by our Scriptures? § 2.

Effect of the Divine approbation of Virtue? § 3.
The necessity for this encouragement, — whence arising? § 3.
No positive gratification from compliance with the dictates of conscience? § 3.
Gracious direction of our natural desire for approbation. § 3.
Scriptural encouragement to Moral Improvement? § 3.
Second point revealed in Scripture in reference to Moral Duty? § 4.
The necessity for this aid? § 4.
To what attributed by some? § 4.
This proved to be erroneous, both by reason and Scripture? § 4.
What does Scripture teach us, in the third place, in reference to Duty? § 5.
What, in the fourth place, is the instruction of Scripture in reference to Duty? § 5.
A moral instructor like an oculist? § 5.

Lesson IV.

The true character of the moral instruction of Scripture explained by a rule of our Lord's? § 1.
Probable cause of the rare application of this rule? § 1.
A literal compliance with the rule sometimes absurd? § 1.
Sometimes wrong? § 1.
Sometimes impossible? § 1.
The right application of the rule? § 2.
First notions of right and wrong not derived from it? § 3.
Its real design? § 3.
Danger against which it is a safeguard, illustrated in the case of David? § 3.
Illustration of the distinct uses of Scripture and of natural Conscience? § 4.
Possible depravation of Conscience illustrated? § 5.
Its due regulation? § 5.

Lesson V.

Peculiarity of the Moral teaching of the Gospel as distinguishing it from the Law? § 1.
Adaptation of the teaching of the Law to the condition of the Israelites? § 1.
What does the Gospel substitute for precise rules? § 1.

Tendency of men to prefer precise rules? § 2.

Internal evidence here afforded of the Divine origin of our religion? § 2.

Instances of this tendency in human nature? § 3.

How guarded against by our Lord in the form of his precepts? § 3.

Moral discretion rendered necessary by literal compliance with some precepts involving contradiction? § 4.

Or by literal compliance involving something wrong? § 4.

Or by its restricting too much the scope of the precept? § 5.

Teaching of Scripture as to the essential character of moral virtue? § 6.

That it does not depend on the outward Act, how shown to be generally admitted? § 6.

In what sense do we speak of an outward act as morally good or evil? § 7.

Two requisites in the intention that makes it morally good? § 7.

Lesson VI.

Distinction between the objects in view in conveying instruction? § 1.

The design of our Divine Master's discipline? § 1.

Essential importance of motive hereby made evident? § 1.

Bearing of this design on good works by proxy? § 2.

And on the supposed merit of good works? § 2.

Error on this point from misinterpretation of some expressions of Scripture? § 2.

Give an illustration of the distinction between the objects for which services are required? § 3.

And an illustration serving to correct a mistake as to the merit of good works, and the *rewards* promised in Scripture? § 3.

Real state of the case? § 4.

Groundlessness of any natural claim to reward evident from the nature of duty? § 5.

And of reward? § 5.

Teaching of Scripture on this point? § 5.

Mistake as to the natural connection between Reward and Punishment? § 6.

Works of supererogation, — how contrary to Scripture and Reason? § 6.

The notion of a self-earned heavenly happiness opposed to Reason and Scripture? § 6. (Note.)

Supposed objection to the need of Christ's atoning work? (Note.)

How may it be answered? (Note.)

Wise saying of Scaliger? (Note.)

Lesson VII.

From what has been said, we find that the law of the land is not to be made the standard of right and wrong, for two reasons? § 1.

And that conscience, or the Moral Faculty, is a part of the human constitution? § 1.

And that man has need of Revelation? § 1.

And that good works can have no merit in the sight of God? § 1.

Two things requisite to form a virtuous character? § 1.

These two things, why alike indispensable? § 2.

Illustration of the several conditions in which either of these requisites is wanting? § 2.

The Apostle Paul's description of one who acts against his conscience? § 2.

This sort of description, how shown not to be limited to those whose knowledge is derived from a divine revelation? § 2.

The notion that Paul, in Romans vii., was giving a literal account of his own state, or that of any one under the Gospel, contradicted by the very next passage? § 3.

As also by the sixth chapter? § 3.

As well as by a passage in 1 Corinthians? § 3.

Paul is describing different and opposite conditions? § 3.

How do some persons endeavor to escape the reproaches of conscience? § 4.

When only can the plea of sincerity be admitted as a palliation of error? § 4.

Effect upon conscience of acting against conscience? § 4.

Design of the teaching of Scripture nullified by bias of the mind? § 4.

Instances of misapplication of Scripture from this bias? § 5.

To what may such students of Scripture be compared? § 5.

Dangerous errors arising from misinterpretation of Romans vii. (Note.)

Lesson VIII.

Is the fact that conscience is not infallible, a ground for disregard of it? § 1.

Paul's judgment on this point? § 1.

Principle laid down by Paul with regard to conscientious scruples? § 1.

Cases in which a wrong principle makes it impossible to act rightly? § 2.

Charity and self-distrust, how called for? § 2.

Teaching of Scripture as to the necessity of vigilant care of the moral character? § 3.

The consistency of the dependence on the Divine blessing with diligent care, illustrated from man's procedure in the concerns of ordinary life? § 4.

Lesson IX.

Increased disquiet of conscience, when an encouraging sign? § 1.

Illustration of the effect of increased enlightenment of conscience? § 1.

In what respect does the Moral Faculty differ from our other faculties and sentiments? § 2.

Exemplify this difference? § 2.

Does virtuous conduct, then, afford no gratification? § 3.

Instances of natural feelings graciously made sources of gratification? § 3.

How are these feelings to be controlled and regulated? § 4.

This control, why necessary? § 4.

Instances of its necessity? §§ 4, 5.

Lesson X.

Distinction between the control exercised by Conscience over *feelings* and over *actions?* § 1.

Illustrated from something similar in the bodily frame? § 1.

This difficulty, how to be surmounted? § 2.

Self-deceit as to feelings, from confounding two different things? § 3.

Feelings, how to be reached? § 3.

This procedure, that of the Sacred Writers? § 3.

Another distinction between the control of feelings and of actions? § 4.

Encouragement to the steady exercise of that control? § 4.

Illustration of the process of moral reformation from grafting? § 4.

Influence of actions on the formation of moral habits? § 5.

Moral improvement dependent on right principle? § 6.

Lesson XI.

Moral improvement, how shown to be dependent upon practice? § 1.

Danger from familiarity with principles not reduced to practice? § 1.

Formation of opposite habits under similar circumstances? § 1.

Mistake on this point, whence originating? § 1.

Give some illustrations? §§ 1, 2.

Instructive emblem in Scripture of a mere professor of religion? § 2.

Persons who only talk of religion compared to an unemployed steam-engine? § 2.

Practice for learning equally necessary in the study of Scripture, and in all pious exercises? § 2.

Chief difficulty in forming good moral habits? § 3.

How may an *act* of virtue be said to have less of virtue? § 3.

In what does virtue consist? § 4.

Why is the term not applicable to the Deity? § 4.

Estimate of virtue in any particular case, how to be formed? § 4.

Distinction between the imitation of our Heavenly Father, and the following of the example of a Being of our own nature? § 5.

Example of the Apostles, how far imitable? § 5.

Mistakes to be carefully guarded against? § 5.

Lesson XII.

Nature of the example held out to us in the Lord Jesus? § 1.

Does the possession of human feelings by the Lord Jesus unfit Him for an example? § 2.

The example of the Lord, why too often disregarded? § 3.

And religious veneration, how misdirected? § 3.

Illustration of both these errors? § 3.

Benefit of our Lord's example not dependent on clear notions of his nature? § 3.

The superiority of our Lord's example over all models, real or imaginary? § 4.

Possible mistake in reference to the Old Testament characters? § 4.

Advantage afforded for the study of Christ's example? § 4.

How may imitation be a departure from, rather than a following of, His example? § 5.

Lesson XIII.

The Apostles in a different position from our Lord? § 1.

And from us? § 1.

Erroneous imitation of our Lord's teaching avoided by them? § 2.

Ground on which our Lord exercised the right of giving or withholding Divine truth? § 3.

Another cause of erroneous imitation? § 4.

Mistaken imitation of the fortitude of the Apostles? § 4.

Suffering, when admirable? § 4.

Self-torment, not the practice of the Apostles? § 5.

Scriptural sense of the word "mortification"? § 5.

Mistaken notion of the system of the early Christians with regard to property? § 6.

What was the real state of the case? § 6.

How is this evident from Scripture? § 6.

Lesson XIV.

Mistakes to be guarded against in studying treatises on Morals? § 1.

What is likely to lead to this mistake? § 1.

Distinction between the arts and sciences, and the moral habits? § 1.

What is meant by the habit of virtue? § 1.

Another distinction between the arts and sciences, and the moral habits? § 2.

One cause of mistake as to this point? § 3.

Instances of apparent and unconnected moral virtues? § 3.

Oneness of virtue evident from the nature of virtue? § 3.

Testimony to this oneness by our Lord and His Apostles? § 4.

It is also maintained by Aristotle? § 4.

Duty with regard to the principle adopted? § 5.

Sense in which we speak of a character as inconsistent? § 5.

Illustrated from the conduct of a farmer? § 5.

Consistent following out of a principle will test the principle? § 5.

The tendency to claim merit for good works promoted by the notion of several distinct virtues? § 6.

Lesson XV.

Different parts of duty easier and harder to different persons. Why? § 1.

Such differences analogous to those in bodily constitution? § 2.

Man's procedure with regard to bodily health often reversed in moral conduct? § 2.

Effect of a strong tendency in judging of one's own character? § 2.

Prudent care of bodily health to be imitated in morals? § 3.

And a procedure of builders? § 3.

How may this be carried too far? § 3.

What may help us to guard against self-deceit? § 3.

What help may we have analogous to that of a physician? § 3.

Specification of virtues not necessary? § 4.

Its absence no ground of complaint? § 4.

Divine procedure in the New Testament instruction? § 5.

The omission of specific rules, how supplied to the Christian? § 5.

Lesson XVI.

Importance of a right understanding of the matter each duty relates to? § 1.

Illustration of that principle on which we should act in our charities? § 1.

Fallacy of the common excuse, "It is such a one's fault"? § 1.

Amount of fault not to be estimated by what it relates to? § 2.

Importance of small matters evident from the design of moral discipline? § 2.

And from the way in which habits are formed? § 2.

Distinction between Selfishness and Self-love? § 3.

The word Self-love how sometimes used? § 3.

Definition of Self-love? § 3.

Give an illustration? § 3.

Self-love a distinct and *positive* quality? § 3.

In what respect like our other tendencies? § 3.

Selfishness a *negative* quality? § 3.

How consequently does it show itself? § 3.

Possible selfishness even in amiable feelings? § 3.

The safeguard against it? § 3.

Mistake with regard to escaping temptation? § 4.

And with regard to self-appointed duties? § 4.

Ground upon which the Apostles acted? § 4.

Opportunity to do good, how to be used? § 5.

Conduct of "the children of this world" an example to be followed? § 5.

Lesson XVII.

Proper sense of words? § 1.

Falsehood may be involved in literal truth? § 1.

Give an instance? § 1.

Our Lord's declaration before Pilate, how proved to have been used in its plain literal meaning? § 1.

As also the precepts of the Apostles about submitting to every ordinance of man? § 1.

Moral falsehood not necessarily involved in a literal untruth? § 2.

Give some illustrations of this principle? § 2.

The rule fixing the true sense of a declaration, not limited to words? § 3.

Illustrations of, and reason for, this? § 3.

The condition of any promise should be expressed? § 3.

Cases in which a promise is not binding? § 4.

How then were the Israelites bound to their promise to the Gibeonites? § 4. (Note.)

Caution against unwarily giving a promise of secrecy? § 4. (Note.)

True import of an oath? § 4.

Official oaths, why superfluous? § 4. (Note.)

A promise no excuse for doing anything wrong? § 4.

The guilt of falsehood may be incurred, though everything said may be quite true? § 5.

This illustrated by partial truth told to a rustic? § 5.

Instance in an inscription discovered at Nineveh? § 5.

And in reserve in stating the doctrines of the Gospel? § 5.

Statement of a falsehood not the only way of partaking of the guilt of it? § 6.

The words of the Psalmist, how applicable to such a case? § 6.

Cause of failure in strict justice of those not indifferent about duty? § 6.

Illustration from a story of Cyrus, and from some supposed cases? § 6.

Cases of greatest temptation to connive at falsehood? § 7.
A double guilt hereby incurred? § 7.
A more accurate appellation for a pious fraud? § 7.
Not to undeceive is to deceive? § 7.
Disingenuous suppression of truth, how disguised? § 7.
Instance of suppressed correction of error? § 7.
Danger of disregard of truth in unimportant matters? § 7.
Evil consequences of deception? § 8.
Paley's remark on this point? § 8.
The ultimate expediency of truth not perceived by all? § 8.

Lesson XVIII.

The sin forbidden by the tenth commandment does not consist in a strong wish for what belongs to your neighbor? § 1.
Illustration? (Note.)
In what does the sin of coveting consist? § 1.
Popular mistakes as to gaming, how favored? § 1.
Its especial characteristic? § 1.
All other objections to it applicable to things not evil in themselves? § 1.
Practical use of being early taught thus to regard it? § 1.
Playing where there is no sinful coveting, why to be avoided? § 1.
Confusion of thought leading to mistake as to forgiveness of injuries? § 2.
In what light is one who has personally injured us to be viewed? § 2.
What is not required by the duty of Christian forgiveness. § 2.
Two things never to be confounded? § 2.
Mistake of Christian humility as regards reason? § 3.
As regards blind following of a party? § 3.
As regards the feelings? § 3.
A breach of humility as to speculative points? § 4.
Two opposite breaches of humility in reference to the reasons of God's dealings with man? § 4, and note.
A good reason for obedience may be a bad reason for giving the command? § 4.
Generic Humility not necessarily implying personal hnmility? § 4.
What real humility consists in? § 4.
Just estimate of one's self no breach of duty? § 5.
To what do the terms Self-conceit and Modesty properly apply? § 5. (Note.)

Caution to the possessor of superior endowments as regards himself? § 5.

As regards others? § 5.

General confessions of sin, when no proof of humility? § 6.

Nor confession without amendment? § 6.

The special, constant exercise of Christian humility, to what compared? § 6.

Evidences of true humility? § 6.

Conduct not to be estimated by the opinions of men in general? § 7.

Maxim of Bacon? § 7.

What does he mean by "vulgar"? § 7.

By the "lowest virtues"? § 7.

By "the highest"? § 7.

Instances of virtues not generally approved? § 8.

Two opposite dangers to be guarded against? § 8.

General practical rule? § 8.

Lesson XIX.

A duty in reference to our moral character taught? § 1.

Proverb applicable to postponement of this duty? § 1.

Necessity of candor in self-examination? § 2.

What ought not to be our standard? § 2.

Greater importance of small faults in ourselves than in our neighbors? § 9.

Candor in self-examination not implying a looking for faults only? § 3.

The opposite opinion a mistaken one? § 3.

Evil consequences of hopelessness of moral improvement? § 4.

Special promise of our Lord? § 5.

Procedure of the Apostles with regard to their converts? § 5.

Hopeful vigilance not to be confined to outward conduct? § 5.

Lesson XX.

Point in which improvement can be most easily marked? § 1.

What part is this of the Christian's business? § 1.

Why indispensable? § 1.

Diligent study of the Bible necessary from the nature of its contents? § 2.

Absurdity of a random perusal illustrated? § 2.

Suggestions for the profitable perusal of it? § 2.

Which of all cautions on this head is the most important? § 3.

Outward acts, not the only virtuous practice? § 4.

Outward acts, how far virtuous or vicious? § 4.

The Apostle's enumeration of the fruits of the Spirit, in accordance with this principle? § 4.

Benefits from the counsel of a friend? § 5.

Proper object of confession? § 5.

Cases in which it may be useful; and to which it should be limited? § 5.

Consciousness of sin, when a promising sign? § 6.

What kind of Conscience ought to be sought for? § 6.

The effect of the operation of the Spirit of God in enlightening Conscience, how illustrated? § 6.

Importance of cultivating a habit of perfect sincerity in confession of sin? § 6.

Enumerate some of the most important points in self-examination? § 7.

CHRISTIAN EVIDENCES.

Lesson I.

What is, perhaps, the most common reason of Christians for believing Christianity?

Has this always been the case?

Why is it impossible that it should have been?

What gods can you name formerly worshipped in the British Isles?

How came our forefathers to cease worshipping them?

What religions, besides the Christian, are there now in the world?

What makes anybody believe in them?

Have you any better reason for believing in Christianity?

What is your duty in regard to having a reason for your faith?

How did the Apostles lead the Heathen to believe in Christianity?

What motives had the Heathen for being unwilling to believe?

Could the evidence offered to Heathens consist in arguments from Christian experience?

Why not?

What treatment did the first converts to Christianity receive from their countrymen?

How do we learn this?

What must we infer in regard to the proofs by which they were convinced of the truth of Christianity?

What evidence was ever offered of the truth of a Pagan religion?

What, then, is there peculiar in the mode in which Christianity was introduced into the world?

What is, then, the presumption in regard to its truth?

Lesson II.

What cause had our fathers and other Pagans for forsaking their religion?

Had their fathers previously forsaken a previous faith?

How were, then, Pagan religions introduced?

What, then, is a Pagan's reason for believing?

Are there, then, no accounts of miracles in Pagan religions?

What is the difference between Pagan and Christian accounts of miracles?

How did Mahomet spread his religion?

What was the character of his asserted miracles?

What, then, is the distinguishing mark in the foundations of Christianity?

Is the study of evidences inconsistent with faith?

What is credulity?

What, Scripture faith?

What renders faith difficult?

What prejudice prevented the Jews from having faith in Christ?

What did they say of his miracles?

By what sort of impostors were they afterwards deceived?

What showed the candid mind of the Bereans?

How, then, shall we deserve the Apostolic commendation?

Lesson III.

On whose word do some say we must pin our faith?

On what account?

But can we have no evidence of the existence of the Bible in the original, and of its meaning?

How do we know that France and Italy exist?

How, that travellers do not deceive us?

How do we know that the earth rotates, or that it revolves about the sun?

How, that the books of the Bible are ancient?

How, that they are well translated?

What analogy to witnesses at court?

What points are thus proved of the English New Testament?

What further evidence concerning the Old Testament?

And what evidence does the Old Testament give concerning the New?

Lesson IV.

On what account are the prophecies more instructive to us than to the first Christians?

What is the magnitude of the change wrought by Christ's coming?

How many nominal Christians in the world?

How many Mahometans?

Why count them in estimating the effect of Christianity?

What contrast between the outward coming of Christ in Judæa and this effect?

What is the usual strain of Jewish prophecy in regard to the Messiah's times?

Has the Jewish nation itself seemed to fulfil this?

Does the spread of Christianity?

What comparison would you make between the argument from prophecy as felt by the Jews at Jesus's day and by us?

What evidence in the New Testament that the argument from prophecy had any force to the minds of men at that day?

Lesson V.

What did those who saw Jesus's miracles do to test his claims?

Is a miracle supernatural or superhuman?

Which name did our Lord himself give them?

To whom did Jesus impart power to work miracles?

Could they impart this power?

What argument shows this power did not consist in the knowledge of a new natural agent?

What conviction was forced on the Jews concerning the works of Christ?

Why did they not, then, believe that God was with him?

What proof of this beside the New Testament history?

If the Jews of our Saviour's day had denied his miracles, whence could this tradition have arisen?

What was the Pagan view of the subject?

What two questions did the men of our Saviour's times ask?

What advantage had they over us?

What have we over them?

Beside the advantage mentioned in the book, what is there in the fact of our not believing in magic?

Lesson VI.

With what modern fact are the miracles of the New Testament connected?

By what natural means can you account for the present prevalence of Christianity?

Which is the least difficult to believe of these three propositions: that an effect came without a cause, that it came from an inadequate cause, or that it came from a superhuman cause?

Which do you believe concerning the change of the religion of Europe from Paganism to Christianity?

What comparison will you make of the presence of sea-shells on inland mountains, and the presence of Christianity in lands far from Judæa?

Why is the credulity of the ancients an insufficient cause to account for their reception of Christianity?

Describe the manner in which a credulous man receives evidences.

How, then, would credulous Jews and Pagans receive the proofs of the authority of Jesus?

What is proved as to the facts by their credulously attributing the miracles to magic?

What are the contents of John ix.?

How does this accord with what we might expect?

What effect, then, would the credulity of the ancients have on the spread of Christianity?

What, then, does its rapid spread prove?

This rapid spread in the face of these superstitious prejudices proves something to us concerning the miracles; what is it?

With what words does the chapter close?

Lesson VII.

What evidences are there of the truth of our religion to be found in its own character?

Why would a Jew of the days of Christ have been of all men most unlikely to invent such teaching as that of Jesus?

Is the evidence of miracle, then, unnecessary?

Why not?

What is the relative value of this branch of evidence to us, and to those of the Apostles' days?

What connection has the difficulty of proving a fact, with the value of that fact (if proved), as evidence?

Illustrate this by the sea-shells on mountains.

Apply it to the Christian miracles.

How might we alter the phrase, "No less a proof," when we remember that the men of Jesus's time believed in magic?

How will the difficulty of believing in miracles compare with the difficulty of believing in the natural origin of Christianity?

How do the outward circumstances of Jesus compare with the outward triumphs of his religion?

What aid would an appeal to pretended miracles have been to the Apostles?

What is the peculiar distinction between Pagan and Christian accounts of miracles?

What is the distinctive peculiarity of the origin of our religion?

What, then, is probable as to the number of miracles?

What confirmation of this in the New Testament?

In what manner are they there mentioned?

From the nature of the case, why could not the Apostles have gained a hearing without miracle?

What effect would the moral character of the Gospel have in obtaining a hearing for it?

What, then, was the first mode of gaining a hearing?

What testimony was afterwards sufficient?

What is the difference in value, as evidence of truth, between suffering for *opinion's* sake and suffering for *testimony* given?

Explain the reason of this difference?

But how should the Apostles first make men listen to this testimony?

Lesson VIII.

Did the prevalent belief in magic make it more or less easy for Jesus to prove his authority by miraculous works?

What passages in John and Matthew are in point?

What is needed in addition to the reality of a wonderful event to make it confirm the authority of Christ or his Apostles?

What sort of miracles does the Koran narrate?

What did Mahomet's wonderful victories really prove?

What did he attempt to make them prove?

What is the true difference between a wonder and a sign?

Illustrate by a sudden calm; by reviving from a trance; by sudden loss of sight.

What may be justly asked of a professed messenger from God?

Repeat the distinction between a wonder and a sign.

Why is this distinction often overlooked?

How did this circumstance operate on the credit given to the Apostles?

What inference do you draw concerning their miracles?

Lesson IX.

What amount of evidence is there in behalf of Christianity?

What men have ever examined it all?

What proportion of the whole amount of proof possible is necessary to convince?

What proportion does the evidence which you have studied bear to the whole?

What is the first evidence drawn from the mere existence of Christianity in countries formerly heathen?

What evidence is drawn from the fact of the Apostles appealing to miracles?

How is this confirmed by comparison with Pagan religions?

What did the people of the Apostles' day say of the miracles?

Why did they not deny their reality?

How do we know that they did not deny it?

What force has this fact of the record being in heathen writings?

What testimony have we that the early Christians suffered in behalf of their faith?

What do you argue from their constancy in suffering?

What do you argue from a man's being willing to suffer for his opinion's sake?

What is the difference, then, between opinion and knowledge?

Why is it unnecessary to understand Greek and Hebrew before attempting to understand the Bible?

What reason have you for believing that our translations are correct?

What reason for believing that the Greek and Hebrew Scriptures are really ancient books?

What particular reason for believing in the Old Testament?

What must be the character of a mind that is not satisfied with the evidence which we have now reviewed?

Can one judge fairly of evidence, when he does not wish the fact to be proved?

How does credulity lead one to regard evidence?

What effect have independent arguments, when they all bear upon the same point?

The arguments of the present Lesson are of force to an unbeliever's mind; why will those of the succeeding Lessons have less force to an unbeliever, though equally convincing to a believer?

Lesson X.

What four suppositions can we make concerning the origin of Christianity?

How is the truth of these suppositions tested by internal evidence?

Why does not this imply that we are to be judges of God?

Of whom may we more judiciously judge?

What is the probability that Christianity came from men?

What would you expect from scheming men as to the books of a new faith?

Which of the Gospels is attributed to a distinguished Apostle?

What was the rank of the other Evangelists?

Why is high antiquity of the books of the New Testament an argument for their truth?

How is a high antiquity proved by the authors' names?

How by the non-use of the word Christian?

How often and in what manner is this word used in the New Testament?

What reason does Whately give for the Apostles using other titles?

How does the validity of this reasoning affect the argument for the antiquity of the books?

What, then, is the reasoning concerning the word Christian?

What was the expectation of the Jews?

How did the pretended Christs fail of fulfilling it?

How did Jesus fail?

What does this prove, in regard to his character, and to his Apostles' character?

What further opposition in Jesus to the prejudices of the Jews?

Why is this unlike an impostor?

Why unlike an enthusiast?

How might these arguments be, perhaps, answered?

What further argument would you bring from the spiritual pride of the Jews?

How is this confirmed by passages in the New Testament history?

How might an unbeliever attempt to evade this further argument?

What answer would you make concerning sacrifices?

What might you add in general on the character of Christianity?

What argument is drawn from the Gospel estimate of zeal, compared with righteousness?

Mention passages of Scripture illustrating this argument.

Lesson XI.

How does the particular kind of moral duties, inculcated by Jesus, prove him no artful or designing man?

Illustrate this by examples.

How is a similar argument to be drawn from his treatment of parties?

What is the peculiar difference between the morality of our Lord, and that of philosophers of that day?

What strong evidence of this is to be found in the conduct of Christians at the present day?

What, then, is the living evidence, to-day, of the Divine origin of Christianity?

What argument is drawn from the style of the New Testament in regard to miracles?

In regard to sins of the Apostles?

What additional force, in much internal evidence, arises from the multiplicity of books in the New Testament?

What is the summing-up of the argument against the human origin of the Christian Scriptures?

Why is it important in this argument to remember that the Apostles were witnesses of the resurrection and life of a man who had been crucified and buried in public?

Lesson XII.

Why does the author decline entering on the argument from the character of our Redeemer?

What does he propose to us instead?

What is the first point to be kept in mind?

What the second?

How does the inability of men to draw a spotless character appear in the spurious Gospels?

When were these books composed?

How have they been received?

What contrast between them and the Evangelists?

What is the third point to be remembered?

Why are reasons drawn from internal evidence better to have than to give?

How do John and Paul allude to it?

Of what value is this kind of evidence?

What kind of evidence is necessary for us to rest our faith upon when our minds are harassed by doubts? to convict us, if we have lost faith by first losing virtue?

If, while in doubt and darkness, we appeal to the internal evidences, where may it lead us?

Illustrate by Jews, by Mahometans, and by Pagans.

What is the true course for an inquiring spirit?

How rapidly will the confirmation arising from experience come?

What evidence of sound judgment in Apostles from their view of Christian experience?

What bearing has this on our estimate of their testimony concerning Jesus and his miracles?

Note A.

What does John represent the officers sent to apprehend Jesus as saying on their return?

What appeal does he represent Jesus as making to the Jews?

Why is it highly improbable that such an appeal should be made by a bad man?

What difference between making protestations of innocence, and inviting the proof of charges of guilt?

What does Matthew say of the witnesses on whose testimony Jesus was condemned to death?

What of Pilate's words?

What does Luke say of Pilate's words?

What does Luke represent Peter as telling the Jews concerning Pilate's view of Jesus?

What does Peter himself say of Jesus?

And why is it most probable that such claims could not have been made *at that time* for a bad man?

Mention circumstances to show Jesus's benevolence; mention such as show kindness; such as show meekness or humility; such as show sincerity; singleness of purpose; moderation, coolness, and warmth of human affection. Mention any other passages you may have read in the New Testament which show our Lord's character.

Lesson XIII.

What refutation of the proof of Christianity do unbelievers make?

How do they explain that so many proofs are offered to establish what they think a false story?

What, then, do writers against Christianity do?

What is the difference between giving reasons for believing a thing, and answering objections against its truth?

Is it wise to shut our ears entirely against hearing such objections?

What inference might be drawn by an unbeliever from such a course?

What danger do some seem to apprehend?

What reply would you make?

Why may you be willing to hear objections which you cannot answer?

What is the difference between an unanswerable objection and a fatal objection?

Illustrate by fossil shells; by the Copernican system; by aërolites; by the history of Napoleon.

The right way of viewing objections consists of two points. What is the first?

What the second?

Lesson XIV.

Granting the truth of revelation, what proportion does revealed truth bear to that not revealed?

What proportion does the past bear to the future in history?

In the soul's life?

How, then, may Christianity be compared to an inland map?

What Scotch proverb is quoted as in point?

What reference to paper-making?

What, then, should we say to things difficult to be understood in revelation?

How will your minds at your present age compare with what they probably will be, if you should live in good health, and be faithful in study, for ten years?

Are all difficulties objections?

Shew how the bad lives of Christians should act on our faith.

But how does it really act on men's faith?

How did Jesus speak of zeal and morality?

What, then, does the bitter zeal of some loosely moral Christians show?

How bear on the evidences of Christianity?

What argument for our religion is drawn from the fanatical enthusiasm of some sects?

What argument may be drawn from the present slow growth of Christianity, compared with its rapid spread in early ages?

What is the object of the Scriptures?

What answer, then, shall we make to those who object to the unscientific, popular language of the Bible?

How does the paucity of information as to a future state prove the New Testament not to have come from impostors?

How, that it does not come from enthusiasts?

If from neither, and certainly not from both, whence came it?

Are the objections now brought forth new or old?

What proof does this furnish?

What hinderance to Christianity in its early spread is now done away?

Lesson XV.

How does Whately think the condition of the Jews affects the evidences of Christianity?

What threatenings and prophecies does their present condition *seem* to fulfil?

When was Jerusalem destroyed?

What became of the Jews?

On what account did Moses threaten them?

On what account do they appear to suffer?

How is this contradiction explained on Christian grounds?

How explained even on Jewish grounds?

Why do the Jews cease to sacrifice?

How does their reason for ceasing affect the question?

The fact that they have ceased, — how explained by the Christian and by the Jew?

What peculiarity in Judaism as to the power of strangers over it?

How does Christianity afford a means of accounting for this peculiarity?

Lesson XVI.

What effect did the destruction of the Temple have on the Jews?

How many of the descendants of unconverted Jews are now living?

What relation do they bear to other people?

How are they kept separate?

What usually becomes of a conquered people?

What, then, do you infer of the prophecies that they shall remain separate?

What other people mix, and yet keep separate?

What keeps them separate?

How do the Gipsies regard religion?

What, then, is the peculiarity of the Jews?

What objection, then, does their state offer to Christianity?

Under what three heads may all the evidences given in this book be classed?

Why does not this evidence convince the Jew, Mahometan, and Pagan?

Why does it not support and strengthen many Christians?

How will you compare an unbelieving Jew and an unchristian Christian?

Lastly, what is the most powerful argument, practically, which you can offer for Christianity? Repeat Matt. v. 16.

THE END.

www.ingramcontent.com/pod-product-compliance
Lightning Source LLC
LaVergne TN
LVHW010202110826
845151LV00002B/584
* 9 7 8 1 4 2 5 5 3 5 9 5 7 *